Praise for *Does it Work?*

An exceptional guide on how to drive results and make a difference in the ever-changing marketing industry. The principles in *Does it Work?* on setting and tracking goals, executing on data-driven creative, and achieving business results, are applicable to a myriad of initiatives and will have a hugely transformative impact on how you do business.

—CAROLYN EVERSON, Vice President, Global Marketing Solutions, Facebook

Highly approachable, pithy, real and very engaging. The beauty of this book is that it's about marketing today, not just being a better digital person. *Does it Work?* is also perfect for any level of experience with actionable insights for strategy development and executional excellence. That combination makes it an ideal reference book, a mainstay in your marketing arsenal.

—KIERAN HANNON, CMO, Belkin International

Marketers continue to face a multitude of decisions around how, where, and when to engage with customers. The 10 principles Shane and Jason share can truly help marketers focus their efforts in the places that will drive their business forward.

—DANIELLE TIEDT, Chief Marketing Officer, YouTube

A yellow brick road of thinking that can help leading marketers take on the fragile balance between the art and the science of digital marketing.

—MICHAEL KOTICK, Brand Director, Nestlé Purina North America

In a world with an abundance of data, much of it free, it is remarkable that creativity and business profits are primarily faith-based. Jason and Shane ride to our rescue in *Does it Work* with ten illuminating principles that will transform your ability to leverage the Big Data opportunity. As you go from zero to ten in the book, be prepared for your business to go from zero to glorious!

—**AVINASH KAUSHIK,** Marketing Evangelist, Google & Market Motive, and author of *Web Analytics 2.0*

Over the years, I've worked with countless marketers who try to measure everything just because they can. *Does it Work?* brings into sharp focus the only real metric that matters. By helping change the focus and conversation, Shane Atchison and Jason Burby are giving CMOs, CEOs and all shareholders THE standard against which every marketing decision should evaluated.

—**JOSH JAMES,** founder and CEO, Domo

How do you best take advantage of the ever changing opportunities that digital offers your brand to connect with your customer? *Does it Work?* provides principles on everything from setting goals, building teams, driving great creative and most importantly understanding actual business value to your organization.

—**JOANNE BRADFORD,** Head of Partnerships, Pinterest

Does it Work?™

10 Principles for Delivering
True Business Value in Digital Marketing

SHANE ATCHISON | JASON BURBY

Foreword by Sir Martin Sorrell, CEO, WPP

New York Chicago San Francisco Athens London Madrid
Mexico City Milan New Delhi Singapore Sydney Toronto

1 2 3 4 5 6 7 8 9 0   DOC/DOC   1 2 1 0 9 8 7 6 5

ISBN   978-0-07-184786-5
MHID   0-07-184786-3

e-ISBN   978-0-07-184787-2
e-MHID   0-07-184787-1

Library of Congress Cataloging-in-Publication Data

Atchison, Shane.
  Does it work? : 10 principles for delivering true business value in digital marketing / Shane Atchison.
    pages cm
  ISBN 978-0-07-184786-5 (hardback) — ISBN 0-07-184786-3 (hardback) 1. Marketing—Management. 2. Internet marketing. 3. Business planning. I. Burby, Jason. II. Title.
  HF5415.13.A877 2015
  658.8'72—dc23

                                                          2015001219

To Terrance, Ron "TJ" Powers,
Dean R., and Scott Greene

CONTENTS

FOREWORD

"DOES IT WORK?" Shane Atchison and Jason Burby's approach to digital marketing comes in the form of a question. And that's exactly as it should be.

I met the authors of this book for the first time in 2005. They were entrepreneurs who had built a digital agency called ZAAZ.

It was a remarkable firm for the time, driven by one simple conviction: data is of value only if it delivers insight; insight is of value only if it inspires ideas; and ideas are of value only if they deliver clear and measurable business results.

WPP acquired ZAAZ in 2006. A year later, Atchison and Burby explained their ideas in a book, *Actionable Web Analytics*, and it won instant recognition. I remember that, in 2007, the book was the overall winner in its category of the WPP Atticus Awards—our influential annual competition for original published thinking in marketing communications.

Since then, dismissive as always of theories that have no practical application, Atchison and Burby have continued to expose their ideas to the ultimate test by putting them into practice: first at ZAAZ and later at one of WPP's largest digital agencies, POSSIBLE. Their ideas worked, and many others in the industry followed them.

At WPP, we've long and publicly believed that digital media and data investment management were key areas for the allocation of thought and investment: both because of their increasing intrinsic importance and also because of the bewildering speed with which they continue to develop.

As initiators of such change—and learning, as always, from the marketplace lessons of the recent past—Atchison and Burby have now taken their sleeves-rolled-up approach to digital marketing one whole step further.

I love this book's title: *Does it Work?* Three small, tough mono-syllables—and a question mark. It's a question we should be asking about every activity stemming from every part of the WPP group.

The book—again, typically—is as practical as a road map; yet that makes it sound too linear, perhaps too methodical to be inspiring. In truth, it's a book that encourages leaps of imagination. It doesn't tell you what to do; it helps you think so freely and inventively that you'll work out what to do for yourself: and that's always the best way.

And it never allows you to dodge that crucial question: Does it work?

I do hope that a great many WPP clients read and apply this book. If they do, it will be so much easier for our companies to make them even more successful.

Sir Martin Sorrell
CEO WPP

ACKNOWLEDGMENTS

First of all, we'd like to thank the many friends and colleagues who have supported our ideas, challenged our thinking, and helped us learn over the years. At POSSIBLE we have the privilege of working closely with 1,300-plus colleagues around the world supporting amazing global brands. In particular, we'd like to thank the following people for their significant contributions to the book: Thomas Stelter, Jason Carmel, Halina Lukoskie, Liz Valentine, Jason Brush, Jon McVey, Brad Gagne, Michael Watts, Nick Leggett, Dmitria Burby, Justin Cooke, Adam Wolf, Anders Rosenquist, Andrew Solmssen, Paul J. Kerr, Andrey Anischenko, Tyler Brain, Alicia McVey, Ben Reubenstein, Danielle Trivisonno Hawley, Darin Brown, Diane Holland, Brandon Geary, Jessica Ostrow, Angela Griffen-Meyers, Chien-Wen Tong, Mike Reeder, Tony Aguero, Elaine Ng, Gus Weigel, Liz Fairchild, Sarah McCarthy, Tony Desjardins, Jamie Pattan, Jim Chesnutt, Justin Marshall, Kenny Powar, Krisztian Toth, Kunal Muzumdar, Lucas Peon, Laura Wolf, Martha Hiefield, and Tonya Peck.

We'd also like to extend a special thanks to Joe Shepter, who helped take our ideas and thinking and formulate them into the 10 principles in the book. A big thanks also goes to Donya Dickerson, Executive Editor at McGraw-Hill, for her enthusiasm about our book and encouragement throughout the process.

Each of the 10 principles in the book has grown out of our experience leading client work for some of the best brands around the world. Over the years, we have had many conversations with clients, friends, and industry thought leaders. Some of them were so productive and influential to our thinking that we decided to interview a number of people when writing the book. All of them helped shape its content and contributed real-life stories to support our points. In that regard, we would like to thank Ali Behnam, Andrew Connell, Avinash Kaushik, Brent Hieggelke, Brian Lesser, Chris Kerns, Chris

Scoggins, Curt Hecht, Dana Cogswell, Dean Aragon, Deep Nishar, Denise Karkos, Doug Chavez, Eddy Moretti, Emily Brooke, Grace Ho, Guido Rosales, Jean-Philippe Maheu, Joe Shepter, John Mellor, Jonah Peretti, Josh James, Kieran Hannon, Lars Madsen, Marc Connor, Mark Read, Matt Mason, McGregor Agan, Mike Fridgen, Phyllis Jackson, René Rechtman, Richard Hyde, Richard Nunn, Nick Nyhan, Mike Dodd, Sam Decker, Scott Lux, Steve Jarvis, Ted Cannis, and Yonca Brunini.

We'd also like to extend a special thanks to Sir Martin Sorrell, CEO of WPP, not only for writing the foreword to this book, but also for creating—together with Mark Read, CEO of WPP Digital—an environment where we can learn, try new things, take chances, attract great talent and clients, and most important, do great work for our clients.

Above all, we'd like to thank our families—Tasha, Keegan, Francis, Taco, Dmitria, Cade, Blake, and Avangeline—for putting up with our frequent travel, late-night phone calls and texts, and everything else you do to support us in chasing our dreams.

HOW TO SAVE LIVES WITH ADVERTISING

In 2013, we all fell in love with a cheeky public service campaign called *Dumb Ways to Die*. Intended to promote safety on the Metro in Melbourne, Australia, it featured a music video that listed the many foolish ways you could die. They included eating superglue, inviting a serial killer into your home, and selling both your kidneys. At the end, the video said that perhaps the dumbest way of all to die is to get hit by a train.

The video went viral. Viewed more than 100 million times, it was declared by many to be the most successful public service announcement ever. *Dumb Ways to Die* went on to win every major advertising award, including the most Cannes Lions (the industry's top honor) of any campaign in history.

But did it work? The simple answer is "of course." As its agency pointed out, it not only won awards, it also generated $50 million in global advertising value. It became so popular that Metro even made money by licensing it to a life insurance company. *OK, but did it work?*

Let's think about that for a moment. What was the Metro trying to achieve? If we take the title of the video seriously, it wanted to save lives by changing the reckless behavior of people around trains. And initially, it claimed great success. Two and a half months after its release in November 2012, the Metro announced that it had seen a change. "The biggest improvement was in the number of collisions or near misses with vehicles and pedestrians at level crossings," gushed one official.[1] She claimed a reduction of 31%.

If you're looking for data to gauge train safety and changes in public behavior, near misses at level crossings isn't a bad metric. They occur whenever a person or driver willfully ignores safety gates and other warnings that a train is coming and tries to dash across the tracks before it arrives. By definition, they measure recklessness. And since many more people narrowly miss being hit by trains than get hit by them, those statistics are less noisy and allow you to make more certain conclusions over time.

Unfortunately for the campaign, however, near misses did not continue their hopeful trend. In fact, they got much worse. By 2014, Transport Safety Victoria issued a warning to the public because such incidents had *increased* by 66% in the year after the ad was released, putting them at their highest level in four years.[2] By that measure, the ad certainly didn't work.

Undeterred, Metro Trains went fishing for data again and submitted the campaign for several marketing effectiveness awards. First, it said "risky behavior" had decreased 20%. Then, its agency released a case study that claimed the ad had reduced deaths and accidents by 32% over the time frame of the campaign. You can find a detailed analysis of the various claims in Appendix B, but here's a brief summary of why they don't add up:

1. **THEY CHERRY PICK.** Transport Safety Victoria (TSV), the authority that collects Metro Trains statistics, tracks nine different categories of incidents. If you take those nine and start looking at different time periods, you should always be able to find something that indicates success. In fact, some of the categories did show improvement in 2013. Others showed the opposite. And if you add up all of the incidents together, they showed almost no change from 2012 to 2013. That doesn't sound effective to us.

2. **THEY'RE NOT STATISTICALLY SIGNIFICANT.** We had our marketing sciences department analyze the data, and even though statistical significance is not a simple matter, the claims clearly do not make the grade. The reason is that safety incidents are rare, and the data is extremely noisy. In some of the nine categories, only 11 incidents occur on average in any given year. While 20% and 32%

may sound impressive, they might only mean a difference of two or three incidents—and fluctuations of that kind are common.

3. THE VIDEO DOESN'T ADDRESS THE REAL PROBLEM. The biggest cause of deaths on Australian trains is not carelessness or recklessness. Rather, suicides account for 80% of all fatalities nationally.[3] In addition, Melbourne young people have a peculiar fascination for riding on the outside of trains, a practice known as "train surfing" or "coupler riding." The campaign addressed neither topic directly, nor does it seem to have improved matters with either.[4]

4. THE CLAIMS IGNORE OTHER FACTORS. Whenever you analyze the effectiveness of a campaign, you have to account for everything that may have moved the metrics. You can't attribute *all* the perceived improvement to a single ad. And prior to the campaign's launch, TSV was already taking aggressive steps to improve safety. In early 2012, for example, it became a partner in TrackSAFE, a national public awareness and training program aimed at reducing suicides and railway accidents. In addition, the agency has made numerous investments in safety since 2010, including upgrading technology, increasing conductor training, improving crossings, and adding fencing to keep people out of dangerous areas. All these activities should have had an impact as well.

Not surprisingly, many experts criticized *Dumb Ways to Die.* A former Metro Trains employee, who had worked for years on level crossing communications, declared its claims for success "social media bulls⁎⁎t."[5][†] A prominent social psychologist deplored "the

---

[†] This and all subsequent uses of this word changed per publisher policy.

myth of stupidity" promoted by the ad.[6] And a 2014 study by the Victoria Transit Policy Institute contended that safety messaging that focused on danger was counterproductive. Public transit, it held, is considerably safer than alternatives such as automobiles, but has an undeserved and exaggerated reputation for danger. Ads that emphasize that danger encourage people to use more risky (not to mention less environmentally responsible) means of transportation. Instead of saving lives, these kinds of messages probably increase the likelihood of death by other means.[7]

In Appendix B, we'll continue our discussion of *Dumb Ways to Die* and look at some of the real problems faced by the Melbourne Metro. In the meantime, let's stop being negative and examine a campaign that saved lives and a lot of them.

> **The beauty of innovation and the beauty of doing things is that it's a trial and error. As soon as you move ahead, you can learn on the things that you did very good and the things that you did bad. You need to understand why you failed and then try to correct the mistake and try to avoid that in the future.**
>
> *—Guido Rosales, Europe Group Integrated Marketing Director, The Coca-Cola Company*

VINNIE JONES TO THE RESCUE

In 2011, Britons saw a hilarious PSA created by Grey London starring Vinnie Jones, an ex-footballer in Europe. Dressed as a gangster and snarling with slang, he demonstrated how hands-only CPR could save the lives of people having a cardiac arrest. The punchline of the ad was that you needed to push hard and fast (which Vinnie had helpfully tattooed on his fists) to the beat of the Bee Gees' "Staying Alive." It was an easy-to-remember lesson that perfectly merged message with purpose.

"Hard & fast."

Did it work? This time, the answer is a resounding yes. Grey and its client, the British Heart Foundation, made that case in a persuasive white paper for the 2014 IPA Effectiveness Awards. It first pointed out that 60,000 people suffer a cardiac arrest outside of a hospital each year in the UK. Your best chance of survival in that case is if you get CPR fast. But at the time, only 25% of people in the UK were confident enough to perform CPR. As a result, only a shocking 7% of cardiac arrest victims lived to leave the hospital.[8]

The British Heart Foundation compared the UK statistics with a number of other places, including Seattle, where every child has been taught CPR in gym class for the last 30 years. There, the survival rate jumps to 50%.[9]

Next, they conducted a survey to learn why so few people were willing to attempt CPR. It revealed that fear and ignorance played leading roles in the problem. Prior to the campaign, 74% of people said that lack of confidence was a factor, while 77% cited a lack of knowledge.

Vinnie Jones struck at both of these problems. With an unlikely character, a catchy tune, and plenty of humor, it disarmed the fears of viewers and delivered useful tools for saving lives. Far fewer people (5 million) viewed the ad than saw *Dumb Ways to Die,* but in the year after the campaign, the British Heart Foundation identified 30 people whose lives were directly saved by it. More important, the larger metrics also moved. The number of UK residents who lacked confidence to perform CPR dropped to 65%, and the number who didn't know how fell to 70%. Since few other major initiatives to teach CPR were under way, a good part of the credit must go to the campaign.[10]

In other words, both the Melbourne Metro and the British Heart Foundation produced brilliant content. In the case of *Vinnie Jones*, that content was effective. In the case of *Dumb Ways to Die,* it wasn't. This matters.

ACTIONABLE ANALYTICS

We've been thinking about the problem of measurable objectives with marketing for a long time. In 2007, we wrote a book called *Actionable Web Analytics: Using Data to Make Smart Business Decisions.* At that time, people were just starting to get their heads around a concept that now seems to be top of mind for everyone: websites and other digital properties have something that other forms of marketing don't. They have memories.

Everything a user does on a digital property can be—or often is, by default—recorded and stored away. Back in 2007, people were starting to look at this information, analyze it, and figure out how well or poorly they were doing. Instead of trusting a "web design guru" (and there were plenty of them around), people wanted to know what their customers had actually done on a website. They would then use that information to boost performance and results.

The biggest problem, we felt, was that by themselves many of the success metrics people were using—such as impressions, page views, time spent on site—were largely meaningless, a position we still hold. A page view matters only if it represents a potential customer or someone who might share your brand with others. A share matters only if a sharer has followers. Followers matter only if they are in your purchase demographic. So we argued that web strategy had to be brought into the overall context of a business. It had to move metrics that matter, not influence meaningless statistics.

A NEW START

We wrote *Actionable Web Analytics* when the digital world was much simpler. Back then, you had some digital technology but nothing like today. There was no social, not a huge amount of third party recommendation, and relatively primitive mobile devices. Since then, things have obviously changed. The highlights include:

- Data and insight have increased exponentially.
- Customers have become vastly more mobile.
- Tablets and second screening are commonplace.
- Social media. Enough said.
- The key 18–34 demographic was raised on digital.
- Transparency has increased.
- Audiences are fragmented.
- CMOs play a much larger role for brands.
- Silos have become a real problem.
- Big Data has arrived.
- Disruptive technologies crop up every day.
- Innovation is now a mandate for marketers.
- Competition is fiercer.
- Location data is available and important.
- Stakes are higher.
- The speed of change is accelerating.
- And no one seems to know what to do with it all.

As all of these have happened, our company has evolved a philosophy that's different from the clean but narrow world of our first book. We call it Does it Work?™. It's a strategy for achieving business success from digital efforts.

OUR METHODOLOGY

We did not come up with Does it Work? on our own. In fact, it was a process involving a lot of people and time. We wanted to make sure it worked not only locally where we live, but also included a wide global perspective. To do that, we relied on four sources of data and information.

OUR TEAM. Our agency, POSSIBLE, has more than 1,300 employees with offices spanning five continents. We selected experts from every digital field to help us understand the nuances of their work. They include smart people in creative, data, brand, social media, mobile devices, technology,innovation, and much more. They also bring different perspectives from around the world.

INDEPENDENT RESEARCH. We also commissioned Forrester Consulting to do research on our behalf. They interviewed 30 global CMOs on what they felt was working or not working in their marketing. The resulting report, "What CMOs Need to Make Digital Marketing Work," appears as Appendix A at the end of this book and is quoted throughout.

INDUSTRY THOUGHT LEADERS. We interviewed and corresponded with more than 50 thought leaders, CMOs, CEOs, innovators, data analysts, venture capitalists, and more. Some came from global corporations, such as Coca-Cola, eBay, Procter & Gamble, Microsoft, and SAP. Others came from leading-edge technology companies such as Google, Bittorrent, and Urban Airship. Their conversations helped shape our thinking and our approach. You'll also find some of their words throughout this book, and their thoughts are collected at the end of each chapter. Of course, they don't always echo our ideas perfectly, and sometimes they disagree with us, but we think different perspectives are always valuable.

OURSELVES. Last and perhaps least, we've been in the industry for 20 years working with a large number of highly respected clients, including Microsoft, Procter and Gamble, AT&T, Sony, and Ford. In addition, we have written or been interviewed about digital marketing everywhere from Fortune.com and Bloomberg TV to *Contagious* and *Communication Arts* magazines.

WHY A QUESTION?

We know Does it Work? sounds a little strange for a business ideology. It is something that we follow and act on, but we use a question to describe it. If you're wondering why, it's because of the pace of change. Disruptive technologies are emerging every day. It would be fantastic if we knew how the world will look in five years. But if we're being honest with ourselves, we don't know what it will look like in five months. Not to mention the fact that it will look different to different people. The future is impossible to predict.

Don't believe us? Every year, the Consumer Electronics Show brings together some of the world's best and brightest minds in technology. Together, they select the products they believe are the most exciting with the greatest chance for future success to present at the event. You might think that this esteemed body would be pretty much right about its predictions. After all, they have so much information at their fingertips. Many of them, in fact, earn a living by telling us what technology we'll be using next year. They must be good at this.

Not so much. They turn out to be vastly better at predicting goats than game changers. From 2004 to 2006, for example, the jury had an unfathomable infatuation with the Zen Vision series of iPod competitors (surely you remember them). In 2009, it touted the game-changing nature of the now-defunct Palm Pre. In 2011, it swooned over the Motorola Xoom. In 2010, they jumped on the

3-D TV bandwagon, a trend that still hasn't caught on. If the most tech-knowledgeable people in the world can be so consistently wrong, what chance do the rest of us have?

In addition, we also have the problem of change. Consumers migrate. Their tastes constantly change. Their ideas of privacy change. The way they use social media changes. And some of your customers may be very different from others, but you need to know how to reach all of them effectively. One size doesn't really fit anyone anymore. So we have to forget prescriptions and the lofty pronouncements of experts. It's time to start asking questions. It's time to admit what we don't know the answers—but we can find them out.

THE "DOES IT WORK?" PROCESS

Below, we'll describe the 10 principles that comprise the Does it Work? philosophy. But in essence you can think of it as having four real steps:

1. SET GOALS. Does it Work? goals are a series of specific objectives that you set both for your business and every project or campaign you do. To them we apply Does it Work? criteria, or solid metrics that define what success should look like. We use these metrics to help us understand progress against our goals, what's working or not, and how we should react.

2. INSPIRE BRILLIANT CREATIVITY. Creative intuition is vital and essential to everything we do in digital. While this book will deal more extensively with data (after all, that's what's new to the marketing world), data must be in the service of creativity. *Dumb Ways to Die* was a great idea if the objective was to get tons of views. *Vinnie Jones* was a great creative idea if the objective was to get plenty of views and also educate the audience. It used data in a terrific way: to identify an area where an ad could achieve something. The data did not hinder creativity; it ensured that it was not just brilliant, but also effective.

3. MEASURE THE RESULTS. Measurement is not a passive activity. It's a process of determining what's working, making adjustments, and learning from the results. You should not merely see if something worked or not. You should know how well it worked and what that teaches you about your customers.

4. MAKE A DIFFERENCE. Rather than simply getting industry recognition, we want to make sure we help brands and businesses meet their goals. Whether we're trying to save lives, boost revenue, or achieve global success, Does it Work? helps us know that we've made a difference.

One of the interesting things we learned from the Forrester study and our interviews is that some regions of the world are much closer to our ideas than we think. Marketers in China tend to set much clearer objectives up front and tie performance and even compensation to whether things work or not. Marketers in the United States and Europe—and especially those operating in stressed economies such as the UK—rarely do so, if at all. Clearly, there is room for improvement.

CORE PRINCIPLES

Does it Work? is organized around 10 principles, which are also chapters of this book. You should see these not as a road map, but as a way to think about data and digital, and how to move your organization to take better advantage of its challenges and opportunities.

PRINCIPLE 1:
BUSINESS GOALS ARE EVERYTHING

Business goals lie at the center of Does it Work? Without them, you can't understand effectiveness, measure progress, or learn anything. Put simply, if you don't know what success looks like, you can't know if you're driving it.

Goals are an overarching concept— they are the aspirations of a company or the outcome you desire for an activity. They are what you are trying to achieve. But they also require measurement, or Does it Work? criteria. A set of metrical targets, they reflect the factors that push a business in the right direction. By measuring progress against them, you can learn what you're doing well, where you need help, and what changes you might need to make.

PRINCIPLE 2:
A COLLECTIVE VISION

If your goals sit in a drawer, they can't do you any good. That's why everyone in a company has to understand and work toward them. Doing this involves making sure that every team, initiative, and campaign has its own Does it Work? criteria that ladder up to one or more of your business goals.

A collective vision is not just essential to making progress toward your goals; it also helps break down silos. Global complexity has increased the need for communication and coordination across different parts of an organization. By making sure we have full alignment, we can build a common understanding of how everyone should work together to achieve our goals.

PRINCIPLE 3:
DATA INSPIRES CREATIVITY

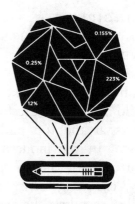

Most of the time, marketers think of data as a success (or failure) metric. In a Does it Work? context, it should not be used simply to evaluate performance. It should also be used to inspire creativity.

Data by itself does not provide solutions—it can only provide a clearer vision of opportunities. It can enable marketers to pursue bold ideas and defend them from those loud voices who always think they're the experts. To do this, we need to take the research and data we have and distill it into simple, powerful ideas that inspire creative people.

PRINCIPLE 4:
FINDING UNICORNS

To create a Does it Work? culture, you need special people, those who are able to use data creatively and achieve real results for your brand. Our answer is to look for unicorns, people born for digital. We'll meet some of them, and see the traits that make them smart, flexible, low-key team players who adapt easily and love to make things work. We'll also look at what they want out of their job. They no longer simply want to be creative, they want to make a difference. Does it Work? channels that desire into concrete achievements, such as building revenue for a brand or making customers' lives easier and more meaningful.

PRINCIPLE 5:
CULTURE PREDICTS SUCCESS AND FAILURE

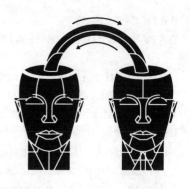

So how do you make unicorns happy? Build a great culture for digital. Culture starts at the top and flows naturally down. In the modern business world, that calls for lack of egos, a flat hierarchy, encouragement of ideas, and the ability to take risks and accept failure. Beyond that, Does it Work? tries to deliver everyone a sense of accomplishment. Our work should do something meaningful for our brands and the wider world.

PRINCIPLE 6:
MEASURE WHAT MATTERS

Today we have plenty of readily available metrics, but we'll never know what works if we stick to them. Instead we have to measure what matters, not what is easy. This means taking on tough topics, such as understanding how digital affects offline transactions and how short-term campaigns can impact long-term brand value. But it also means being realistic about measurement. We have many things we can measure, but we should only measure them if we can act on them. Measurement without action is a waste of time.

PRINCIPLE 7:
WHAT IT'S WORTH

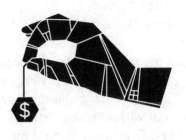

With Does it Work?, we don't merely want to know what works and doesn't. We also want to know what works better than something else. Every marketer has 10 things she can do, but if asked to choose just three, she has a difficult time.

The answer to her dilemma is relative-value modeling, or the process of assigning dollar values to activities and behaviors. These values don't have to be absolute—and often they aren't—but they still can be extremely useful. The reason is that today, we don't always have clear insight into the value and effectiveness of things we do. What is a tweet worth to your brand compared to an Instagram like? Models can help you bridge this gap, understand the relative value of activities, and prioritize between them.

PRINCIPLE 8:
NEVER STOP IMPROVING

Are digital properties ever perfect? Quick answer: no. Even the most seasoned UX expert can get things drastically wrong. Yet most marketers simply launch projects and leave them to their own devices. Huge lost opportunity. A project is merely a hypothesis of what might work, and it's probably not 100% correct. That's why we should always leave room (and budget) for improvement.

Technically speaking, this is known as "optimization." That's a fancy way of saying you test out what's working—and not—on your digital properties. Ask if a headline about free stuff works better than one about cash back. Then test. When you get the results, you can act on your learnings and improve your understanding over time.

PRINCIPLE 9:
ONE SIZE FITS NO ONE

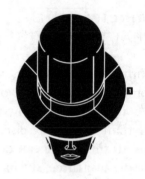

Customers are not all the same and don't want a generic experience—especially in a personalized digital world. Some find motivation in some things, others in others. One Size Fits No One shows how we can identify and target different groups with different experiences. The end result may be a lift in sales, but it could also simply provide a much better experience for your loyal customers.

PRINCIPLE 10:
FRAMEWORK FOR INNOVATION

In the current environment, innovation is simply part of the job. You'll always need to learn and do new things. From a Does it Work? perspective, innovation is an ongoing process based on solid principles: goals, measurement, and action. We want to make sure that our innovation process drives better results.

We also need to understand what happens after we build new things. Make an app? You're entering a new arena with different expectations. You now have a relationship with your customers—a real relationship that has real consequences if you don't maintain it. You have to develop true product management processes to ensure that your brand stays fresh and relevant to the people you value most.

As we introduce each principle we also include a link to a short video to bring the principle to life. These can be found on the first page of each chapter. For example you can see the link "POSSIBLE.com/ principle1" on the opening page of the "Business Goals Are Everything" chapter.

THE PURPOSE OF "DOES IT WORK?"

Much of this book will focus on areas that may initially seem distant from the most important things to the marketing industry: ideas and creativity itself. *This is an illusion.*

This book is about a field that relies on brilliant ideas and creativity. Data and process can never replace imagination. They can't remove risk or do your homework for you. They can, however, help create the conditions that allow magic to happen.

You should look at almost every Does it Work? principle through the lens of creative ideas. We set business goals so we know what those ideas should do. We build a collective vision so that every person can be on the same page and contribute to creative solutions. We need unicorns because they're the kind of people who aren't afraid to think out loud and either come up with great ideas or help those who do. We need to measure what matters because measurement itself can be creative and can help suggest new ways to approach marketing.

At the same time, you want creativity to be effective. *Dumb Ways to Die* is great creative. But the awards it received should have come from the *film* festival at Cannes, not the advertising one. With Does it Work?, brilliant ideas achieve business objectives.

FINAL THOUGHT

Does it Work? may seem an easy thing to adopt, but it's not. It mandates a long-term shift in how you approach digital and marketing and your customer relationships overall. It will change not merely how you look at data and creativity, but how you staff your organization, prioritize among initiatives, and organize and incentivize your people. It will change your relationship to agencies and clients, and maybe even with customers, too. Changes like that don't come quickly; they take a strong commitment to making things better. But the good news is, you can start implementing these ideas today. Just start asking, "Does it work?" The answer may surprise you.

THOUGHT LEADERS WEIGH IN

At the end of every chapter, we'll include quotes from the thought leaders and POSSIBLE experts who helped shape this book. We've tried to include people from around the world and across industries so that we could present different perspectives on our topics. Some of these perspectives echo our own; others show another take on the issues. Hopefully, they'll all help trigger additional thoughts and ideas. You can find biographies of all participants in the Contributor Bios section at the back of this book.

> The temptation with digital platforms like social media is to treat them with a certain degree of reverence, simply because of the technological upgrade to what is essentially "human connection." It must have the same criteria as any other channels which connect us as people. It must fascinate. It must engage. Ultimately, it needs to stimulate the response that is sought by your brand and/or business goals. We often get lost on the technology front, thinking that we have to maneuver in some special way, rather than focusing on why it's worth anyone's time.
>
> —**DEAN ARAGON,** VP CX Brand and CEO, Shell Brands International AG

> The thing that ad agencies struggle with is they're very good at doing things that are cool, but they find it very hard to do things that work.
>
> —**MARK READ,** CEO, WPP Digital

Data or insights by themselves don't mean anything. You need to activate people and motivate them to do something, and the way we've been able to do that is through really crystallizing our findings into evocative stories, rich with components that then leave the creatives with so much to go after.

—PHYLLIS JACKSON, VP, North America, Consumer & Market Knowledge, P&G

They cared tons about awards. I didn't give a s**t[†] about them. It was a huge divergence. I could tell that their creative was almost geared towards getting them an award, and I didn't think it was effective for driving our business. It was a huge problem for me. I am fine with awards as a secondary goal, but it has to drive our business first and foremost.

—STEVE JARVIS, VP, Strategy Global Tour & Transport, Expedia, Inc.

The best ideas don't come just from the designers. They come from the designers, and they come from the creative people and user experience, but they also come from end users, and they come from the analysts, and they come from the janitor and anybody. And so encouraging heuristic evaluations process, encouraging this whole idea that everybody is empowered to create the most crazy-ass idea and that we can put a naked Richard Branson on the home page and see what happens, we just control for risk by showing it to maybe 1% of the people.

—AVINASH KAUSHIK, Marketing Evangelist, Google & Market Motive, and author of *Web Analytics 2.0*

[†] This and all subsequent uses of this word changed per publisher policy.

I was in grad school at the MIT Media Lab. Sometimes, we would create brilliant ideas there that really were impractical and that couldn't actually live in the world, but they were an amazing demo . . . Other times, there were things that were less impressive demos that actually you saw and you thought about it for a little while. You said, "Oh, I see how this could impact culture. I see how this could have a sociological impact." . . . Those are the kinds of ideas that I like. When you see something and you say, "Wow, why doesn't this exist? Why doesn't this obvious thing exist?" Those are the ideas that really are exciting to me. They're the ones you can usually put into action.

—**JONAH PERETTI,** Founder and CEO, BuzzFeed

Insights can come out of data, but they're required to drive amazing ideas and creativity that engage consumers.

—**CURT HECHT,** Chief Global Revenue Officer, The Weather Company

I couldn't tell you what the next social platform is, or commerce platform; however, it is critical that we stay immersed in up-and-coming capabilities and be prepared to act if it supports our customer vision.

—**SCOTT A. LUX,** VP eCommerce & Multi Channel, Diesel

Most companies still profoundly underleverage what digital can do for their business. The tops of companies are still filled with people who came to power and control in the offline world, and they still very much think with that lens on.

—**AVINASH KAUSHIK,** Marketing Evangelist, Google & Market Motive, and author of *Web Analytics 2.0*

Stories let us balance our left and right brain. They bring our emotions and everything together to unlock us as human beings so we want to address the tension that sparks really great creativity and advertising.

—**PHYLLIS JACKSON,** VP, North America, Consumer & Market
Knowledge, P&G

[This] book is really about setting out what you're going to measure very clearly in the front end and as you go, finding the right people to put on your bus to innovate and spot the channels and different digital things that are succeeding.

—**ANDREW CONNELL,** CMO, Western Europe, Devices Business,
Huawei Technologies

01
BUSINESS GOALS ARE EVERYTHING

POSSIBLE.com/principle1

INTRODUCTION

Business goals are the foundation of this book. Without them, you can't begin to understand your effectiveness, gain insight, or improve anything. Each goal is the "it" in Does it Work?

Today many brands have business goals, but a far smaller number are using metrics to back them up. Still fewer are using data to evaluate their marketing efforts on an initiative-by-initiative basis. This may not seem important, but it is. If you don't set good goals up front and measure progress against them, you'll never understand what works. You'll simply look at your efforts in a rearview mirror.

In this chapter, we discuss what good goals are, how to establish criteria for evaluating them, how to measure them effectively, and how to use the results to learn and grow.

> **Marketers can be very much focused on the marketing goals and sometimes forget: What is the business goal here?**
>
> —*Kieran Hannon, CMO, Belkin International*

> **We have to ask, "What are the goals and what are the strategies that we're going to use to go attack those objectives?"**
>
> —*Avinash Kaushik, Marketing Evangelist, Google & Market Motive, and author of* Web Analytics 2.0

A MILLION DOLLARS FOR NOTHING

Ask Alex Tew, and he'll tell you it's good to aim high. As a 21-year-old student at the University of Nottingham, he came up with an ambitious goal: raising enough cash to cover the cost of his education. To reach it, he hit on an unlikely idea: he'd get people to give the money to him.

Tew's idea was simple: he'd sell a million pixels of space on a web page for $1 per pixel. You could buy them in blocks of 100 for $100 apiece and put anything you liked on them. The idea was (perhaps) to sell all million, or at least enough to pay for his education.

The Million Dollar Homepage, as it became known, is a great example of setting a goal and having a plan and metrics to back it up. Tew's goal: pay for college. His metric: cost of college education. He would easily be able to understand success if it came, and failure if it didn't.

In the event, things went well for him. A friend bought a block of pixels for $400, and Tew sent out a press release about it. The release was picked up by one news outlet after another, and momentum grew. Tew sold more and more blocks of pixels and became an Internet sensation along the way. Thanks to coverage in major news organizations around the world, he soon blew past the amount of money he needed. In fact, demand mounted so high that he surpassed his goal, and racked up more than $1,000,000.[1]

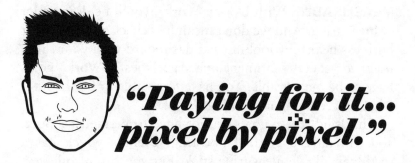

"Paying for it... pixel by pixel."

SMART GOALS

So what are goals? Goals are outcomes you want to achieve or aspects of your business that you want to improve. For example, say your brand is universally recognized in North America; you may want to build similar mindshare in Europe. You may want to lift your sales by 30%. You may want to become the biggest reseller of wing nuts in the world.

Not all goals, however, are good goals. To set ones that work, we rely on a specialized version of one of the oldest business goal frameworks around: SMART. The basic idea (though not the acronym) first appeared in Peter Drucker's 1954 classic *The Practice of Management*. It states that goals should be specific, measurable, achievable, relevant, and time-bound. Let's look at what these mean in a digital context:

SPECIFIC. Goals outline an objective you want to achieve. In Tew's case, he wanted to pay for college. Brands may want to increase revenue or decrease customer service calls by 10%. Or they may want to increase brand equity by 20%. Such goals are specific. What's not a specific goal? To be the best. To strive for excellence. To crush the competition. To live the dream. Those goals may be meaningful to you, but they are too vague to provide a business with direction.

MEASURABLE. With Does it Work?, you'll be doing a lot of measuring. And we don't mean just checking in on your business health by looking at a dashboard with your sales, users, or social sentiment analysis. Does it Work? goals have to be measurable. You have to be able to figure out if what you're doing is working or not.

That said, these goals do not have to be metrics. Sure, you can have a goal of boosting revenue, which has a readily available measuring stick. But you can also have a softer goal, such as improving the customer experience. If you do, you need to establish a matrix of criteria (we call them Does it Work? criteria) that reflect progress toward that goal. For customer experience, you could use metrics such as retention rate, social advocacy rate, customer satisfaction scores, and so on. These harder metrics, taken together, can tell you how you're progressing toward your softer goal.

ACHIEVABLE. If your team can't realistically reach a goal, don't set it. Even the best brands get this one wrong. In 1971, for example, Lee Iacocca set a goal for Ford's engineers to create a car, the Pinto, that weighed less than 2,000 pounds and cost less than $2,000. In order to meet a tight deadline, the team cut corners on safety checks. As a result, the car's gas tank had a structural weakness that caused it to burst into flame on impact, and 53 people died.

The problem with Iacocca's goal is that it wasn't achievable. Unrealistic goals lead to poor execution, unethical behavior, and overworked employees. We'll discuss this problem in more detail below.

RELEVANT. This is the easiest one. You have to make sure your business goals ladder up to success. You can have a goal, for example, of having the most popular Instagram page in your category. But to do so, you'd probably have to attract lots of noncustomers, which wouldn't help your bottom line. The goals you set should ultimately drive revenue or reduce costs.

TIME BOUND. Goals need deadlines. It makes a huge difference if you try to increase your customer base by 10% in one year or ten. A deeper problem occurs when you set goals and put off their achievement until some vague time in the future. In that case, you may never get anything done.

MAKING GOALS SMARTER

Does it Work? differs from standard SMART goal setting in one big way: this approach has a wider business context. With SMART goals, you set objectives primarily for teams. One team within a company may have goals that differ radically from another, and the two may not necessarily mesh. In Does it Work?, you first set overarching goals for your business. Then you set group and project goals that ladder up to them. In this way, business goals serve as a guiding framework for everything you do.

Of course, not all teams and projects equally support all goals. A sales team is much better positioned to support a revenue goal than a customer service team is; while both can work toward a customer experience goal. That's fine. But every effort should at least support one business goal.

Does it Work? also differs from SMART in the purpose of the goals. Ordinary SMART goals are motivational hurdles you want to leap over or tools for performance evaluation. You either beat them or you don't. You get a reward, or you don't. You get to keep your job, or maybe not.

Does it Work? goals don't operate this way. They are not signposts or mile markers. They are careful estimates of expected outcomes. They are what we think should happen if we succeed. As a result, they can serve as touchpoints around which we can build understanding on whether things are working or not. Done right, they increase our knowledge and help us navigate a complex and rapidly changing environment. In the next section we see how.

> **Before launching a product we always discuss what success looks like. Only then can we have an objective answer to understand if it works. That type of disciplines allows us to know if we are successful.**
>
> —Deep Nishar, SVP, Products and User Experience, LinkedIn

VARIANCE AND DOES IT WORK? CRITERIA

You often hear that the digital world is changing rapidly. So how do you keep up with it? There are two major ways. First, we have to be observant of the changes and try to adapt ourselves to them. The second is that we can use Does it Work? goals to help us understand how change affects our brands and our audience. It's nice to know that a sharing economy has arisen, but how exactly does that affect our brand? We can learn that by forming hypotheses about our projects and measuring them as they move along.

"We can't stress the concept of variance enough."

To do this, we have to embrace a concept called variance. Variance indicates how close any given effort comes to a goal. If we set a goal of shipping 2,000 units and we miss it by 10, our variance is only −0.5%. Even though we missed our goal, it would be silly to criticize ourselves for such a slight lack of performance. On the other hand, if we exceed our goal by 200, our variance now becomes +10%. That's big—and possibly provides a learning opportunity.

For example, let's say you have a chain of restaurants with an overall business goal of increasing sales. You look at your numbers, compare them to industry data, and realize that your midweek lunch sales are lagging behind the averages. This should tell you that lunch is an area where you have a good opportunity to achieve lift, or improvement.

You also know that your most loyal customers are your best bet for increasing sales. It turns out that most of them have downloaded and installed an ordering app that your team created a year ago. So you create an in-app promotion that offers a free order of French fries for anyone who stops by for lunch Monday through Friday.

Next, you need to figure out what success would look like. Luckily, you've been doing in-app promotions for a year and have plenty of data. Based on a review of that data, you conclude that you can probably drive 1,000 extra lunches.

You then run the promotion. For the purposes of argument, let's say that 1,200 people take advantage of it. Congratulations, you did well. But remember, we aren't simply evaluating your performance on this effort. We also want to learn. So you look at the variance. In this case, it's +20%. This is pretty significant and means that you should figure out why.

To do this, you first need to make sure that your initial estimation was not too low. Then you look at the images, copy, and other creative elements to see if you can find anything significantly different from past promotions. You realize that the pushed headline "Free Fries" drove a much higher open rate than previous promotions. The learning? Your customers like simple messages that tout free items. You'll want to confirm that with tests in the future, but now you're at least working toward a better understanding of your customers.

On the other hand, let's suppose you had only 960 lunches. This is a variance of −4%. Do you fire the team for not living up to your expectations? Of course not. You didn't miss by much, and you don't want them to think of your measurement program as a sword of Damocles hanging over their heads. Instead, you want to determine if something caused the miss or if it was simply noise. In this case, you notice that you dropped most of the promotions on a Sunday evening. You then look at similar promos sent out on Sunday evening and realize that anything sent at that time underperforms expectations. Again, you have learned something.

We can't stress the concept of variance enough. To figure out what works for your brand, you need a measuring stick to go by, and it should be as accurate and useful as possible. You can't simply rely on available metrics that seem to show success.

For example, a few years ago, our agency did an online video for Samsung about a young guy who doesn't realize that his stuffed dog isn't real. He takes the dog to the park, introduces it to strangers and neighbors, and even lets it play with another dog that tries to mate with it. The underlying concept was that a real premium monitor like Samsung's always beats a fake one.

The video blew up, getting more than 2 million views. That may seem like a massive success, but what if our target expectation was 5 million? Then we failed pretty miserably. Or what if we expected only 1,000? In that case, we crushed it. In fact, as you've probably guessed, our major criteria on the project had more to do with pushing sales than getting eyeballs—the eyeballs were just a bonus. Sales did improve, but nothing like the gaudy view total would suggest. In fact, as you get into viral-crazy territory, the quality of your audience inevitably declines. You may affect your brand positively—and that's always a good thing—but your sales will not rise in lockstep with the variance in your views.

LEARNING WITH GOALS

You may not realize it, but you already employ Does it Work? goals and criteria all the time. Let's say, for example, that you want to shave five minutes off your commute time and have heard about a possible shortcut. You'll invariably use a Does it Work? process. Here's how:

GOAL. You want to reduce your current commute time.

DOES IT WORK? CRITERIA. You believe success would be achieved with a five-minute reduction in driving time.

IDEA. You think you may have found a shortcut.

TEST. You drive to work using the shortcut to find out.

RESULTS. Either you shave off some time or you don't.

LEARNINGS AND ACTION. You either start taking the shortcut every day or not.

This is an intuitive process, and a big way we learn. For example, if you want to grow a garden in your backyard, you will probably do the following. The first year, you will do a little research up front about what plants grow in your area. You may take soil samples and add some fertilizer. And you'll plant seeds and hope for success.

That year will be very unpredictable, as all your efforts will be at the beginning of any Does it Work? process. You lack information and data—you have no idea what will work and how well. But you go ahead and plant; some things thrive, and some don't. The next year, however, you'll come armed with a different understanding of the game. You'll plant the things that did well, try out analogous things, and have more solid expectations as to what will happen. In most cases, your garden will do better. From there, you will continue to use Does it Work? each season to improve it.

GOALS AND ACCOUNTABILITY

In the study we commissioned from Forrester Consulting, researchers asked whether marketers thought it would be fair to incentivize agencies based on performance. The answer split geographically. "In Western markets, accountability is more qualitative than quantitative," Forrester wrote, "and few marketers tie remuneration to market performance. Agencies are expected to deliver on project objectives, and some marketers conduct annual reviews. For some, renewing the relationship is its own measure of success. But marketers in China institute more formal contracts that link their agencies' revenue to their own, with both upside and downside potential."

The reasons Western marketers gave for their reluctance were predictable. As a marketing manager at a major US retailer put it, "There's no way to hold someone accountable in an environment that changes on a semiannual basis."

This seems overstated. There is chaos in the system, and it can be wildly unpredictable at times. But not always. And not usually. When we're optimizing a social media presence, for example, we can predict the results within a fairly close range. Similarly, we have a fairly good idea of the impact of a campaign based on a particular spend.

Are these predictions always right? No, but here's the beauty of it: even when we're wrong, we can benefit from that. We can adjust our expectations slightly based on what we've experienced, so that we get better at prediction over time.

Most marketers look at data as a reflexive tool—a way to understand their current situation. They have dashboards populated with metrics: social media outreach, Twitter impressions, mobile map search results, and so on. While such things are useful, many marketers seem afraid that numbers will tell them they're not doing their jobs well. With Does it Work?, data is nothing to be feared. Instead, you look at failed initiatives as learning opportunities. Every project enables you to understand your audience and their motivations better, even if the central learning is that you shouldn't have done the project in the first place.

Last thought: you have the biggest opportunity to make mistakes with Does it Work? when you have outsized success. With our Samsung ad, we knew we had done something great. It was a great creative idea. But we shouldn't conclude that stuffed dogs and dopey owners are always a winning formula. Instead we should look at what conditions allowed our team to come up with that great idea. After all, it's the ideas that we're looking to foster—and much of Does it Work? involves making sure you have the right elements in place to allow more magic to happen.

> **I don't run marketing like a function. I run marketing like a business. Everything we do, we need to have clear idea and accountability for why we're doing it, how we are doing it. We need to know the business outcome that we are aspiring to achieve whenever we do something.**
>
> —*Grace Ho, Managing Director, Marketing, SAP Asia Pacific Japan*

GETTING ACCOUNTABILITY RIGHT

In the beginning of this chapter, we saw how ethical problems arose when Ford set an unrealistic goal for its employees. Clearly the designers and engineers felt their jobs were in danger if they did not hit their targets.

Goals won't do you any good if they drive your best people away. They'll hurt you if they make people afraid to come up with bold ideas. That said, we also want to know if our ideas are really working or if adjustments need to be made. If a brand hires an agency and it misses reasonable targets again and again, that's a problem. Perhaps the agency is a bad fit or not as creative and idea-focused as it first appears. Or maybe it needs to modify its approach to the brand. In either case, you'll want to know.

Accountability requires balance. First, we should be brutally honest about initiatives. If something is not working, stop it and figure out why. Not every idea will be brilliant, so you must recognize failure quickly and act on it. Second, make sure your performance evaluation relies more on incentives than punishment. We think agency compensation, for example, should reflect accomplishment in some way, but refusing to pay vendors will not work long term.

> **Marketers rely heavily on their agencies to help them navigate the rapidly evolving digital marketing space. But performance evaluation has not evolved. Most marketers evaluate their agencies by a more subjective assessment of doing a good job rather than on direct business outcomes.**
>
> *—Forrester Consulting, "What CMOs Need to Make Digital Marketing Work," September 2014 (a commissioned study conducted by Forrester Consulting on behalf of POSSIBLE)*

Last, we have to recognize that digital is a chaotic world, and sometimes things don't work for reasons beyond our control. We once dropped a significant initiative on the day of a terrorist attack. It did spectacularly poorly—as it should have. If you can point to an external factor, do so. And remember that a single failure means nothing. A string of similar failures, however, may indicate an underlying problem.

BALANCING THE SHORT AND LONG TERM

As we've said, goals should have time limits, but you should be wary of relying too much on short-term goals. This is not always easy. We can measure short-term goals more accurately, and they provide a stronger indication of success. You can know you did X and got result Y. Long-term goals can be fuzzier and harder to quantify. As a result, we often find that goal-driven organizations gravitate toward the short term. This is a mistake. To see why, let's look at a business that nearly killed itself off with an extreme short-term focus.

Chicago spa/salon Blo was a bit of an oddball. Businesses in its field usually market themselves on luxury and tranquility. They talk about relaxation and regeneration in calming, organic environments. For most people, such places and their services are a treat, something you spend money on because it's worth it—and this is the typical focus of the industry's promotions.

Blo marched to a different beat. Just like a diner or a discount store, it used promotions to bring new business in the door. Its Refer a Friend program, for example, let you give one of your buddies a card worth $20 off their first visit. If your friend took advantage of it, you also got $20 off on your next visit. Men have never been great spa-goers, so Blo gave them $10 off on Tuesdays and Wednesdays. It even had an eye toward building a future customer base: students with a valid school ID received 20% off.

Blo also delivered good service. Its loyal customers proudly spread the word on social media sites such as Yelp. In particular, customers loved something called a Blo Out, a hair treatment that left them feeling like a supermodel for a few days.

Then Blo discovered Groupon. With its penchant for discounts, the daily deals site was a natural fit for the spa. Unfortunately, Groupon had a dangerous quirk at the time: it didn't allow you to limit the number of people who purchased your deal. If your deal was too good, you could sell way too many of them. A related problem was that Groupon encouraged its retailers to offer at least 50% off as a starting point. For a seasoned discounter like Blo, even that was too low. Its Groupon enabled people to pay $40 for $110 worth of services, or nearly 65% off.

Over the next few weeks, Blo sold a whopping 3,915 Groupons. That put the spa in an enormous bind. It could hardly fit, let alone serve all of those customers in a year. Either quantity or quality had to give, and in the event both apparently did. On the quantity front, Blo stopped answering its phone to ensure that it made fewer appointments. On the quality front, it apparently sped up any service to the absolute minimum time required.[2]

We can track the results via Yelp. Pre-Groupon Blo had a positive rating on the site. People loved the idea of getting good service for a little less, and the Blo-Outs were popular. Post-Groupon, customer sentiment nosedived. Regulars now saw the staff as distracted, rude, and clueless. They complained of difficulty in getting appointments, hasty service, waiting too long, and being left in chairs for hours.

Their grumbling, however, paled in comparison to that of the new Groupon customers. Those people had never had a good Blo experience and had nothing to compare it to. They seemed to revel in having discovered the very worst spa on the planet. And being Internet savvy, they let everyone know.

"Frankly, this place blows," wrote one of them, using the obvious pun. "I went here with my Groupon and got a nice dye job and then a TERRIBLE haircut. It took all of 5 minutes. This is not an exaggeration."

"I bought the groupon - like so many others - and was extremely disappointed," said another. "I could not get a hold of anyone at the salon for 5 continuous days of calling. I even set my alarm for 7 a.m.

so that I could call as soon as they opened, and yet the lines were still busy."[3]

Blo had imagined that its Groupon promotion would pull new customers in the door, some of whom would be converted into long-term ones. Instead, the service gave them a massive influx of unfriendly customers who paid little, complained loudly, and never visited the spa again. Meanwhile, it angered its existing customers and drove many of them away.*

In other words, you need to balance short-term goals with longer-term brand objectives. While you may want to kick up revenue, you don't want to do so in a way that damages your business over the long haul.

> **We have limited resources and budgets. Our biggest challenge is to work on long-term strategic plans when faced with often unplanned short-term tactics.**
>
> *—Global marketing communications manager at a large European CPG firm, as quoted in Forrester Consulting, "What CMOs Need to Make Digital Marketing Work," September 2014 (a commissioned study conducted by Forrester Consulting on behalf of POSSIBLE)*

VANITY METRICS

In creating goals, you should also be wary of something we call vanity metrics. Certain numbers are easy to get: fans, app downloads, Twitter impressions, and check-ins. If we focus on these things, we may not be helping our business. Instead, we end up with positive digital scorecards (visits to product pages are up 40%!) that don't reflect actual sales or other business metrics (then why are sales down by 15%?). We'll discuss this problem in greater detail in Chapter 6.

---

*Blo survived the disaster, but later went out of business.

HOW TO SET BUSINESS GOALS

Now that we know about good business goals, let's take a brief look at how to set them. To do so, you'll need to designate a team. In doing this, it may be helpful to have someone outside your company take part as well. People inside a company tend to know the politics, listen to certain people not others, and allow their career path to influence their thinking on goals. In such a situation, someone with no stake in the game can often prove useful.

The actual process of setting business goals consists, roughly, of four steps: research, analysis, goal setting, and adoption.

1. RESEARCH. First, you need to find data and other information to determine what is important and achievable. You then get input from all stakeholders. Typically, when we're leading goal-setting exercises, we sit down with each person one-on-one in their office (this helps eliminate groupthink). We then ask a series of questions about what that person believes the business should be trying to achieve.

2. ANALYSIS. Next comes analysis. You need to sift through the data and interviews and identify the most important challenges or opportunities facing the brand. You should not look for consensus, which can produce weak goals; find data that produces smart and actionable ones.

3. GOAL SETTING. We typically suggest setting three to five goals. If you have only a single goal, it's often too general and makes it hard for all parts of an organization to feel like they can contribute. Having too many goals is equally problematic—such organizations usually are working on so many things that they might as well have no goals at all. After that, you should identify specific metrics, called Does it Work? criteria, for evaluating progress against them. Each goal needs at least three supporting metrics, unless the goal itself is a metric.

4. ADOPTION. At this point, you need to align everyone in the organization to those goals. This is an ongoing process that never really ends, and we discuss it at length in Chapter 2.

CASE STUDY: ONE FORD

Although we used Ford's Pinto as an example of the problems with bad goals earlier in this chapter, that's ancient history. Today, the company has become one of the most successful goal-setting businesses in the world. Since 2007, it has pursued a plan called One Ford. Essentially it means merging the company's design and technology efforts to produce a single line of cars for all markets. Let's look at their goals and metrics.

ONE TEAM
- People working together as a lean, global enterprise for automotive leadership, as measured by: Customer, Employee, Dealer, Investor, Supplier, Union/Council, and Community Satisfaction

ONE PLAN
- Aggressively restructure to operate profitably at the current demand and changing model mix
- Accelerate development of new products our customers want and value
- Finance our plan and improve our balance sheet
- Work together effectively as one team

ONE GOAL
An exciting viable Ford delivering profitable growth for all[4]

We can translate this to show how it fits into a Does it Work? framework. To do so, we'll add our own imaginary criteria (Ford has not published its actual metrical targets, but they can be implied from the plan).

Goal 1
Become one global team

Does it Work? Criteria
· Work together to increase customer satisfaction scores by 20% over five years
· Raise employee satisfaction to 70% in two years
· Drive stock price and investor value 10% per year
· Increase supplier satisfaction 5% per year

Goal 2
Rally around one plan

Does it Work? Criteria
· Build cars our customers want and value with improved customer retention rates (+10% in five years)
· Restructure to achieve profitability at current demand levels even with new structure
· Decrease development time of new models by 4% every year
· Improve our balance sheet by $1 billion in assets vs. liabilities in five years, while financing the changes

Goal 3
Achieve one goal

Does it Work? Criteria
· Build an exciting, viable Ford, measured by increased social sentiment of 2% per year

· Increase brand value by 10% per year
· Grow revenue by 10% per year
· Increase ROI by 2% per year for the first five years

These goals have a number of great features.

THEY'RE SMART. We may have put in imaginary, achievable, time-bound targets (Ford kept them confidential), but it was easy to do.

THEY'RE SIMPLE. Nothing could be clearer than One Ford. It consists of a single overarching concept with a three-part plan to achieve it. At the same time, it's comprehensive, covering every aspect of the company's business. Everyone in the organization can contribute to the success.

THEY HAVE SHORT- AND LONG-TERM CRITERIA FOR SUCCESS. If you look under each goal, you'll find measurable objectives with both short- and long-term targets.

THEY ARE STILL EMOTIONAL. Numbers keep you honest, but they don't inspire. That's why One Ford is infused with plenty of emotional words such as "exciting," "working together," "want," and "value." People can strive solely to influence metrics, but they prefer to be part of something bigger. One Ford helps them feel that way.

THEY LADDER UP TO INCREASED PROFIT. We should never forget why we're in business. If your goals don't lead to a financially more successful company, they should be changed. One Ford envisions a company that increases its efficiency in order to concentrate innovation on a smaller number of models. That should lead to better cars and increased profit.

Does One Ford work? Does it ever. Since its implementation, Ford has seen its stock price roughly double—while those of competitors GM, Toyota, and Honda have remained essentially flat.[5]

DOES IT WORK FOR YOU?

At the end of every chapter, we'll set out a few questions to help you start a conversation about Does it Work? in your company. These should make it easy to see how far along you already are to Does it Work? thinking:

- Do we have short- and long-term business goals?
- Are they specific and relevant?
- Are they supported by achievable, time-bound metrics?
- Do all other activities and projects have criteria that ladder up to our business goals?
- When we undertake an activity, are we making reasonable predictions about success?
- Do we use variance, or are our goals performance targets?
- If we succeed or fail, are we able to learn from that?
- Are we incentivizing ourselves and our teams to reach our goals?
- Do we have a process to create and reevaluate goals?
- Do our team members know the Does it Work? criteria for all projects and initiatives up front, throughout the process, and upon completion?

ADDITIONAL THOUGHTS

I think when you start with something, whether it's digital or any other commercial project, it's really key to have a clear objective. What are you trying to actually achieve? Because otherwise it becomes almost impossible to understand what you need to deliver.

—**LARS MADSEN,** Business Strategy & Development Director, Canon Europe

We're all thinkers. We love to look at things different ways. Who knows who can crack the nut when they're told the ultimate goal rather than focusing on an element of that goal?

—**KIERAN HANNON,** CMO, Belkin International

You have to set a target up front. If you don't have a target, the analyst doesn't know when to declare victory.

—**AVINASH KAUSHIK,** Marketing Evangelist, Google & Market Motive, and author of *Web Analytics 2.0*

The thing about business objectives and the digital channel is that the conversation either revolves around constant optimization or around doing things that blow up in culture and go viral. The real art form is developing strategies that leverage both but that also come from understanding the real needs of the business . . . think transformational and incremental.

—**DARIN BROWN,** CEO EMEA, POSSIBLE

Most organizations fall down in not having leaders repeating and tying all conversations back to goals and objectives so that everyone and every discussion doesn't go off course.

—**SAM DECKER,** Chairman, Clearhead and Entrepreneur, Investor, and Board Member

I think the brands that are doing it right aren't creating separate social goals. They're looking at their overall corporate goals, and they're saying, "What are we trying to achieve?" And social should help feed each one of those, whether it's increased revenue or reducing costs or getting the brand out there, as far as brand awareness.

—**CHRIS KERNS,** Director of Analytics/Research, Spredfast, and author of *Trendology*

During 18 years in this business, I've seen clients shift from complaining "I don't have enough data" to "I'm drowning in data." Collecting data isn't enough; brands need to define goals and KPIs, then focus on evaluating a smaller number of more important criteria.

—**ANDREW SOLMSSEN,** Managing Director, POSSIBLE

The setting of concise business goals at the beginning of an initiative often isn't given enough time. This is really how you create your hypothesis about what you want the whole campaign to do.

—**ANDREW CONNELL,** CMO, Western Europe, Devices Business, Huawei Technologies

Having clear business goals helps me . . . push to get better value from our partners. But I also know that if I bring someone in, there's that reverse accountability. I can hold them accountable; at the same time I can also go back to our CEO and say, "Here's why we're doing this, and you can hold me accountable for it because of X, Y, and Z."

—SCOTT A. LUX, VP eCommerce & Multi Channel, Diesel

I have a card on my desk that reads, "A goal without a plan is just a wish," and I completely agree with this. I think about it all the time. Business goals are the most critical piece on our business plan. For me, it's all about measurement and how we get there. So it's very important that goals be relevant to the project, impactful to the brand, and understood by all involved. Without really thinking and debating and implementing, you're just hoping something works.

—MIKE REEDER, SVP, Brand Strategy & Insights, POSSIBLE

I feel in many cases digital marketers simply throw money at problems, because they feel like they need to be doing something. Six years ago, it was "I need a Facebook strategy." Now it's "I need a Twitter strategy." But in fact they don't really have any business goals in mind. All the other CMOs are doing it and therefore they have to do it. A good example of that was when every brand was trying to outdo each other with the number of likes that they had on Facebook, not actually understanding what the goal of a like was or what the value of a like was.

—BRIAN LESSER, Global CEO, Xaxis

At the end, you have to sit down with your team and go, "This is what we did successfully here. Here's where we learned something." You need to feed that culture of learning. You need to bring it to innovation and [bring] everything else in so that you close the loop, and the next time you try something, you've moved your organization onto the next level.

As a company we live or die by achieving goals. We do this through an annual, tried-and-tested strategy of goal setting and budgeting. This is then set in stone in the bible and distributed amongst the team. Each and every team member is given six or seven goals against which they are incentivized. I believe you can actually achieve anything within your capability with a goal. Without a goal, chances are, you will not achieve anything.

—**PAUL J. KERR,** CEO, Small Luxury Hotels of the World

Recently, I asked a client for a well-known start-up brand what he was trying to achieve by the end of the year, and his immediate response floored me: "Grow Twitter by 50K followers and Facebook by 100%." I love these types of responses, because it calls the insatiable curiosity in all of us to keep asking the question, "Why?" and continue to ask until you find the answer.

—**JUSTIN MARSHALL,** Business Development Director, Americas, POSSIBLE

Sometimes people ask, "What if your business goals are actually driving you in the wrong direction?" Sure, that can happen. But the important thing is that you have an organization that knows how to work in a direction. You can always change that direction if you need to. But if you don't know how to work towards a goal, you'll never be able to respond decisively when disruptive change comes.

—**JOE SHEPTER,** Freelance Marketing/Advertising Writer and Strategic Consultant

02
A COLLECTIVE VISION

● POSSIBLE.com/principle2

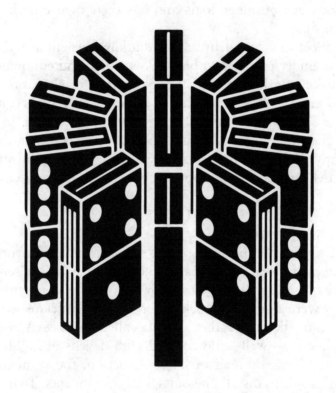

INTRODUCTION

If you've ever set a goal for fitness, you know how hard it can be to stay with it and keep it top of mind. Businesses are no different from people in this respect. We may have fun creating goals, but not so much fun getting everyone working toward them. That's why we have to build a collective vision. We have to make sure everyone understands our business goals and has their own criteria for supporting them.

A collective vision delivers an additional benefit as well. Today, brands are under pressure to break down silos and eliminate bottlenecks between marketing and other parts of an organization (or even within different parts of a marketing group). Getting everyone on the same page can help you take a big step in this direction. In the first place, it gives everyone a starting point for any conversation. More importantly, it can unlock creativity across your organization and help you deliver a consistent, positive experience for your customers.

A SILO FAIL

We often say marketing isn't rocket science, but our favorite story about alignment deals with real rocket scientists and a screwup so massive that it dwarfed the yearly revenue of many companies.

They were a group of Lockheed Martin technicians working on a $233 million–dollar weather satellite called the NOAA N-Prime. It was a tall, shiny—well—silo covered with dozens of highly delicate instruments. Near the end of its construction, the team needed to turn it on its side to install one of its final components. To do so, they slid a special turnover cart under it and bolted it to an adapter plate. Unfortunately, they failed to notice that the adapter plate itself was not bolted to anything. When they started to turn the satellite over, it slid off like a wayward birthday cake and smashed to the floor. Luckily, no one was hurt. Except the American taxpayer. The damage to her wallet topped $100 million.

"We're screwed."

Because of this, the US government conducted an investigation. Its final report totaled 113 pages, but its findings were exactly what you'd expect. The people who were working on the satellite and those who maintained the turnover carts were on completely different pages. The maintenance people thought that the plate was not part of the cart and had removed its 24 bolts for storage. The technicians thought it *was* and never bothered to check to see if it was properly attached. In other words, they shared a tiny but vital touchpoint, and they never talked to one another about it.[1]

This may be the simplest and most costly example of misalignment you'll find. Not all companies pay such a steep price for a lack of communication, but misaligned organizations are common these days and always have been. They live in silos, lack agreed-upon goals, fail to communicate, and work at cross purposes. A collective vision is the answer.

> **I say that my team is my creative agency, because for me, the creative agency is all part of the marketing team in the Coca-Cola company.**
>
> —*Guido Rosales, Europe Group Integrated Marketing Director, The Coca-Cola Company*

A COLLECTIVE VISION 101

The first step in getting on the same page is to publish and share your goals. Unfortunately, that's also many organizations' last step. Goals are easily forgotten in the day-to-day grind of getting work done. They need constant reinforcement and incentives to be successful.

To do this, you should first set additional Does it Work? criteria for every group and every initiative. These criteria should always ladder up to at least one business goal. Naturally, not every group, department, or project you undertake will contribute to your goals in the same way. A packaging company may set a target for improving worker safety, but the finance department probably won't help with that, outside of signing off on tools and training. It will be able to support other goals, however.

The good news is that while many companies find overall goal setting a challenge, teams usually find it easy to figure out how their activities can support business goals. So what are we talking about?

SETTING GROUP AND ORGANIZATIONAL CRITERIA

Each department and group in your business should set its own criteria for what it is trying to achieve. For example, in the last chapter, we looked at how Ford set overarching goals and success metrics for its business. One of them involved maintaining profits while investing in change. Here's how different parts of the business might contribute to it:

> **SALES.** This team will want to increase sales and decrease the cost of sales for their organization.

> **DIGITAL MARKETERS.** This group will again want to hold the line on expenses, while increasing the social conversation and driving sales.

FINANCE. This group should seek to balance funding in a way that maximizes ROI, while looking for smart ways to save money.

HUMAN RESOURCES. They need to attract and retain top-quality talent—while keeping within budgets.

ESTABLISH CRITERIA FOR EVERY ACTIVITY

Next, we move down in scale to projects and other smaller activities. Here, we'd advise setting criteria for pretty much everything. To see why, let's look at the biggest necessary evil in business: meetings. Most meeting planners rely on blocked-off time slots, where everyone goes into a room with an agenda of things to discuss. They think a meeting is successful if they get through all the items on the list. Such meetings tend to drag on until their time frame is complete, wasting time that could be better spent elsewhere. Or they end up with the participants only getting through part of the agenda.

Does it Work? meetings are different. Instead of an agenda, we have outcomes we wish to achieve. We don't say that we will "brainstorm on possible approaches." Instead we say, "We leave with three viable approaches." We don't "update everyone on status." We ensure that "everyone understands where the parts of the project stand and what the next steps are." These may seem like trivial distinctions, but they provide you with focus and a clear endpoint. That pushes the pace and ensures you don't spend too much time discussing any one thing. And once you get to your objectives, everyone can get up and leave (or talk about football).

We'd advise using this model for every major activity. At our agency, for example, we use Does it Work? criteria for all of the following:

· Intake briefs
· RFPs

- All projects
- All internal meetings
- All client meetings and presentations
- Quarterly account reviews
- Team/employee onboarding
- Reviews and promotions
- Prioritization of initiatives
- Ongoing success measurement
- Case study creation and storytelling
- PCN (project change notices) discussions
- Prioritization
- Cross-office collaboration
- Handoffs across craft teams
- Initiative launch reports
- Postlaunch recommendations

ACTIVELY USE GOALS AND CRITERIA

We also advise bringing up the overall business goals and criteria in active situations. They should be mentioned at the start of presentations and serve as a touchpoint with any activity. They should come to life in conversations and feedback. In meetings, for example, we start by repeating our business goals and criteria and saying how the meeting fits into them. If you can't easily explain why you're having a meeting, you shouldn't be having it.

ALIGN OUTSIDE YOUR COMPANY

The Forrester study we commissioned to help us with this book revealed that agencies "remain a critical partner for marketing leaders. But in a world where CMOs are increasingly expected to deliver revenue results, most of these marketing leaders—particularly in the US and Europe—are reluctant to hold their agencies equally answerable."[2] As we've mentioned before, it went on to point out that Chinese companies tend to hold their agency partners to a much higher standard, tying compensation to performance.

We think they're ahead of the game. Too often in Europe and North America, success means completion, not achievement. The former should be a given, the latter the goal. While agencies can be hired guns who perform a task, they're more effective when they're part of a team and are able to bring their expertise to bear on the underlying problem, not just the solution.

Unfortunately, we hamstring them when they don't understand the desired outcome. If they know that, they may come up with creative ideas that will work better. They may be able to innovate with new solutions rather than executing existing ideas. They can never innovate, however, if they don't know what they're trying to achieve.

Besides, left to their own devices, many agencies and other vendors revert to their own goals, such as winning peer recognition. Awards are great, but not all award-winning projects work and make a meaningful difference for brands. We saw this with *Dumb Ways to Die*. The agency created the perfect piece of content for its purposes, but it may not have made a dent in the more mundane objectives of its client.

INCENTIVIZE PEOPLE TO PERFORM

Want people to help you achieve your goals? Give them a reason. Incentives are a great way to keep your goals and criteria top of mind for employees, managers, and agency partners alike. You can also use your criteria in reviews or as an evaluation tool for promotions.

ASK "DOES IT WORK?"

Of course, whenever we set criteria, we continually ask the following:

- Will it work?
- Is it working?
- Did it work?
- Why did it work?

You should ask these questions whenever a campaign launches, on an ongoing basis, after a meeting, during a performance review, and so on. Then use the answers to learn and improve.

> **The thing about alignment is of course all about good communication, and really clear communication. I think it really boils down to being clear, concise, and actually quite simple about what it is you're trying to achieve. If you can't explain what you're trying to achieve in a 30-second elevator pitch, or even less, then it becomes really difficult to get people aligned around it.**
>
> —*Lars Madsen, Business Strategy & Development Director, Canon Europe*

SILOS AND ALIGNMENT

Let's assume you're perfectly internally aligned. You have a complete collective vision: strong goals and criteria perfectly tailored to everyone's role in the organization. At every meeting you have success criteria, and every project ladders up to larger objectives. So what could go wrong? Just about everything. The reason? Silos. Let's see how that can happen.

Imagine you have a company that mows lawns. You set three overall goals for your people: cut grass, take away the clippings, and be completely attentive to customer needs. You align all your various departments to understand these goals. They come up with their own criteria that ladder up to them, and everyone goes off and does their thing.

Six months later, you conduct a survey of what your new customers think—and find that they hate you. "What happened?" you ask your senior managers. "We've had meetings about this. We've taped a 'Be nice' sign to the underside of everyone's baseball cap. What gives?"

Luckily, you call up an agency that understands how to break down silos. They analyze your communications and quickly pinpoint the problem. Whenever you get a new customer, you smother them. Multiple parts of your organization, all intent on being completely attentive, start triggering communications. The first is an assessment team that you dispatch to the customer's house to determine its cutting needs. The second is a maintenance team that actually does the lawn cutting. Then, a week after service starts, a customer relations team sends a welcome packet, calls up to find out how things are going, and finishes everything off with an automated survey. Each one also piles on the e-mails and text messages to ensure that they are being completely attentive to customer needs.

About halfway through this bombardment, your client has received so much well-meaning attention that she's sick of you and wondering why she didn't just hire the freckle-faced kid with the push-mower down the street. Each of your teams knows nothing about what the others are doing, and as a result you're ruining any chance at repeat business.

This is not a theoretical problem. We once worked with an international telecom company that offered everything from TV to Internet to cell phone service, all in an array of different packages depending on customers' needs. They were spending a lot of money on customer service, especially on calls to new customers. We analyzed their communications to find ways they could teach customers how to resolve basic issues on their own.

What we found was surprising. They were already sending out plenty of communications that did that very thing. The instructions were clear, and we could not really improve on them. The problem was that so many different groups were sending these communications out, and customers were receiving so many e-mails from the company that they stopped reading them.

This happened because their different business units had no idea what the others were doing. They all were trying to help, but their tasks overlapped to the point that if customers picked exactly the right services and installation options, they might receive 100 communications in the course of two weeks. Clearly, those silos needed to come down, and the messaging needed to be more focused.

The flip side of this happens when one group assumes the other group is communicating and it's not. An example would be when a customer asks a question on social media. The social media team refers it to customer service. But the customer service representatives don't think they should do anything in social, because they don't see it as their responsibility. So the question goes unanswered, and the customer becomes angry. Instead, the two teams need to come together and work out a better process.

> **We definitely share common goals with colleagues in other departments. Our ultimate goal is to expand and strengthen our corporation. The goals of the corporation are closely related to the goals of each employee.**
>
> —*Marketing director at a Chinese high-tech firm, as quoted in Forrester Consulting, "What CMOs Need to Make Digital Marketing Work," September 2014 (a commissioned study conducted by Forrester Consulting on behalf of POSSIBLE)*

RECOGNIZING THE PROBLEM

Companies have always had these problems, but they've become much more acute in recent years. Almost every week we read of some meltdown in communications from a major company (see sidebar on page 61 for some of brands' greatest Twitter hits). Here's why:

FRAGMENTATION. We communicate today on a much greater number of platforms, which allows us to target our audiences more precisely. Sometimes that's great. But it also means that you have more people talking to a much more dispersed audience. You need to make sure they are all on the same page.

TRANSPARENCY. Digital has turned nearly every business unit into a customer-facing part of your company. Whenever an engineer writes a blog or a salesperson gets rude with a customer, it can go viral. Almost everyone has become a potential company spokesperson. They can make you look great, or foolish.

BRAND AS CONTENT PRODUCER. Many companies use their own digital properties or other platforms to reach their customers. Again, this produces more avenues for content, which in turn means you have more places where employees can go off the reservation. Brands need to have a filter for ensuring this content stays within guidelines.

TWO-WAY CONVERSATIONS. Through social media and on third-party sites, brands now engage in conversations with customers on a regular basis. These conversations often involve nontraditional players in the communications game, such as engineers and product developers. That makes them de facto marketers and forces brands to look at their activities as well.

UNCONTROLLED MESSAGES. We no longer have the same control over our brand conversation we once did. Other people can shape perceptions of us, and we have to respond the best we can.

> There are so many people involved in a campaign these days. Alignment is all about keeping it simple. It's important to have one rallying cry behind the campaign, whatever it's all about. You must have a specific vision of how you're going to measure success so you can all be aligned with that vision.
>
> —*Denise Karkos, CMO, TD Ameritrade*

A COLLECTIVE VISION UNLOCKS CREATIVITY

A further and more important digital challenge comes with creativity. In the old days, of course, advertisers often followed a traditional model where most—if not all—creative ideas came from teams composed of a single copywriter and art director. This has never really been the case in successful digital agencies. As technology has advanced, we've learned that creativity can come from anywhere. Your technologist might know a new way to wow your audience. An intern might have seen something cool at a club that would work great in a different context. A data analyst might notice an emerging trend that points to a different solution. This might not happen every day, but we want to capture imagination and ideas from anywhere they are.

Twitter nightmares

If you're not convinced of the problems faced by brands in an environment in which everyone can be a spokesperson, look no further than Twitter. It just may be the most dangerous social media platform out there because the people who tweet for brands also tweet for themselves. And they sometimes tweet without thinking. For examples of how it can go wrong, check out the following:

CHRYSLER. A contract employee, thinking he was on his own account, tweeted: "I find it ironic that Detroit is known as #motorcity and yet no one here knows how to f**king† drive."[3]

KENNETH COLE. Responding to the Egyptian riots in Tahrir Square: "Millions are in uproar in #Cairo. Rumor is they heard our new collection is available online . . ." Thousands of people took the brand to task for its tastelessness on social media.

KENNETH COLE, PART TWO. Apparently Ken did not get the memo on not making lighthearted comments on serious news events in the Middle East. During the Syrian crisis, when many believed the West might attack, Cole returned to the fray with this tone-deaf tweet: "'Boots on the ground' or not, let's not forget about sandals, pumps and loafers #footware."

THE AMERICAN RED CROSS. Apparently no one parties like the Red Cross. One of their employees mistook the organization's account for a personal one and tweeted, "Ryan found 2 more 4 bottle packs of Dogfish Head's Midas Touch Beer . . . when we drink we do it right #gettngslizzerd"

---

† This and all subsequent uses of this word changed per publisher policy. In reality, the brands were much naughtier.

NOT THE AMERICAN RED CROSS. Luckily, the organization came back with one of the best replies ever. "We've deleted the rogue tweet but rest assured the Red Cross is sober and we've confiscated the keys." Dogfish Head then used the hashtag to encourage donations to the Red Cross. Here's to #gettngslizerd.

NOKIA NEW ZEALAND. Some brands keep it simple. "F**k you," Nokia New Zealand tweeted one day to no one in particular.

THE STRAITS TIMES. Same theme, slightly elaborated: "omg. f**k you all. seriously."

STUBHUB. This brand offered its own unique take on TGIF: "Thank f**k it's Friday. I can't wait to get out of this stubsucking hellhole." Next time, tell us what you really think about your company's culture.

TESCO. During a scandal in which the supermarket was found to be selling horsemeat as ground beef, it tweeted, "It's sleepy time so we're off to hit the hay! See you at 8 a.m. for more #TescoTweets."

SUSAN BOYLE'S PR FIRM. It's always important look at your hashtag as a 16-year-old boy might. In order to promote an album release party, they created the hashtag #susanalbumparty. Read it a few times and channel your inner teenager. You'll get it.

The bottom line? Too many brands assign careless and clueless employees to tweet. You need make sure your social team has solid people who will not mix personal and business accounts. Beyond that, avoid sensitive topics. People may love your brand, but that doesn't mean they want to hear your opinion on the latest upheavals in the Middle East.

ALIGNING MARKETING

In the beginning of this chapter, we looked at a simple communication failure at Lockheed Martin. Two different groups were working on the same project, but they weren't talking together. They shared the same touchpoint but needed to get on the same page.

Marketing is similar. To make everything work, we need to build a unified view of our company's communication activities and then exploit the opportunities we find. While we have no magic bullet for doing this in every organization, here are a few of the tools you can use to overcome the problems:

TOUCHPOINT MAPS. These show all the places where a brand interacts with its consumers and evaluates the current state and potential opportunities/future state for each channel. You can use them for communications or just about any activity where the interests of two different parts of your company intersect.

MINDSET AND MOMENTS OF INFLUENCE. These are places on a touchpoint map where a brand has an opportunity to improve or enhance the customer experience or influence customer actions.

CONSUMER ACTION MAPS. This is a forward-looking document that models the future, or how your entire organization can improve the customer experience over time.

MESSAGING HIERARCHIES. This is a separate document that indicates the major points a brand wishes to communicate about its products and services. Some brands may find this less useful than others. Consumer brands will often find that their ability to control the conversation is so limited that it's best to simply be transparent and let their customers do the talking. However, brands with new, innovative, or more complex products and services can use these tools to speak with a single voice.

If we have a consistent view of who the customer is, we have a lot more stakeholders in the process. That way, you can act is an organism rather than an organization. If we can come to the table and say, "We have a common view of the customer," it overcomes the issue of addressing a problem from within our own departments or self-imposed silos. If we can bring multiple lenses with shared goals, that's where all the innovation comes. Then you have a rapid creation of teams that are *not* bound by an organizational structure.

—*McGregor Agan, Director of Marketing Corporate Affairs Group, Intel Corporation*

TOUCHPOINT MAPPING

If you're going anywhere as a brand, it's good to have a map. Touchpoint maps list out all the places where your brand interacts with a customer. Needless to say, for some brands that can be a lot of places. That's why it's often better to have multiple maps covering different areas of a customer's experience. For example, you might have a touchpoint map covering mobile, location-based services or one looking at your in-store experience. The key is to get the touchpoints down and get the people who share them to start talking.

The advantages of these maps are clear:

· They allow us to see at a glance how a customer experiences our brand.

· They get people out of their own siloed viewpoints to see the role they're playing in a broader experience.

· They allow different silos to understand where they share touchpoints and where opportunities for them might lie in communications they don't own.

· They help eliminate duplicate efforts.

Touchpoint mapping is also one of the more eye-opening things we can do as marketers. The reason is that to create them, we often have to be customers. Anytime we create a touchpoint map for a client, for example, we put on our trench coats and fedoras and go into full detective mode. We become customers. Or you could say we become investigators in search of understanding what it's like to be a customer.

We sign up for their services, we ask questions, and we try out their products. We also construct personas for different types of customers and see how they interact differently with the brand. We see if a website knows if we've been there before or if it even knows we're a customer. We make up problems, we contact customer service, we try to answer questions from a support website, and we use their chat services if they have them. We also do traditional analysis and customer interviews to understand the mindset of people experiencing the brand.

We then pour all of this information into our touchpoint map, a color-coded spreadsheet that lists out every touchpoint and what happens there. Typically it contains:

- **TOUCHPOINTS.** We list all customer touchpoints for the brand or service.
- **CURRENT EFFECTIVENESS.** We rate the current effectiveness of each touchpoint by measuring brand awareness, consideration, conversion, and advocacy—and the level of opportunity we have for each one.
- **MINDSET.** We establish the customer's mindset at the time.
- **MOMENTS OF INFLUENCE.** We determine whether this is a place where we can make an impact and how.
- **MARKETING ACTIONS.** We suggest a particular marketing action (it could be as simple as displaying an ad or adding a sentence).
- **MESSAGING CONTENT.** We specify what message that action should contain.

Let's look at some of these in more detail.

MINDSET AND MOMENTS
OF INFLUENCE

In 2002, the British bank HSBC overlaid Heathrow airport with a campaign called Heathrow Domination. The goal was to make it impossible for travelers not to notice the brand. To do so, HSBC stuck its branding and logo on hallways, walls, escalators, gates, jetways—just about anything.

It was great. Imagine walking down an HSBC-branded jetway and seeing an HSBC-branded garbage can, and you get the point. However, you can go too far, and the rest of the industry did. Over the next five years, copycat banks put their logos on everything: elevators, escalators, floors, exterior building walls, bridge overpasses, city buses, and even bathrooms. By 2007 it was hard to find a single item that had not been emblazoned with a bank logo.

The predictable followed. The trend was ridiculed. Parody sites emerged. Branding experts demurred. So did it work? For HSBC, probably yes. Overall, not really. The problem was relevancy. No one naturally connects elevator doors or stairwells with banks. Few people will remember the ad, and still fewer will act.

To get around this, we needed to add something to our touchpoint map: mindset and moments of influence. In other words, we don't just list out the touchpoints, we evaluate them to see if they are also places where a brand has an opportunity to make progress on its goals.

How do we do this?

1. SPECIFY CUSTOMER MINDSET AND ACTIVITIES.
You'll want to figure out what a customer is thinking at different moments in the journey. For example, a customer in a hotel has many different mindsets. When she is checking in, she is often engaged with the clerk and open to a positive brand experience. When she's calling the complaint hotline about a clogged bathtub, you should probably just send over a plumber.

2. ASSIGN MARKETING ACTIONS. Once you establish mindset, you have be smart about what to do at every touchpoint. For example, we found that it's a good idea for digital storefronts to offer first-time visitors free shipping. The reason may be that they're shopping around, and if you can give them a better deal, you'll win the sale.

3. SUGGEST MESSAGES OR STORIES. As we've said above, the final column of your spreadsheet should tell a story that will affect the customer positively at that point in the journey.

4. DON'T FORGET PERSONAS. Not all your customers are the same. You may find it necessary to split up your spreadsheet and provide different experiences for different kinds of customers.

Personas

When we're trying to understand the experience of a customer, it's important that we see it through their eyes. But, of course, not all customers experience products and services the same. Instead, they fall into different categories, or what marketers call segments. A segment is simply a subset of your customers who respond to your marketing in a similar way.

Typically, you can isolate segments using surveys or other data. For example, you may know that 40% of your audience are moms with young children, or 20% of them are male golfers. And you may know some of their traits. 65% of the moms are on Facebook more than once a day. Or 90% of the male golfers have downloaded apps to their smartphones.*

*For more on segments, please see Chapter 9, "One Size Fits No One."

The problem is that it's hard to leap from data like this to a more emotional quality like mindset. Numbers are simply too abstract to help you understand motivation.

That's why you need a persona. A persona is a fictional character that represents a significant segment of your audience. Traditionally, personas have been a single page with a picture and a list of characteristics. While this is better than nothing, it's far better if they're much more alive. You should know them by their voice, their fears, their hopes, how they use your product, how they use it with friends, and how their use changes over the course of the day.

Let's take a look at a simple persona that brings to life a male customer segment for an upscale activewear company.

REZA

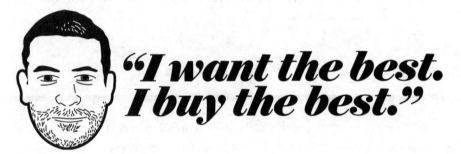

"I want the best. I buy the best."

AGE: 42

INCOME: $250K +

JOB: Entrepreneur

FAMILY: Married to Marie Anne; two kids—Jamie, 8; Samir, 10

CLOTHING HABITS: Needs to have the best clothes and gear, regardless of cost

INFLUENCER: Yes, has an influential blog; talks frequently at conferences, where he likes to wear sporty (nonbusiness) attire.

STORY: Reza came to the United States for college and stayed because he loves building things. Since then, he's been a serial entrepreneur, creating small companies that develop niche technologies that he then sells to larger companies. Married with two kids, he is perpetually in motion, getting more done in one day than most people do in six. But ten times a year, he hops on a plane, flies his family first class to a major resort, and skis for several days straight. While he's a mediocre skier at best (and has no illusions about his athletic prowess), he likes to have the latest and best stuff, including wearable technology. He'll haunt blogs and industry pubs to find the latest information on performance clothing, so brand is not as important as specs. An impulsive shopper, he'll buy on his phone, on his tablet, and in store.

When he's not skiing, Reza stays active. He has a mountain bike and takes a few trips to Hawaii each year. Though surfing is outside his skill set, he's trying to learn. Other than that, he spends a lot of time hanging with the wife and kids. They endure his grilling but love when he's around, because his enthusiasm is always infectious.

From here, we would normally outline a number of scenarios that showed how Reza interacts with the world, shops for clothes, uses devices to buy things, and so on. Usually when we do this, we allow Reza to tell us in his own terms. We let him speak with his voice. For example, let's say our data shows this segment cares about social justice, dislikes salespeople, and prefers online shopping. You can thread that all together this way:

> *You know what I don't like? Shopping in person. It takes too much time, and I don't have time. Just send me something over the Net, and if it doesn't look cool I'll send it back. Actually, I usually just keep it, which drives my wife crazy because there's all this stuff piling up in the closet. We donate it all eventually, but in the meantime, it's a mess."*

This type of persona has a number of advantages over a typical one:

RICHNESS. We relate to people only if they seem real. You shouldn't know them by characteristics; you should know them by who they are.

RELATABILITY. You have what their vulnerabilities are. A persona is not a Facebook page offering a rose-colored view of one's life. It's a realistic person whose characteristics reflect but do not slavishly repeat segmentation data. There are very few people in Reza's segment with his particular background. You should be very careful to avoid stereotypes, especially around moms.

PEOPLE IN ACTION. If you tell a story about a persona, the people it represents become much more relatable. By seeing personas in action, you'll understand the segment better, which helps ensure that the enhanced experiences you'll provide will resonate with your audience.

VOICE. You should let personas talk in their own words. That will differentiate them from a generic segment.

When you're making personas, make them real. That way everyone on your team will get a much better feel for them faster than they ever would with raw data alone.

CONSUMER-ACTION MAPPING

Touchpoint maps are great at telling you where you are. But you also want everyone to know where your brands and products should be in the future. That requires a different tool: a consumer-action map. Its purpose is give everyone a collective vision on what comes next.

The consumer-action map shows the experiences your customers will have in the future—and hopefully how those experiences will make them feel. These maps are much more emotional in nature than touchpoint maps. They describe desired outcomes, rather than specific stories told or actions taken. As a result, they don't look much like touchpoint maps. While each one is different, most resemble a flowchart that indicates how a specific experience is supposed to make people feel. Let's see why, using a simple example.

You have a candy company. You want to institute a revolutionary loyalty program for your customers. It will link the fun they have eating candy to other kinds of fun. Because candy has an unhealthy reputation, and that's a barrier to sales, you decide to make those activities healthy. Gain enough points and you get a free one-day gym pass. Or a downloadable fitness app. Or a coupon at a sports store.

The problem is, you don't know exactly what those activities will be. You haven't partnered with a fitness store or a gym. You haven't decided to create an app or work with an app maker. So do you stop? No, instead you make up a story for each experience. Maybe you say it's a gym pass or a coupon for a health food store. It doesn't really matter. What matters is how the experience should affect people. That way, even if you can't create a particular promotion or experience, you know that you want to make one that has the same outcome. That gives you a map moving forward to help your people create experiences people love.

The process for making a customer action map is long but really boils down to a few key steps:

RESEARCH. To the degree you can, gather all the relevant data and third-party reports that relate to your industry and your opportunities.

SPECIFY MARKETING AND BUSINESS OBJECTIVES. In other words, set your Does it Work? criteria. What do you want to achieve from the outcome of your three-to-five-year vision?

OUTLINE STRATEGY. Lay out the vision for success.

ALIGN RESOURCES. Determine which resources you'll need and what silos will have to start talking with each other to make this happen.

CREATE A MAP. Usually the map looks like a flow-chart—a series of interconnected experiences that show key moments of influence, the emotional reactions people have. You can also trace likely customer paths through them.

Last point: the consumer action map takes some work to create, but it's a very powerful and useful tool. It's great to provide an organization with clear goals and criteria around them. It's even better to map an organization's activities so that everyone understands holistically how different silos are interacting with people. But the most interesting and important challenge of all is to create a collective vision that enables the organization to create a better future experience for its customers.

MESSAGING HIERARCHIES

Let's take a slight detour and discuss more complicated products and services for a moment. You only need great ideas to sell doughnuts, but some people sell jet aircraft. That often takes something else.

It's natural to look at products through a "narrative" viewpoint, to talk about them through stories and use cases rather than looking at them from a holistic standpoint. If you've developed a new kind of frying pan, you'll often talk about the kinds of things it's good for (frying an egg, because you fry eggs a lot) rather than the overall benefit of the product (nonstick capabilities that give customers the freedom to cook the foods they like more easily).

With simple products, this isn't usually a problem. Much of the conversation around your brand will be driven by people in the marketplace, and having a coherent story may not count for much. But for new and innovative products and those with complex capabilities, good old communication still matters. So you'll need to make sure everyone in your organization understands the product story. What is the product, what does it do, and how does this help people? For this, you need a different tool, and one that's been around a long time: a messaging hierarchy.

This document organizes a brand's thinking around a product— or multiple products. It gives everyone a collective vision of how to explain the different features and benefits of a product. Let's take a look at a simple hierarchy for a product that allows you to control a garage door with your smart watch. It has a number of features that make it attractive: security, the ability to turn on a light, the ability to check whether it's open or closed from anywhere, and so on. The hierarchy organizes all these advantages into a single, coordinated view that everyone in your company can understand.

VALUE PROPOSITION	WristDoor gives you peace of mind knowing you have full control over a key entry point to your home, wherever you are.		
KEY BENEFITS/ REASONS TO BELIEVE	Securely control your door	Access from anywhere	Simplify your life
FEATURES THAT SUPPORT BENEFITS	Encrypted, hack-proof radio communication channel. Ability to check and make sure you never leave your garage door open again. Remote light feature lets you see if anyone is hiding in your garage before you enter.	View & operate your garage door from anywhere. Secure, convenient web and mobile apps. Open before you get home. Close from your bedroom using long-range remote.	The door can be set to raise automatically when you are within four feet of it. The product's API plugs into existing home automation systems for a single point of control for your entire home.

A good messaging hierarchy gives you an almost at-a-glance overview of what you want to say about the product. Here are the different parts.

VALUE PROPOSITION. This is a single statement that gives the key consumer takeaway about your product or service.

KEY BENEFITS. This section breaks down the main reasons a customer might like your product. It's very important to remember that we're focusing on the customer here. So while you may be including a raft of features to demonstrate your brand's innovative spirit, your customer only cares about what the product can do.

FEATURES. These are the nuts and bolts of your product or the reasons to believe in the topline benefits.

You should never look at a hierarchy as a rigid script, but a story you tell to explain a product. Obviously contexts vary, and your people should adapt that story to them. Even so, the hierarchy at least gives everyone an understanding of how they should be discussing a product.

Not surprisingly, messaging hierarchies can take weeks or more to develop. These exercises often produce surprising results, not least because they make it impossible for marketers to hide from the deficiencies of a product. But in the end, they are great tools for helping everyone understand what they should be saying and why. Even if your customers always have the ability to take the discussion in a different direction.

DOES IT WORK FOR YOU?

Businesses without a collective vision simply don't work. To find out if yours is good, bad, or on the road to recovery, ask yourself these questions.

· Does our organization make its goals clear?
· Is it clear how groups within our organization should support those goals?
· Do we have success criteria for projects that ladder up to our larger goals?
· Do we know why we're doing the things we're doing?
· How bad is the silo problem in our company?
· Do we have any tools for breaking down silos?
· Would touchpoint maps and similar tools work for our organization?
· Are people from across our organization and agency partners focusing on goals that ladder up to our consistent overall business goals?
· How do we, as an organization, plan for the future?

ADDITIONAL THOUGHTS

Most marketers work toward the same set of high-level company revenue goals as their peers, and some are incented by formal bonus structures tied to annual performance reviews. But for many CMOs, individual contribution to these results is loosely measured, especially in the US and Europe.

—FORRESTER CONSULTING, "What CMOs Need to Make Digital Marketing Work," September 2014 (a commissioned study conducted by Forrester Consulting on behalf of POSSIBLE)

When your collective vision isn't about driving total brand growth, you can have different factions that are focused on great initiative success, and you can have a great initiative that can be very successful, but you lose so much out of the base that the net for the brand is no good.

—PHYLLIS JACKSON, VP, North America, Consumer & Market Knowledge, P&G

There's a real aversion to accepting responsibility for things that are outside of our control. But in upper management, there should never be just one person taking responsibility until they feel like they've passed the baton on to the next person, because where that pass happens is where all the trouble and misinterpretations exist.

—JOSH JAMES, Founder & CEO, Domo

One of the things I learned at Dell when I implemented their customer centric strategy was that alignment of the groups alone could drive that. If one group was way out ahead in their policy or capabilities, and another wasn't, you created dissonance for the customer."

—SAM DECKER, Chairman, Clearhead and Entrepreneur, Investor, and Board Member

There's a difference between a collective vision and integrated campaigns. Too often we judge an integrated campaign on its ability to provide matching luggage for each channel. A shared vision or collective vision allows brands to have a North Star—that's important. But each partner agency needs to bring their specialized skills set to the work with all their strength. This allows them to interpret the overall vision into the channel they know best.

—DANIELLE TRIVISONNO HAWLEY, CCO, Americas, POSSIBLE

Ads are like riding a tandem bike: if you're not doing it together, it's a more difficult effort. Even though I'm putting all the effort in up front, you could be hitting the breaks in the back. Or you could be leaning the wrong way when you're trying to make a turn. Who knows? The point is that it's hard for everybody. At the end of the day, there's so much advertising in the marketplace. There are 2,600 different ads someone sees on a daily basis. You have to be working together to break through.

—KIERAN HANNON, CMO, Belkin International

Alignment is a critical component to a shared organizational vision. When the client's efforts are aligned internally and externally, at a practical level we gain efficiencies, but at a strategic level we gain clarity and momentum. It is at this level we begin to see emergent opportunities and position the organization for the greatest chance of success.

—ANDERS ROSENQUIST, PhD, Director of Emerging Media, Strategist, POSSIBLE

Our approach—because we have so many third parties involved—is that we need them to be aligned with us. We can't have 30 different cultures and 30 different ways of working for our 30 suppliers that are involved in our customer channel business. We need them to work in a way that fits in with us, rather than the other way around.

—**CHRIS SCOGGINS,** CEO, National Rail Enquiries

In absence of having a holistic strategy, we found we were competing for the same customer with the same product across our distribution channels.

—**SCOTT A. LUX,** VP eCommerce & Multi Channel, Diesel

Clients that arm us with a thorough understanding of their short- and long-term business goals as well as challenges and vulnerabilities allow us to do our best work. With clear goals that we can measure and optimize against, we can evaluate our creative objectively and pivot when needed. Our strongest partnerships are with clients that have a healthy respect for both qualitative and quantitative data in addition to moving creative.

—**LIZ VALENTINE,** Cofounder & CEO, Swift (a POSSIBLE agency)

The problem is that so many organizations are so siloed in their structure that, when initiatives are cascaded down, the business objectives become disconnected from the real business needs. Goals get set that don't truly deliver real business value. A shared vision is one that aligns everyone around the ultimate business objectives—internal stakeholders, agencies, and everyone else.

—**DARIN BROWN,** CEO EMEA, POSSIBLE

When people on your team are trying to drive alignment, you need [to have] the right goals and [to] ensure that people are spending most of their energy on executing those things.

—**MIKE FRIDGEN,** President & CEO, Decide.com (acquired by eBay)

Some of the greatest leaders I've ever worked with were able to align multiple teams by doing one thing: clarifying the win. They defined the vision—the score on the scoreboard (grow revenues by 20%, eliminate all cases of malaria, pay off our debt, etc.)—with ultimate simplicity, allowing the team to know when they can look at each other and say, "We won!"

—**JUSTIN MARSHALL,** Business Development Director, Americas,
  POSSIBLE

How important is it to have everyone aligned? If you have the right strategy and a team that's aligned, you're guaranteed to win. If you have a questionable strategy and yet a team that's aligned, you still have a shot. If you have the right strategy and a team that's misaligned, you're guaranteed to fail.

—**ALI BEHNAM,** Cofounder, Tealium Inc.

True alignment is poetry in motion; a hot knife cutting through digital butter. An organized, prioritized, focused, and aligned team will be two to three times more digitally effective with less effort than a bunch of well-funded, talented busy fools.

—**JUSTIN COOKE,** CEO, UK, POSSIBLE

03
DATA
INSPIRES
CREATIVITY

POSSIBLE.com/principle3

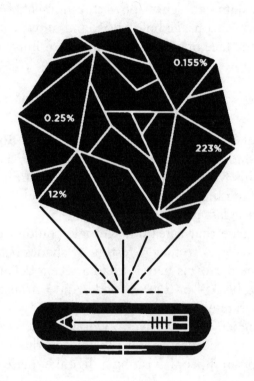

INTRODUCTION

Creative people have often cringed at data, and sometimes they have every right. Historically, marketers have used data primarily to test and verify projects, which does little more than stifle creative ideas. On the other hand, we're not huge fans of appointing all-powerful creative directors who work purely on their own intuition. Instead, we believe that data can deliver powerful moments of truth that can inspire creativity, encourage bold ideas, and allow you to hang on to your vision in the face of subjective opposition. But you have to learn how to use it right.

THE THREAT OF DATA

In 2009, Google's first visual design lead, Doug Bowman, quit in spectacular fashion. Fed up with what he perceived as too much interference in his work, he posted a 600-word manifesto, "Goodbye, Google." In it, he railed against the company's habit of testing everything down to the last pixel.

"Yes, it's true that a team at Google couldn't decide between two blues," he wrote, "so they're testing 41 shades between each blue to see which one performs better. I had a recent debate over whether a border should be 3, 4 or 5 pixels wide, and was asked to prove my case. I can't operate in an environment like that."[1]

Most designers do not have to worry about a company testing 50 shades of gray, because it's not possible for them to do so. If you only have a thousand people visiting a digital experience every week, you don't get a statistically significant amount of data to test anything but major elements. You can check the performance of a call to action, but when you drill down to the brightness of a secondary image or the pixel width of a logo, you won't get a clear answer in a short period of time.

That said, success has its privileges. With 115 billion searches and 1.5 billion users per month,[2] Google can test just about anything it wants. And it's right to do so. With that scale, even a tiny change can have a huge return. Google is also culturally inclined toward numbers. Its algorithms for targeting ads are among the best in the world, and it provides sophisticated targeting and testing tools for its advertisers. The company is just very good at putting data to work to make a difference.

That's probably why for its first seven years, it had no classically trained designers. Its first logo, interestingly enough, was created by founder Sergey Brin and was quite similar to the one used today. Rather than relying on design experts, Google seems to have made UX decisions by incremental testing. Want to change something? Test it. If it works, go for it. If not, back to the drawing board.

Such an iterative methodology may not produce visually spectacular results, but it has helped Google build some of the best user experiences around. Unfortunately, it is also everything a classically trained designer would hate. Excellent designers come up with bold ideas that involve changes across entire properties, both online and offline. Their goal isn't to make a single page element perform better; it's to have a consistent system, *whose net effect makes everything perform better.*

Bowman obviously chafed under data used this way. Toward the end of "Goodbye, Google," you can sense his frustration:

> Reduce each decision to a simple logic problem. Remove all subjectivity and just look at the data. Data in your favor? Ok, launch it. Data shows negative effects? Back to the drawing board. And that data eventually becomes a crutch for every decision, paralyzing the company and preventing it from making any daring design decisions.[3]

This is perhaps too much. Merely because you can overdo something doesn't mean you shouldn't do it at all. And data is not like heroin—a little doesn't lead to a lot and make you an addict with no chance to escape. Instead, you have to have a guiding set of principles and strategy. As we wrote in *Actionable Web Analytics,* "It's important not to get too excited about what analytics can do in the short term. Analytics without a comprehensive . . . strategy is like a ship without a captain. The mates, sailors, and everyone else can run around making minor improvements to the ship's performance, but they may end up beaching it in the long run."[4]

In fairness, Google is successful with data. And Bowman, who is the current creative director of Twitter, has also created great experiences. Both of their approaches have their merits. But imagine if you could put them together and make them work happily toward one goal. Then you'd be on to something.

> Creative people don't come up with brilliant ideas in a vacuum. The whole "data's evil" and all that s**t—it's really the wrong attitude. The best work is the work that's been researched and that you've learned about before you start. The best ideas are usually born from a deep understanding of the problem you are trying to solve or a familiarity with what your audience really wants. Data is not about a right or wrong answer. Data is not prescriptive. It's just a way to understand the behaviors and patterns that might ultimately inspire you.
>
> —*Jon McVey, Chief Creative Officer, POSSIBLE*

CREATIVITY WITHOUT DATA

Data and creative work are not natural enemies. They've just been deployed the wrong way.

To understand why, let's look at how creativity happens in the absence of data. Imagine that you're an account director for a large agency and you have a corporate client who wants a new digital strategy. You go over the brief with your team, discuss how you could approach it, and finally send them off to do what they do best. That typically means coming up with a range of ideas that you present.

You'd think that this would encourage daring thinking. After all, you have complete freedom within the confines of the brand and brief. No one says you can't do X or Y, and you have a blank slate for solving the problems the assignment presents.

Unfortunately, this ignores a significant factor in discussions of marketing: the human decision-making process. We love to shout from the rooftops about start-up mentalities and going for broke, but that runs up against human nature. Once people get involved, freedom can run into a number of problems:

SELF-CENSORSHIP. Creative people usually dream up a large number of concepts for any idea, some of which are really out there. Sooner or later, they have to make a decision about which ones to present to their creative director. Sometimes—and especially in more conservative situations—they take out the most daring one.

MANAGERIAL CENSORSHIP. Intermediaries, such as a project managers, can also evaluate creative options before they are passed on to the decision maker. And so, they can base feedback not on what they like, but what they think a higher-up will like. So before a decision maker even sees the ideas, you may lose a good one.

THE BIG DOG STEPPING IN. Ultimately, most design decisions in a data-free process are made by the person with the loudest voice in the room. We call this the "big-dog syndrome." It is not universally a recipe for disaster; the loudest voice may come from a visionary like Steve Jobs. But it is often someone who is very far from the target audience in terms of age, income, and lifestyle. Such people *might* have good intuitions, but often do not.

How can data help? First, as we'll see below, it can help you inspire and generate good ideas. But it can also give you the ability to overcome the reluctance of people to embrace them. Big ideas are often risky or unusual. So rather than try to win people over with aesthetics or an argument, you can offer data instead. In this way, it can help the reluctant embrace the bold.

"mmmfffm."

In 2013, for example, a large electronics company came to us wanting a video about a high-resolution monitor. We examined the brief and dug into the potential. One half consisted of people who simply like having the best technology out there. The other half were creative people—photographers and illustrators who actually needed it to do what they love to do. Eventually, we realized that these two audiences had completely different motivations. The one cared about cool factor, the other about creativity. An idea that addressed both audiences would be weak. We knew we could come up with better ideas for each one in isolation. And so we proposed to do two videos instead of one.

Normally, when an agency asks a client to double the scope, it doesn't happen. But our contacts at the client saw that we were on to something. Thanks to the data, they were able to sell our approach internally. We eventually did both videos, each inspired by a completely different idea. Both reached a wide and responsive audience, with one of them having less than 1% negative comments.

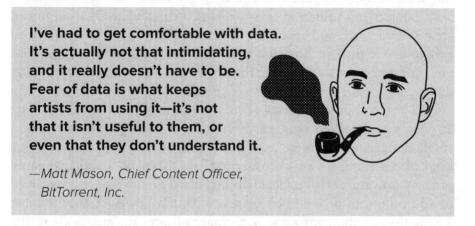

I've had to get comfortable with data. It's actually not that intimidating, and it really doesn't have to be. Fear of data is what keeps artists from using it—it's not that it isn't useful to them, or even that they don't understand it.

—*Matt Mason, Chief Content Officer, BitTorrent, Inc.*

THE PROBLEM OF SUBJECTIVE INTERFERENCE

An additional problem with a data-free process has been happening even longer. Sometime, say, 5,000 years ago at Sumer in present-day Iraq, a workman was nearing the end of a busy workday, etching pictographs on walls. (The Sumerians invented a kind of writing that's considered the first in the world.) As he chipped away, recording the season's weather, his boss—who was likely some dull bureaucrat put in place by his uncle—leaned in and said, "You know, Ekur, I really don't like the way you're doing the pictogram for mountains. It just leaves me . . . how shall I say it . . . flat. I want more verticality in that pictogram. We're talking mountains, Ekur. It should be bigger than the others, shouldn't it?"

Likely the stone designer argued that while, yes, the pictogram could be spiked up a bit, the overall composition of the piece would likely suffer, and the excessive focus on the mountain didn't fit with its relative unimportance in the grand scheme of things. And he likely lost the argument. Luckily, in addition to developing the first system of writing, the Sumerians had also invented beer. So Ekur could probably do what creative people have done ever since: order a cold one with a couple of colleagues and bitch about their boss's stupidity.

Subjective evaluation is an enormous challenge in any kind of creative endeavor, and especially digital. While you'd think we digital people are logical in how we approach things, individual opinions always matter. At some point, they come up—and they can do great damage.

The worst problem of all occurs in a slow-moving, insidious way: an idea gets attacked by a string of people, each of whom demand small changes to a project as it goes along. Creative people call this kind of destruction "Frankensteining." In a typical Frankensteining process, you start with a clear, unified idea. Then you suddenly need to add a button, or lengthen text, or create a new section. "It's just a little thing," someone says. But sooner or later the aggregate of the additions makes a monster.

The best example of this, you'll probably remember, was a video called "Microsoft Redesigns the iPod Packaging." It started with the sleek lines of the original package and eventually covered it with starbursts, special offers, and incomprehensible marketing speak. The end result was pretty bad, and quite reminiscent of the packaging prevalent at most software companies in those days. The surprise came when the source of the video was discovered. It was produced by Microsoft packaging designers who were sick of internal clients Frankensteining their work. Interestingly, their vision eventually prevailed at the company, which now makes beautiful things too.[5]

"No better way to overpower a trickle of doubt than with a flood of naked truth."

"A HOUSE OF CARDS"

So let's see how data can work really well. On February 1, 2013, a TV series called *House of Cards* debuted on the video streaming service Netflix. Directed by David Fincher and starring Kevin Spacey, it proved an immediate hit. A few months after its debut, it had logged an 8.8 rating (out of 10) on popular entertainment website IMDb from more than 65,000 reviewers.[6] Those numbers place it in the same category as *Avatar* and *The Sopranos*, but this success, some said, was guaranteed in advance. Why? Because Netflix had used all the Big Data it had collected on its viewers to determine what they might like to see. In other words, data had inspired the creative direction.

This approach produced strong reactions. "What?" asked some. "You used data to make a TV show I loved?" Some thought the entire world audience would be reduced to a pack of zombies, doing whatever Big Data told them to do.

OK, slow down. It didn't happen that way. First, much like Google, Netflix has a lot of data. Currently, it has 33 million customers worldwide and spreads a very wide net to collect data on them. As a commentator in 2011 wrote: "Netflix stores 50 different files for every viewable media asset, including 3 copies of every movie, ten years of user ratings, extensive user account info and metadata including complex licensing rights for everything."[7] What's more, the site also logs something it calls "user actions." These include the times of day people watch horror movies (not before breakfast) and when they watch humor. It also logs when you start and stop viewing, what you rewind to watch again, whether you watch on a TV or iPad, and so on. It even looks at pirate movie sites to determine what's trending.[8] This, theoretically, gives them very deep insight into peoples' taste in entertainment.

Why would Netflix do this? The simple answer is marketing and customer service. If viewers tend to watch thrillers late in the evening and TV serials in the morning, you know what to promote to them at those times of day. If Netflix knows you've watched and highly rated *Dude, Where's My Car*, they know you're probably more interested in a flick like *Half Baked* than Sir Lawrence Olivier in *Richard III*. In fact, they can even use this data to serve more relevant ads. (*Dude, Where's My Car* = Doritos; Sir Lawrence Olivier = Grey Poupon.)

If you have a problem with Netflix doing this, you should probably read the terms of use of your favorite online store again.* Nearly every e-commerce site deploys techniques like this to increase sales and make better experiences for their customers. But where it gets interesting is that with *House of Cards*, Netflix was not using data retroactively to make suggestions for content. It was proactively using data to figure out what its customers would like to see in the future. As a *New York Times* article explained:

> [Netflix] already knew that a healthy share had streamed the work of Mr. Fincher, the director of "The Social Network," from beginning to end. And films featuring Mr. Spacey had always done well, as had the British version of "House of Cards." With those three circles of interest, Netflix was able to find a Venn diagram intersection that suggested that buying the series would be a very good bet on original programming.[9]

In other words, they knew that their customers on average really liked Mr. Spacey. They knew they really liked Mr. Fincher,[†] and there was interest in the British version of *House of Cards*. They also knew that people who liked Fincher also liked Spacey—and if they liked both, they typically liked shows such as *House of Cards* (in statistics, this is called a strong correlation). Based on that information, the execs at Netflix plunked down $100 million for two seasons. It was a bold bet for a company that had little experience in original programming—but since they were a data-driven company, the decision was logical.

This approach, however, was not universally well received. Rather than looking at what Netflix had actually done, many critics

---

*We discuss guidelines for marketers using this kind of data and targeting in Chapter 9, "One Size Fits No One."

†Please note: Fincher only directed the first two episodes, setting the tone.

focused on the possible creative abuses of data. One of the loudest, Andrew Leonard, wrote in *Salon* that this trend represented a near apocalypse for creativity. If Big Data is to rule the choice of a show, a director, and an actor, what will prevent a company from determining whether a show has quick cuts or saturated cinematography? What would prevent it from basing all creative decisions on a detailed analysis of what had worked in the past? Would we ever see groundbreaking shows like *Breaking Bad*—which are, by definition, *not* reflections of things we'd seen before?

"I'm guessing this will be good for Netflix's bottom line," he wrote, "but at what point do we go from being happy subscribers, to mindless puppets?"[10]

The short answer is that you can always turn off your TV and pick up a book. We also think Leonard grossly misrepresents what Netflix has done. Netflix did not weigh in on creative questions at all; its executives did not explain that films with short pithy dialogues tend to be more successful than those with long philosophical soliloquys. In fact, contrary to what Leonard says, *House of Cards* did feature a lot of Kevin Spacey talking directly to the viewer—a tactic borrowed from the British version of the show, but highly unusual for an American television program. It was not paint by numbers. Netflix merely used data to set some broad creative guidelines—ones that, in fact, were looser than Fincher had experienced earlier in his career.*

Used the same way, data (or, rather, the insights gleaned from data) can help drive almost any form of creativity. By setting the contours for success, it can release creative teams to do what they do best—in full confidence that what they do will likely be well received. Let's face it: nobody wants to fail. They want to know what will be successful ahead of time, especially if you're not restricting them in the most important ways. In this way, data enables creative freedom, rather than defeats it.

---

*With *Zodiac*, for example, Fincher made a film much shorter than he wished, due to producer interference.

Netflix's success was based on following a few simple rules that should guide anyone trying to use data to inspire a project. Let's look at them in detail.

> **People often believe that testing and data and quantitative analysis means that the gut feeling of quality goes away. You test the nth blue color, and that's the typical boogeyman that people hate on. The reality is that I have always framed inside companies that data inspires creativity, because we will bring more people than just the "experts" into the fold and get them to do things, to provide their ideas, and get them to inspire their team to go out and do new things.**
>
> —*Avinash Kaushik, Marketing Evangelist, Google & Market Motive, and author of* Web Analytics 2.0

FOCUS ON BIG IDEAS

You can't micromanage creatives. It doesn't work. Instead, you have to distill your data into simple, easily understood insights. You can't hand a creative a sheaf of spreadsheets and expect magic. You have to come up with a single, true statement that they can use.

You also shouldn't be restrictive or detail focused. In 2013, for example, Yahoo developed a (widely panned) new logo for the company. To do so, the company smartly decided to conduct a survey to find out what people might like.

The first mistake was that they polled only employees, who may or may not reflect customer opinion, and usually don't. Next they used narrow questions that relied on self-reported opinion, a no-no in the data business. Among others, they asked if people liked serif typefaces. Most said no.

This sort of direction—even though it was derived from a survey—is too much. It takes almost half of the typographic world out of play simply because people felt the logo looked too old-fashioned. Serifs do not make or break a creative direction; they simply denote a typographic category. Contrary to what Yahoo thought, they are also not necessarily old-fashioned. Adobe Garamond, for example, is a popular, progressive serif typeface produced more than 30 years after the Optima that Yahoo eventually chose (and which is also a beloved typeface). Creatives need more freedom than this.*

The new design launched to heavy professional criticism. While it does not seem to have harmed Yahoo long term, it was not a positive step.

Netflix's approach was much better. The company used data, yes, but it came up with a relatively simple brief that focused on big ideas. The directive was: Fincher, Spacey, political revenge drama, TV series. These guidelines allowed the series' creators to work within wide boundaries, wider than you see in the kinds of pitches that film and TV makers typically make to investors.

EMPOWER

Once you establish the guidelines of your project, you have to let your creatives go. This is extraordinarily important. Data does not,

---

*In one sense, however, the new logo worked brilliantly. The discussion of and controversy over it garnered Yahoo a huge amount of free publicity. No one much cared for the design, but everyone talked about it.

contrary to what some think, provide intricate creative direction. It doesn't provide a solution. It can only tell you a small number of things:

WHAT IS NOT WORKING OR MIGHT NOT WORK. Data can certainly pinpoint when something is frustrating people. It can tell you that your numbers are low, certain demographics dislike what you're doing, or you're more popular in some locations than in others. Learning that can help you extrapolate what won't work in the future.

WHAT IS WORKING OR WILL PROBABLY WORK. This is the flip side of the previous point. You can learn how you're doing, benchmark it against the performance of others, and understand whether you have room for improvement. Data can also tell you what your users like and might want to see more.

A HYPOTHESIS FOR WHY EACH IS WORKING OR NOT WORKING. When Netflix used data to set up *House of Cards*, they had a hypothesis that a collaboration between Spacey and Fincher would be a success. They did not have proof. The two could have flopped. They could have had bad chemistry or bad ideas. You can't judge the series simply by its success—you have to realize that there was always an opportunity for failure. That said, data had given Netflix confidence that *House of Cards* was less likely to fail than a concept chosen at random.

AN UNDERSTANDING OF YOUR AUDIENCE THAT INSPIRES IDEAS. The insight Netflix derived was perfect for inspiring brilliant creative. Simple yet insightful, it allowed creative people to understand what their audience wanted and how they could fulfill that.

Data never tells you how to solve a problem. People still have to generate brilliant ideas. The execs at Netflix understood that a drama with certain characteristics would likely be a success, but they also knew they weren't filmmakers themselves. So they gave Fincher the green light to make it work in whatever way he felt best. Likewise, once your data suggests a direction, trust it. Your brief should no longer be a list of subjective asks, but a framework for objective ideas. So long as your creative team stays true to them, they should have the freedom to do what they do best.

SWORD AND SHIELD

At our agency, we sometimes discuss data and creativity using a "sword and shield" metaphor. The sword part talks about how data can help argue for much more daring approaches. The shield allows you to defend those ideas against subjective interference.

Of course, you have to be willing to let the data speak, and sometimes it will tell you things you don't want to hear. That was the fate of Rhett Reese and Paul Wernick, who had written the most successful zombie movie ever: *Zombieland*. They wanted to continue the story by turning it into a TV series. The project was funded with great fanfare by Amazon Prime Video, which announced that it would put the pilot to an online test, allowing users to view it for free and then crunching the data it received. The thinking was that fans would love the reboot and want to continue the story.

Unfortunately, it didn't work out that way. The pilot received 5,500 reviews, more than 1,200 of which had only one or two stars. And this being the online world, fans also unleashed a truckload of venom in the comments thread. Amazon eventually determined that the show was unlikely to be a success and backed a competing show, *Alpha House*, which received much more favorable ratings. Reese, in particular, took the decision hard. "I'll never understand the vehement hate the pilot received from die-hard *Zombieland* fans," he tweeted. "You guys successfully hated it out of existence."[11]

If you live by the sword, you sometimes die by it.

> What you're seeing now is that creative people are starting to embrace data, because you can try more ideas and you can more quickly see which of your ideas really work. That enables you to increase your creative output. That's what's really exciting now, the art and science coming together, and the ability to do more creative ideas, because you have data that's actually helping you to know what works and giving you feedback. Then it can inspire your next idea.

—*Jonah Peretti, Founder and CEO, BuzzFeed*

DEFENDING IDEAS

Everyone loves to play creative director from an armchair. No matter how well you write your brief, subjective opinions will always crowd into the process. In that case, you can also use data as a shield to protect your ideas. If you can prove something is working or not, you can make a great case for it.

For example, we once had a client that had hired a celebrity spokesperson for a boatload (actually, an ocean-liner-load) of money. Naturally, they wanted us to incorporate him into their digital properties. Problem? He was off brand, and our team thought that focusing on the company's products made more sense. So we did some user research and presented solid data on this point to our client. Things went fine for a while, until the big boss finally noticed we'd de-emphasized the celebrity. "Where is he?" he fumed. "We paid a lot of money for that guy, so we'd better be using him." Without data, our creative team would have had to run back, wash out their ears, and change everything. But since we were able to back up our conception with solid numbers, we managed to stick to our vision.

> The best creative talents I've worked with use data more as a sword than a shield—to champion the boldest, most disruptive creative ideas so that they have a chance to see the light of day in an otherwise risk-averse environment.
>
> *—Jason Carmel, Global SVP, Marketing Sciences, POSSIBLE*

Case study: Blaze

As a product design student at Brighton University in 2011, Emily Brooke fell upon a statistic that shows exactly how data can inspire brilliant ideas.

At the time, she was in her final year and tasked, like all her classmates, with creating a new product from start to finish. An avid cyclist, she wanted to do something that focused on safety. And so, she spent six months researching the problem with bus companies, statisticians, a driving psychologist, and other cyclists.

"There was one stat that really stuck in my mind and inspired the project," she says. "Seventy-nine percent of cyclists hit are traveling straight ahead when a vehicle maneuvers into them. I wanted to make the cyclist seen when they're otherwise invisible. I had the problem really clear in my mind at that point. I was cycling around town and realized that a white van just in front of me couldn't see me. If he turned suddenly at that point, I'd have been squished. I wished I was just five yards ahead. That was my eureka moment."

Inspired by this data point, Emily came up with a great innovative idea: a laser that projected a bright green image of a bike on the pavement in front of her. She built a prototype and launched it as a Kickstarter project in the fall of 2012. Soon Blaze was in business. To date, the company has sold thousands of its lights around the world.

For more information about this story and to see how Emily used data to drive her product design please go to "POSSIBLE.com/blaze."

DOES IT WORK FOR YOU?

Used correctly, data is a creative idea's best friend—or at least, its trusted bodyguard. It bypasses subjective opinions, zeroes in on potential areas of success, and frees up smart people to use their imagination to its limits. Here are a few things to think about.

- Does our organization view data primarily as a tool for evaluation?
- Are we hemming our creative people in by using data only to tell them no?
- Are we using data to identify key insights for creatives?
- Once we find insights, do we get out of the way and empower our creative people to do what they do best?
- Do creatives in our organization seek out data to better understand the marketplace, audiences, competitors, etc?
- Are our creatives supplied with actionable insights and stories from the data or do we merely give them raw data?
- Do we use data to defend against subjective interference?

ADDITIONAL THOUGHTS

Data has always existed in the world of innovation and creativity. And in Asia, we are experiencing an explosion in the desire to create the best designed experiences based on data that provides the most compelling brand engagement and strategy as a competitive strategy. This can only happen when data is distilled to its simplest human truth wrapped around a idea that transforms the brand and business.

—PAUL SOON, CEO Asia Pacific, POSSIBLE

Data drives everything we do. Our creative is informed not just by qualitative data provided by our analysis team, but also by consumer insights uncovered by our planning and community management teams. We often try and tap into existing social behavior in an authentic way, and those behaviors may be discovered and up-leveled by our planning and community teams, and then verified as significant by our analysis team. The Starbucks #sipface campaign is a great example of all three disciplines coming together to inform a campaign direction.

—LIZ VALENTINE, Cofounder & CEO, Swift (a POSSIBLE agency)

Our approach at BuzzFeed is coming up with creative ideas for the raw material. The analytics and data allow us to see which of those ideas are resonating with an audience. When we see someone do something they're really proud of and people start sharing and engaging with it in a deeper way, then we know we've had the right impact, and it's a success.

—JONAH PERETTI, Founder and CEO, BuzzFeed

Traditional agencies are idea-driven organizations by definition, whereas digital agencies were generally started by entrepreneurs and they're often results-oriented organizations. The key is bringing both of those together. It's not a popular thing to say, but I think it's true.

—MARK READ, CEO, WPP Digital

Too often I see creatives shy away from data. They fear it will put them in a box. They have to get comfortable with it. They have to know how to leverage data to inspire their creativity and perhaps more importantly, build the story around those ideas in a way a decision maker can get behind. If you get used to data, you start to care about more than winning awards. You care about changing behavior and impacting lives.

—DANIELLE TRIVISONNO HAWLEY, CCO, Americas, POSSIBLE

It's amazing how many marketers and agencies you see where the conversation doesn't start with consumer insight.

—CURT HECHT, Chief Global Revenue Officer, The Weather Company

You can convince clients to take risks not just by basing it all on your intuition, but also by using data to support and help you sell what your intuition is clearly marking as the right idea.

—LUCAS PEON, Executive Creative Director, POSSIBLE

Data by itself is in isolation; it's a point. We are looking at data for insights. Those all can come from anywhere, whether it's qualitative or quantitative or ethnographic, or social conversations, data mining, public census data, you name it. All of that data counts.

—PHYLLIS JACKSON, VP, North America, Consumer & Market Knowledge, P&G

Creativity supported by data analysis is extremely important in recession-torn markets like Central-Eastern Europe, where client budgets are still suffering from serious cutbacks. Clients need and deserve to understand what results they can expect from your ideas—the less cliché the idea, the more proof is needed. Radical collaboration of data, creativity, and art gives birth to beautiful projects.

—KRISZTIAN TOTH, CEO & Chief Creative Officer, Carnation Group (a POSSIBLE agency)

When you get to a certain scale, if you don't use data, then you will not be able to grow faster and even bigger. Data is fundamental. But I also think that the creative idea, the whole naive, disruptive, funny, or super-creative idea is just as important. Data without the idea is worth nothing.

—RENE RECHTMAN, President, Maker Studios

Data is really just a way to help us understand human behavior. One of the many ways we use data is with our community management practice. They allow us to spot consumer trends and get incredible insight into what's resonating with people interacting with a brand in real time.

—ALICIA MCVEY, Cofounder & Chief Creative Officer, Swift (a POSSIBLE agency)

Data unleashes more creativity in organizations than less. But there is this weird belief that if you quantitatively analyze everything, you are trying to limit creativity. But if you set them up right, you set them up to allow more ideas to come in and [to] let the customer help us understand which one meets the business goals. If you set it up right, I think the data can inspire an enormous amount of creativity, and it's not as much of a threat as some people make it out to be.

—**AVINASH KAUSHIK,** Marketing Evangelist, Google & Market Motive, and author of *Web Analytics 2.0*

Data helps us prove that creative proposals which might be out of a client's comfort zone traditionally work for their audience and can build the brand. In Russia, we can show that creative ideas and execution for a campaign can and should be considerably different for each of the three major social networks in Russia: Vkontakte, Odnoklassniki, and Facebook.

—**ANDREY ANISCHENKO,** CEO, Grape Digital (a POSSIBLE agency)

The leadership of any creative process needs to really be courageous and willful. Often, what should be genuine consultation morphs into excessive intervention. Far too many hands stirring the pot; far too many views blurring the obvious. The work is at risk of becoming Frankensteinish, with a little bit of this and that. It also renders the whole creative process rather impotent, and its product . . . nothing more than a compromise. The creative leader, assumed to have the most experience and savvy, must singularly drive and decide on the work.

—**DEAN ARAGON,** VP CX Brand and CEO Shell Brands International AG

The old juxtaposition of data vs. creative is like saying marketing is all about TV spots and copy-testing. Sure, there is still some of that, but haven't we moved well beyond it as well? Smart creative people are using data to expand their thinking and get clients to take more risks, not less. It's just like how politicians use polls. Some use it to play it safe, but some use it drive their agendas. It all depends on the person who has the data in their hand, really.

With the growing availability and complexity of data, we must move the data and insights up in the creative process. You need people who can translate the data into insights and stories instead of dropping a spreadsheet or dashboard in a creative's lap. Smart creatives are starting to embrace data as a must have instead of seeing it as taking power away or limiting them.

—NICK NYHAN, CEO, WPP Data Alliance and Chief Digital Officer, Kantar, a WPP Company

Can we bridge that gap between marketers and data scientists to collaborate in a productive way? Because that's where the magic happens—when you get people with these massively diverse skill sets, whether it's a designer, a marketer, or a data scientist in the room on a whiteboard trying to solve a problem and able to communicate and understand each other.

—MIKE FRIDGEN, President & CEO, Decide.com (acquired by eBay)

Creativity is really the backbone of emotion. We like to talk a lot about data and firmly believe that data drives the experience, but creativity is what pays it off. Creativity is that emotional connection that you get with the audience. No matter how good your data gets, the emotion is always the payoff.

—JOHN MELLOR, VP, Business Development & Strategy, Adobe

The important piece that we've really seen unlocking and inspiring creativity is when that data and those insights come together to form a story that's particularly compelling, that brings the emotion to it, and helps people that haven't been immersed in the data journey to really get at and immediately understand what the tension is and what the elements to leverage are.

—PHYLLIS JACKSON, VP, North America, Consumer & Market Knowledge, P&G

It's amazing to see the mindset shift of great creative leaders today. They are finding that data can be incredibly empowering—inspiring great ideas, rather than hindering them.

—KUNAL MUZUMDAR, Managing Director, POSSIBLE

You can think of Twitter as what is happening right now in your world, or what is happening right now in the world in general. The amount of data that we aggregate via Twitter can be very useful for the creators, for the creative agencies, for brands to engage with consumers in what we call live storytelling.

—JEAN-PHILIPPE MAHEU, Managing Director, Global Brand & Agency Strategy, Twitter

The best creative connects with people; it has meaning for them and makes their world a better place. However, it's hard for creatives to know if and how, exactly, their work is hitting its mark. Data gives creatives a precious window into how ideas work, why they work, and what can be done to make them even better. Unlike a focus group, data tells you what people really react to in the real world, at scale.

—JASON BRUSH, Executive Creative Director, POSSIBLE

Especially coming from the analytics and data perspective, data is becoming more democratized. People have worked very hard to get more data out there to create hybrids of creative and data, and the insights are available across the organization.

—**CHRIS KERNS,** Director of Analytics/Research, Spredfast, and author of *Trendology*

If we can use data to convince our clients to take a calculated risk on something that has the potential to change the game for them or the industry at large, then we are realizing the true potential of data as a partner to brilliant creative.

—**JASON CARMEL,** Global SVP, Marketing Sciences, POSSIBLE

04
FINDING UNICORNS

● POSSIBLE.com/principle4

INTRODUCTION

Talent. If you could pick the one thing that CMOs fret over, it's not the landscape, budget, or even time—it's those bright people they need to make it happen. But great digital talent differs substantially from the kinds of people formerly found in marketing departments or at traditional advertising agencies. They are not tyrants or prima donnas. They aren't necessarily always geniuses—but they trust the process and know how to make things work.

Digital is a mindset as much as a skill set. The world has many people who can be good at it. You don't need necessarily need a degree in marketing or a background in technology. You don't need brilliance or arrogance. You need people with passion, curiosity, creativity of all kinds, and the ability to get beyond their own egos and work on a team. We call them unicorns—and finding them may be the most important key to success.

> **When interviewing candidates, I look beyond pure smarts, since we can filter for that in writing samples. I look for the "fire in the belly" and if the person has a curious personality and a history of curiosity in their career path. Candidates with a strong sense of curiosity always end up having a great conversation instead of an interview.**
>
> —*Doug Chavez, Global Head of Marketing Research & Content, Kenshoo*

JESUS MAKES A CRAIGSLIST AD

A few years ago, a 20-something named Joe decided it was finally time to let go of his car. It was a wrenching decision, but not because the car was any great shakes. He'd had it since high school, and even he admitted it was a complete piece of crap: a 1995 teal Pontiac that had just blown its head gasket. He had nursed it through many a crisis before, but this latest breakdown forced him to face reality. After all, he was making far more money than he needed to buy a new car. He just hated to give anything up.

Given the state of the Pontiac, it had virtually no trade-in value. So Joe asked a friend, Kyle, to help him put an ad on Craigslist to sell it. Kyle had just started his career as a graphic artist at a content management company. Though he lacked formal training in design, he knew enough about Adobe Creative Suite to spiffy up sales materials—and presumably he could make a Craigslist ad stand out. Kyle agreed to help. He had his own motivation. He hated the car.

Less than two hours after being asked, Kyle wrapped up with what turned out to be the perfect parody of a car ad. Leading off with the headline "Jesus Tap-Dancing Christ," it featured sunbursts, unicorns, and copy that described the pile of rusting metal as an awesome chick magnet, perfect for any dude manly enough to score. "Every previous owner has had a beard," he wrote.

Kyle sent it off to Joe, went to bed, and thought nothing more of it.

THE UNICORN PARADOX

What Kyle didn't know is that people with any sort of digital talent are in high demand these days. A 2012 survey by the Economist Intelligence Unit found that CMOs listed hiring and retaining talent as the number one barrier to success in marketing.[1] The situation is so dire that global digital agencies have started hiring chief talent officers, responsible for finding, growing, and retaining qualified people.

The reasons for this scarcity are many, but a chief culprit is the disruptions that have roiled the marketing world in the last five years. We usually praise disruption and new opportunities, but they come with a staffing headache. New technologies create new needs. If 25% of a major brand's customers are using Social Media Network X and that network has only been around for eight months, it's hard to find someone who knows enough to help out.

In early 2013, for example, we noticed an interesting trend on Amazon. The site, which accounted for 13% of all e-commerce transactions, also accounted for a third of all e-commerce consideration in North America. In other words, people were using the site not just to buy, but also to find out about products before they purchased them elsewhere. That made it into a marketing platform—and a big one that our clients needed to pay attention to. We realized we had to find someone to develop an Amazon practice area at our agency. But how do you find such a person? After all, you couldn't have experience in this field; we'd just invented the job. Needless to say, it took us months to identify a candidate willing to take on the task.

It also doesn't help that we all now compete for talent with a vast pool of corporations and start-ups looking for the same kinds of people. Talented people can often go where they like, and they do. Faced with an intense demand for their services, digital employees are extremely likely to seek a new position once the old one starts to feel too stale or demanding. That makes it very tough to build a team that hangs together. If a good technologist resents a manager's critique or simply wants more money, nothing can prevent him or her from taking a similar or perceived superior position elsewhere. In fact, promotion by job hunting is a common practice.

So what does a digital marketer do? Find the right people, wherever they are.

WAKING UP TO A NEW WORLD

When Joe opened Kyle's e-mail, he laughed and decided to post it. He thought it would make a few people giggle, but nothing more than that. And who knows, it might even sell the car.

But if he went to bed expecting a good night's sleep, he was mistaken. At 3 a.m. he awoke to the sound of his cell phone ringing. Someone wanted the car.

"My car?" Joe answered, scrambling to find a pen to write down the name. After all, if there was a person on earth crazy enough to buy his Pontiac, you'd kind of expect them to call at 3 a.m. He couldn't pass up an opportunity like that.

Joe promised to get in touch and set the phone down. A few minutes later, it rang again. He took down a second name. Then he shut the phone off. He thought it must be some kind of joke. Maybe it had been dreamed up by his friends.

It hadn't. When Joe finally got up for work, he turned on the phone and saw that he had received more calls. His voice mailbox was full. And the phone immediately started ringing again. By the middle of the morning, his mother would call his office landline, unable to get through to him on his cell phone.

Meanwhile, Kyle had started his own morning routine. On the drive to work, he turned on a morning talk radio show. The crew was laughing over some tidbit of news or gossip. Kyle liked a good laugh, so he turned up the radio and heard the words: "Every previous owner has had a beard."

TRAITS OF GREAT DIGITAL EMPLOYEES

Kyle is what we call internally a unicorn (we took the term from the unicorn in his ad). Typically, they merge talent with a personality that's made for dealing with an ever-changing, uncertain world. Skill set is important, but not decisive. You can learn skills. You can't learn to have the following traits:

> **LACK OF EGO.** Ask Kyle to tell you the story of his ad, and he often begins by saying, "Evidently, absolutely nothing was going on in the world that week." If you're going to be racing against the clock with a bunch of other people, you can't have your own agenda. You can't be jealous if someone else gets assigned to an account that you want. And more important, you can't mind too much if a team decides to run with someone else's ideas and not your own.

CURIOSITY. Lack of ego goes hand in hand with an interest in the world around you. Unicorns are observant, and delighted when they find something new. It takes a lot of work to stay on top of a digital discipline, and if you're not interested in what you're doing, you just won't take the time to investigate everything you need to know. Unicorns are also changeable. They don't necessarily stay in the same role or position—if a challenge comes along, they like to take it.

PASSION. As anyone in a creative field knows, you can get to 80% right pretty quickly, but it's much harder and less fun to get to the final 20%. If you have passion, no problem. You want things to be perfect, and no one has to ask you to stay late to make that happen. Unicorns care more about the end result than their own part in it. If someone way down the corporate ladder happens to flash them an idea that's brilliant—this happens more often than you'd think—they are open to it.

OPTIMISM. In digital, we often end up doing things we've never done before, and that requires people to have the confidence that things will work out. Pessimistic people tend to get stressed and overwhelmed thinking about all the reasons something won't work. You just waste energy doing that. Optimists, on the other hand, focus on finding solutions.

But there is one additional trait that's not revealed by Kyle's story. To discover that, we'll have to meet another unicorn.

We can teach the staff we hire techniques, but they must
have the necessary mindset first.

—*Marketing director at a Chinese retailer, as quoted in Forrester
Consulting, "What CMOs Need to Make Digital Marketing Work,"
September 2014 (a commissioned study conducted by Forrester
Consulting on behalf of POSSIBLE)*

THE BARISTA STATISTICIAN
NEXT DOOR

In late 2012, no one who knew Alex would guess he was not completely satisfied with his life. The assistant manager of a coffee shop,
he liked his job. He liked making exotic lattes; he liked walking the
city streets in the early morning; and, most of all, he liked talking
with people. In the past few months, he'd gotten to meet a lot of
them, and especially the friendly crew from some kind of creative
agency next door, across the street.

Pouring coffees was not how Alex had imagined his life would
go. A year earlier, he had wrapped up his master's degree in psycho-
linguistics and quantitative statistics. His thesis had shown promise.
But Alex knew that he didn't want to spend the rest of his life in
academia. He didn't like writing, he didn't like politics, and he didn't
like working all the time—which is, more or less, the definition of an
academic life. When his sister found him a short-term research gig
where she lived, he jumped at the chance.

The job ended after a few months, and Alex found himself at
loose ends. He sent out résumés to technology and research companies, but no one seemed interested. They wanted people with specific
experience to fill roles, and while his skills were obvious, his résumé
was practically blank. Eventually, he settled on the job at the coffee
shop. It paid the bills and left him a lot of time for dreaming up challenges. Math challenges to be precise.

His first dealt with the coffee shop's tip cup. Alex wanted to see if he could predict the dollar amount of the change from his weekly change tips based solely on the weight of the cup. To do so, he took samples from the bag of coins and noted the frequency of each coin. For example, there might 25% nickels, 10% pennies, 40% quarters, and so on. That allowed him to create a model distribution of coins. And because each coin had a different weight, he was soon able to predict the value of any given tip cup with about a 5% margin of error. Once he got that far, however, he needed something new to occupy himself.

His next challenge was to see if he could predict the daily revenue at the coffee shop before a single customer had arrived—a much more difficult statistical problem. To do so, he began logging every day's revenue and modeling the effects that external factors had on it. On very rainy days, for example, fewer people would come in. Mondays were less heavy than Wednesdays. Days after a long weekend were light because many people would choose to take an extra day off. Certain holidays were dead. And so on.

Alex didn't content himself with these observations. He was a scientist by training and wanted to create as perfect a model as he could. He needed additional data and realized he already had a rich and interesting set of it in his regulars. He had an excellent memory, so he remembered what each of them ordered every day. If they failed to show up on a day, or ordered something different, he could ask them why and use the answers to improve his model.

Alex also had a big personality and became something of a local celebrity for his remarkable skill at knowing what people wanted. Soon, some people from the agency across the street started to take notice. It wasn't merely his memory that caught their attention; it was his questions about why people changed their orders. He seemed to be building a predictive model—something they knew a lot about.

They asked him about his background, and when they found out he was a highly trained statistician, they became very interested.

Now, you're combining the art with the science and under-standing the implications with social. So it's no longer, "I can just do numbers or I can just be creative." There's a hybrid process emerging.

—Richard Nunn, Brand & Web Director, Legal & General

STATS VS. CUSTOMER SERVICE

While marketers are hungry for data, quantitative statisticians are not, by themselves, particularly interesting to them. The academic world has plenty of statisticians, but few of them would work out in a marketing setting. Marketing data is vastly more muddy and uncertain than the clean, structured, and painstakingly gathered sets they are used to. With marketing you're often modeling noise.

Digital marketers also don't just need numbers crunched. If you read too many news stories, you might get the impression that by analyzing Big Data you can find amazing patterns that can tell you exactly what buttons to push with your customers. You might think that Big Data itself looks at what your customers are doing and tells you how to serve them better. Not true. Data doesn't tell you anything by itself. In fact, you can only get interesting answers from it if you know how to ask interesting questions. For that, you need more than math. You need an instinctive feel for what people want.

That's why Alex was so attractive to the agency across the street. Not only did he have the quantitative chops, he was great at customer service. He knew everyone's orders, he knew what they liked, and he knew how to make them feel special. If he could do that, he could very likely look at a data set and understand what kinds of questions he should ask of it.

This merging of quantitative sensitivity and customer service is a central feature of the unicorn. It doesn't mean that Alex needs to be a creative director (he's not). Or that Kyle has to be good at math (he's actually not bad). It's that they have to be comfortable in a world where data people know how to ask the right questions, and creative people work with parameters set by the insights they uncover.

> **Hire for data enthusiasts and interpreters, not just data processors. Digital marketing provides a wealth of data never before available. But data without insight will not move business forward. You need two types of data-savvy hires. First hire for people who can mine the data you have to turn it into valuable business-building insights. Then hire for data-friendly marketers who can take those insights and turn them into action.**
>
> —Forrester Consulting, "What CMOs Need to Make Digital Marketing Work," September 2014 (a commissioned study conducted by Forrester Consulting on behalf of POSSIBLE)

This last point does not mean that creatives have to become data-driven, as we saw in the last chapter. It simply means that they have to learn a new way of doing things. Formerly, they worked off of qualitative creative briefs and an understanding of what works built up over years in the field. This does not ensure failure by any means; experience matters a lot. But today we should take advantage of the full insight we have. We can use data to suggest directions, set boundaries, and defend our ideas against subjectivity. Those are big pluses, if you have people who can work with them.

So what do you do with a unicorn once you find one—especially one that has never worked in digital? This is a bigger problem than you might think, as we'll see.

HOW TO HIRE SOMEONE YOU KNOW NOTHING ABOUT

In case it's not clear, Joe and Kyle became overnight Internet stars. Gawker named their ad the greatest ever run on Craigslist. ABC,

CBS, *Time*, and *Ad Age* all ran features on it. Joe's phone rang so often he would eventually have to get a new number.

Surprisingly, some of those calls turned out to be job offers. Tenders for Kyle's services poured in from all over the world. Like us, many agencies recognized his potential. Each one offered him a chance to work for a top team serving the greatest brands in the world. Fortunately for us, this approach was a turnoff. Kyle was not interested in working for something like a digital agency, not least because he wasn't quite sure what one did.

Besides, Kyle had no practical experience with advertising. He'd served a single year as a creative in a company that hardly bothered with it. But one big reason he refused the offers was simple: none of them had an office where he wanted to live.

After a week or so, a group of guys in our office got into the bidding war for the car. That led them to Kyle, and about a month later, one of our creative directors shot him an e-mail: "Dude, that was funny. Want to come in for a chat?"

Kyle was reluctant and even skeptical. He liked his job and life, and he was modest enough not to trust all the attention he was getting. He believed his success was a fluke, and that other agencies were overestimating his skills. What was the point of doing an interview for a job he'd never get? But our approach worked. Here's why:

IT WAS REAL. You want to make sure you don't overwhelm anyone. Our laid-back attitude (and our office in his hometown) let Kyle put his guard down. It was authentic and realistic. Why not, he thought.

WE DIDN'T ASK MUCH. One problem a lot of companies have when they land an Internet star (or barista star) is that they assume he or she can dive right in and be instantly successful at the higher levels of a marketing department. Nothing could be less true. You don't want to put new people into roles for which they're not ready. Any job requires acclimatization. If a big agency gave Kyle a huge job and said, "Go make magic, killer," it would have set him up for failure. Likewise, if we dumped Alex straight into a major account, he would have struggled. Digital is its own world, and it can be a bewildering one for someone unfamiliar with it. It has to be OK for talented people to feel their way in and make their own place.

IT WAS TRANSPARENT. You want people who are a good fit with your culture; you don't want to sell them on a place where they may not belong. It'll waste everyone's time and your money.

Kyle walked in our door with very low expectations. He didn't need a job, and he also had plenty of offers. Besides, he had no idea what we did. So he arrived, sat down to wait, and picked up a book we'd written about our culture back then.

Lucky for us, he opened to the page with everyone's favorite line: "If you're offered a Jaeger shot, take it." Kyle continued reading, and soon found he liked what he saw. Our differentiator, if we have to pick one, was that many digital agencies aren't that great if you want to have a life. When we founded the company, we didn't mind working hard occasionally—or even a lot—but we also like nights, weekends, and vacation. Kyle liked those things too.

The problem was that he was not stupid. Even if he hadn't heard of digital agencies, he certainly knew that companies could write any kind of nonsense about themselves. So we interviewed him, it went well, and he asked if he could just look around. We said sure. So he walked through our offices and noticed that no one seemed particularly stressed or tired. He generally liked the vibe. We suited him, and he suited us.

HOW UNICORNS ACT

Beyond a good hiring process, what do unicorns want? It's an easy question to answer. They want to build things that work. They want a place where they can thrive, and where their talents are recognized for what they are.

Don't believe us? Let's look at another person to see what we mean. At eight years old, a little girl named Bianca was amazed by a new technology. She learned that if you typed some instructions, known as code, into a computer, you could make pictures and messages on a page. Additional code might put stuff in different places on the page or make them blink. And then, if you wrote some other code, everyone else in the world could see it.

Her initial efforts at web design were, of course, awful. Most eight-year-olds lack a sense of composition. Their feel for narrative is quite limited. Luckily, Bianca's dad worked at a graphics shop and decided to encourage his daughter by installing a copy of Photoshop in her computer and giving her some basic instruction.

She stuck with it. She not only became proficient at HTML and JavaScript, she soon learned Flash and its associated technologies. She also pored through graphic design books and developed her visual abilities. After high school she went to Pratt Institute and eventually graduated from the University of Washington with a degree in philosophy. Along the way, she developed a number of respected social media projects, including a programming tool (API) that brought her to the attention of several of our people, who started following her on Twitter.

Out of college, she got a job making Facebook apps. The work was great for a recently minted philosophy major but was a little boring to Bianca. Even her boss urged her to find a new job, and she tweeted out her desire for one. We tweeted right back.

SENSING A PROBLEM

Let's say you're thinking about Bianca's role at your company. One way, of course, is to think of her as an inexperienced but talented kid, fresh out of college. Or you could realize that she's actually been doing this stuff much longer than half your staff and give her a more senior role. We don't like either of those ideas. Instead, it's better to have a culture where she could figure out her own level. Kyle chose his job, and as we'll see, in a way, so did she.

As it happens, Bianca was talented enough that we soon moved her to one of our major, highly visible accounts. Once there, as sometimes happens, we had a problem. The senior art director on the project simply wasn't working out. He was a talented guy, but not a real leader. So without anyone asking and without her even realizing what she was doing, Bianca began doing his job. She gave strategic advice, offered helpful criticism, and before long, we had all 22-years-old of her in front of a Fortune 100 company presenting work. Somehow, two years out of school, she had just become a creative director.

Of course, we wouldn't normally have someone as young as her in a leadership role, but youth can be relative. Bianca didn't have just three years' experience. She'd been doing this since she was eight and lived in a family that did such things. It was dinner-table conversation to her. She was ready.

> That's really my personal mission, to be able to say that the work that I do contributes in some meaningful way, in order to make the world a better place.
>
> —*Deep Nishar, SVP, Products & User Experience, LinkedIn*

UNICORNS AND DOES IT WORK?

In addition to job growth and finding their level, people such as Kyle, Alex, and Bianca all like accomplishing things. "I like to know when we've made a difference," says Bianca.

Smart and low-key team players aren't really into making noise for themselves. The reason Bianca jumped into a creative director's chair was not ego, but her sense that someone had to. Things weren't moving correctly and she felt they had to, even if that meant jumping into a different role and taking over.

In 2002, Richard Florida wrote a highly influential book called *The Rise of the Creative Class*. In it, he discussed how the economy was now driven more by creative ideas than industrial power. He urged the creation of idea centers in cities to bring together smart people and foster innovative collaboration between them. Though this idea (like all ideas eventually) has found its critics, we like it.

But we'd like to extend it. While unicorns certainly belong to the Creative Class, they sit in a special part of it: the achievement class. They want to accomplish things in the real world. They want their actions to have positive effects. They want to be able to achieve things, to have results they can stand by.

That's why a Does it Work? mentality can be so important to unicorns. If you ask any of our people why they like working for us, somewhere on the list, they'll bring up the fact that we evaluate our projects using data. With data, you can prove effectiveness. You can demonstrate achievement. Awards are given out by the bundle in our industry. While awards are one way to measure unicorns' success, they typically prefer proof that they have made a real difference. Recognition is nice, but results are real. And that's the secret of the unicorn.

Headcount blues

The study we commissioned from Forrester Consulting revealed an obvious problem with the idea of quickly building a team of unicorns: headcount. Most organizations can't simply hire whenever they want. We had to wait quite a while, for example, until a position opened up for Alex to come on board.

"I'd like to say my staffing changes," said the marketing director at a US healthcare organization, "but it does not."

The solution? Forrester concluded that you should hire digital talent whenever you can, using digitally savvy hires to replace departing staff. "As natural turnover opens up new positions, hire people who are more digitally savvy, whatever the role—whether it's PR, product, or promotion—and raise the digital game of your existing team."

ARE ALL SUCCESSFUL DIGITAL PEOPLE UNICORNS?

No, not everyone is going to be like that. You're always going to have plenty of perfectly awesome employees who aren't Internet stars and don't want to go from the crib to the boardroom. In fact, many of our top people don't fit the description. You don't want everyone to be like that. Some people will rise without having the odd and bizarre background or the mutability. Some digital people are writers who want to be writers and nothing else. They're valuable too because they will very likely be among the best writers you have. Some people love to create and hate to manage. That's fine; they can be terrific at the tasks they like to do.

But having a few unicorns is great. They tend to be charismatic and well liked, and while they don't all vault into the upper ranks of management, they make the people around them better. They help make teams work and enjoy themselves—and that's maybe their best trait of all.

TRAITS OF THE UNICORN: A SUMMARY

In this chapter we've met a handful of unicorns and looked at some of their traits. Here's a blueprint for finding unicorns:

SMART. Knowledge is not as important as simply being able to learn.

NO EGO. They have to be able to work with others and accept the best solution, not their solution. They're great on a team.

PASSIONATE. They will do anything, even step outside their roles to ensure that things get done right.

OK WITH DATA. They may not be math geniuses, but they have to respect data and work from the insights it gives them.

ABLE TO ROLL WITH THE PUNCHES. Unicorns are always ready for changes and often eager to change their job title if the chance comes.

SENSITIVE AND INSIGHTFUL. If you're going to ask the right questions of data, you have to understand people too. A good data unicorn will have an intuitive sense of what people want.

ACHIEVERS. They want to get things done and make a difference for brands and in the world as a whole.

"Groom me."

As you're implementing Does it Work?, you're going to have to find the right people. Not everyone on staff needs to be a unicorn, but they should have some of the traits and all of the passion. And a few of your people will need to have that special something that brings teams together and moves them forward.

Advice for unicorns

So what if you are a unicorn and no one recognizes it? Imagine, for example, if Alex had not landed in the coffee shop across the street from us. The answer is that he'd very likely never have seen the interior of a marketing company.

Some people are different. They know they have the right stuff and just can't break through. Or they desperately want an entry-level job in marketing and lack the connections to get one.

Andrew was one such unicorn. In 2012, he was working at a good agency across the town, but whatever his reasons, he really wanted to work for us. Problem is, he was a search engine marketing specialist, and there happen to be a lot of those running around Seattle. Every time we put out an ad, we would get flooded with more résumés than we could read, and somehow we never read his. After about a year of fruitlessly answering our ads, he came up with an idea of his own.

He created his own Facebook ad featuring himself pointing to our job listing. Then he microtargeted the ad so that it only showed up whenever a POSSIBLE employee logged on to Facebook. In other words, he used the tools of his trade to make himself visible and relevant to us. It was the best résumé he ever could have sent. Naturally, we hired him.

DOES IT WORK FOR YOU?

Is talent keeping us up at night? It should be. But maybe the solution is to stop looking for it in the usual places—and find it all around you instead. Some questions to get you started:

- Do we merely look at résumés to find employees?
- Are the people we hire team players who will set aside their egos to do the right thing?
- Do we have creative people who like what data tells them?
- Do we have data people who can look beyond the numbers to provide the real human insight that our creative people need?
- Are our people leaders, ready to step in when things aren't working?
- Are we providing a place where they can know they've made a difference—either for our clients or the world at large?
- Are we relying on our top employees to help us find future top employees?

ADDITIONAL THOUGHTS

I think it takes really, really strong management to say, "OK, this person fundamentally is entrepreneurial. They're going to want to have a lot of different experiences, and I need to know and nurture that." I think that [unicorns have] a two-year window, and I think smart organizations should start to have talent development schemes for people they think fit that profile. There's not a lot of them, but we've got to keep an eye on them to make sure that they're not suddenly at three years doing the same thing. Because they may come into your office one day and say, "That's it."

—**CURT HECHT,** Chief Global Revenue Officer, The Weather Company

I think it is about finding those people, making the positive example of them, either through recognition or promotion or whatever, getting people like that in charge. Then over the years, it's going to be a slow arc, but as you build up you're going to have the right people in leadership that have those principles.

—**CHRIS KERNS,** Director of Analytics/Research, Spredfast, and author of *Trendology*

I believe that the roles of teams and individual functions are changing and have been changing rapidly. It's essential to find people and create a culture where we define our roles and the opportunities in the broadest context, and not in a limited way.

—**DANA COGSWELL,** Executive Director, Targeted Marketing & Customer Lifecycle Management, AT&T

A brilliant idea is one that steps out of the muck for a second to see a bigger trend or a bigger pattern. It takes a larger scope, a larger time frame. A brilliant idea will contextualize something that's happening now with recent human history, and the human history we're about to make. That takes someone who can see the forest for the trees and come up with an idea that strikes you as exposing a previously unseen pattern in daily life.

—**EDDY MORETTI,** Chief Creative Officer, VICE Media Worldwide

People have to be psyched about the challenges and the opportunities they see in front of them, from the quality of the work to their career opportunities and opportunities for growth.

—**MIKE FRIDGEN,** President and CEO, Decide.com (acquired by eBay)

I'll take an A team and a B-minus product over an A product and a B-minus team any day.

—MIKE DODD, Partner, Austin Ventures

You can find unicorns when you least expect it. Observe behavior, listen carefully, and look for that unique proof point in how they've done something unique and amazing in the past—and more importantly, what they would bring to your organization for the future. One of my favorite interview questions: If you had multiple offers on the table, what are your top three drivers and why? This question tells a lot about someone's motivations, what's most important to them, and how/why they fit within your org.

—MARTHA HIEFIELD, President Seattle, POSSIBLE

The ideal marketing professional is the one who's able to connect with their and others' humanity. These are those who understand and calibrate the balance of the left and right brain. There is always an irrational reason for why we think, decide, and behave in a certain way. We must fuse rather than confuse *what we buy* vs. what we *buy into*.

—DEAN ARAGON, VP CX Brand and CEO, Shell Brands International AG

Nothing motivates staff more than trust and responsibility. Giving people autonomy to problem solve and work through a challenging assignment individually or with a peer sends a clear message that they are valued. Of course, feedback and direction is a part of the process, but this initial independence is a key motivator.

We look for individuals with grit, a hunger to expand their knowledge and skill set, as well as the ability to think fast on their feet. The ability to take feedback from clients and peers is also a key characteristic. A thick skin is invaluable.

—LIZ VALENTINE, Cofounder and CEO, Swift (a POSSIBLE agency)

What I'm looking for in people is their general attitude, passion, commitment, drive. Because the stuff people work on changes all the time, but the underlying capabilities of people need to just be in place: their willingness to learn, develop their careers, and try new things.

—**LARS MADSEN,** Business Strategy & Development Director, Canon Europe

The first thing about retention is attraction. Before a leader has retention, they have to be able to hire strong, quality individuals. One of the first qualities I look for in hiring any exec or CEO is, do they have a following? Do they have a network of individuals who trust, believe in, and want to work with them?

—**MIKE DODD,** Partner, Austin Ventures

We are living in a beautiful age! I believe that we have full multi-instrumentalist talents by default in our age. Especially the younger generations (under 25). They are great. In the old ages, great ideas came from "professional" copywriters and art directors—and that was great for the ad industry. I am not interested in the regular "agency/media" guys anymore; I always am looking for peeps who are relentless, curious, and crazy enough to invent new things every day.

—**KRISZTIAN TOTH,** CEO & Chief Creative Officer, Carnation Group (a POSSIBLE agency)

I think in the next 5 to 10 years we will see the creative community be more empowered than ever, with no gatekeepers to decide who's good and who's not. For me, that's something that touches a core value of what I want to do. I want to change the world, not only by disrupting an industry, but something much bigger than that.

—**RENE RECHTMAN,** President, Maker Studios

Attitude and aptitude are my two very rough rules of thumb that I typically use to assess very quickly whether the individual will potentially be a fit. I look for a person with the right attitude to watch the business, the market, and also the team dynamic. Then, when a person describes his or her experience or what did they do to overcome certain business challenges or resolving conflicts, I look for aptitude. A lot of times, that is harder to tease out until you actually have a situation where you can see how the person performs and behaves.

—GRACE HO, Managing Director, Marketing, SAP Asia Pacific Japan

I have a theory that unicorns are attracted to other unicorns. That is, it's very rare to find these richly talented people working in isolation. They tend to be collaborating and interacting with other like-minded people. For me, it's all about creating environments and systems that encourage unicorns to flourish. And I'm of the belief that there are more than we think there are, and that if you empower one, you may empower many. People need at bats, empowerment, and a way to work. When you can create this environment, the unicorns, in many ways, come to you."

—MIKE REEDER, SVP, Brand Strategy & Insights, POSSIBLE

05
CULTURE PREDICTS SUCCESS AND FAILURE

POSSIBLE.com/principle5

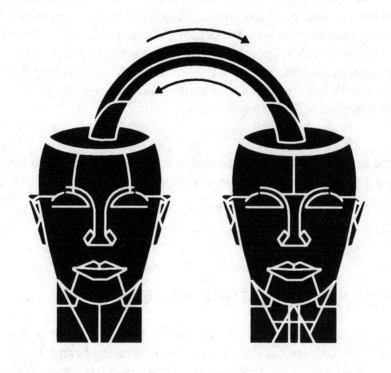

INTRODUCTION

So you've found unicorns. You may find that keeping them around is more difficult than you think. Part of what makes them so change-able and interesting can also make them restless. If they don't find themselves happy, challenged, and making a difference, they're not going to stick around and wait.

That's why you need to build a great culture around them. You can have the best products in the world, but in the end, if you have a terrible culture, you won't succeed. Culture is not about Ping-Pong tables or parties. It's something that happens when people like work-ing together and love the work they're doing. It's the feeling that they have opportunities to learn and grow. And most of all, it's that feel-ing of doing something that matters.

> **The ground zero of your brand is really the culture you actu-ally live in your company every day.**
>
> —*McGregor Agan, Director of Marketing Corporate Affairs Group, Intel Corporation*

CULTURE VOYEURS

There is a story about a small agency in Los Angeles that was sur-prised to win a huge bid for a major manufacturing brand. For weeks, they walked around marveling that they must have beaten out the best agencies in the city.

Then the work started. They learned that in spite of having a globally recognized name, the client's team was invariably behind schedule. They made incoherent requests for changes. And even though they were often the ones dragging their feet, they demanded the agency work late nights to meet their deadlines. Then, when the agency failed to perform miracles, the client refused to pay for work it didn't like (and it didn't like anything). Eventually, it fired the agency and asked it to send back all of the files it had.

Fortunately, this was in the days when agencies often hosted servers for their clients onsite. So the agency came up with a creative approach. They unplugged the machines, put them in the back of a van, and made a pyramid of them on the lawn in front of the client's offices. On top of it they put a huge sign warning others not to do business with the company. Later, the agency learned that all its bigger competitors knew about the manufacturer's reputation and had not responded to the RFP.

Of course, this wasn't us, and the agency's actions were pretty childish. But like all agencies over the years, we have cut ties with clients who had terrible cultures.

In fact, culture is something we look for every time we enter a relationship with a new client. Most clients are fine. But there are a few who will drive your team crazy with unreasonable demands, last-minute requests, and disorganized processes that lead to panicked sprints that tie your people up weekend after weekend. You simply can't have that. Their culture will become your culture at some point, and you have to keep your culture safe and intact.

> **Every organization is only as good as the people that work there. People make the culture real through their daily choices and organizations sink or swim on it. The best-performing companies, like Red Bull, know this and hire people that match the culture while bringing unique value that complements the existing team.**
>
> —Marc Connor, Managing Director, Brand, Build-A-Bear

THE ELEMENTS OF GOOD CULTURE

So how can you build a flexible team of people who can work together great and move seamlessly to new ideas and process? You'll find many different kinds of cultures, but for digital, we think these are the most important steps:

STAY FLEXIBLE. Digital is not a place where job titles should limit individual contributions. If you're going to come up with great ideas, you need a continuous learning environment with flexibility and a certain disdain for roles. No one should ever be allowed to say, "That's not my job description" or "Who asked the engineer for his opinion?" Instead, you should give everyone plenty of chances to step up and be everything they can be.

HIRE LEARNERS. You want your team to be curious and willing to learn things on their own. Software coders are famous for this. Because their tools and platforms are always changing, good development teams are also collaborative learners. Marketers need to adopt this model so that their organizations have an innate flexibility to meet change when it comes.

EMPOWER PEOPLE TO SHARE. Everyone's opinion matters because brilliant ideas can come from anywhere. As a result, people have to feel comfortable bringing up bold ideas. You should encourage them to speak up, share their thoughts, and help push projects forward. And seriously listen. Even that brilliant creative director you have once interned somewhere.

ENCOURAGE THINKING OUTSIDE ROLES. If the data guy has an interesting way to look at a design problem, you want the art director to hear it. Your project manager may have a good creative idea. That's certainly possible, since she hangs out with creative people all day. Your technologist may have uncovered a process that can feed into a cool creative idea. You want to capture every perspective.

MAKE SURE PROBLEMS COME WITH SOLUTIONS. Every company has a group of whiners who can point out what's wrong. But they spend all their time complaining and none of it actually addressing the problem. This is not how unicorns (or anyone else) should operate in digital. Digital always brings new challenges. We need to find ways to solve them.

TO DO THAT, YOU HAVE TO START SOMEWHERE. So you should never allow people merely to point out problems. Instead, they should come with a proposed solution. Even if it doesn't work, it might trigger better ideas from someone else.

MAKE IT OK TO FAIL. As we've seen before, failure promotes learning, and the faster you can fail, the better. Organizations that don't accept failure make it difficult to shift gears and come up with new ideas that work.

FOSTER A CULTURE OF ACHIEVEMENT. If you ask any of our people why they like working for us, somewhere on the list, they'll bring up the fact that we have Does it Work? criteria. At the end of a day or a campaign, they know if they've made a difference. They can prove they've achieved measurable results. Awards are given out by the bundle in our industry, and while awards are one way to measure effectiveness, people know they are an imperfect measure. That's why it's important to give them real data that shows they've accomplished something. Recognition is nice, but results are real.

> You have to make good examples and promote people. You show other people that this is the right way to go. But I think we've all been in organizations or had a view into organizations where selfish behavior and territorial disputes get people something. That's why they perform that way.
>
> —*Chris Kerns, Director of Analytics/Research, Spredfast, and author of* Trendology

WHERE CULTURE COMES FROM

How do you create culture? Simple answer: from as high up in the organization as you can. In fact, if you ever want to know if you'll be happy working somewhere, we have a simple suggestion. Find a video online of a very senior member of management. It doesn't matter if you'll be invisible to this person or will never meet them in your life. Just watch the video. Do you like the person? Does she seem fake? Would you be interested in having coffee or lunch with him or her?

Your answers will probably tell you a lot about the company's culture. If the person seems cool and funny and not too taken with herself, chances are the workplace environment will also be relaxed and easy to handle. If the person seems like a bombastic egotist, you might want to think twice. In an ideal situation, the CEO sets a great tone and cares tremendously about culture.

That said, we should be honest about something. In some cases, terrible culture succeeds. Legendary Hollywood producer Scott Rudin is said to have created an extremely difficult work environment. According to a *Wall Street Journal* profile that dubbed him "Boss Zilla," he once went through 250 assistants in just five years. Rudin, however, is a terrific success. He's produced many,many hit movies and is the only producer to have who have won Emmy, Grammy, Oscar, and Tony Awards. People eagerly line up to work for him.

"E.G.O.T. What you got?"

But Hollywood is not digital marketing. Over the years, our industry has become much more collaborative. Great ideas come when people work collaboratively together. Tyrants find it very hard to excel in an environment where teamwork is essential.

Final point: What do you do if your CEO doesn't share your values and inspire your team? In that case, you have to remember that you can always take responsibility for whatever part of the company you run, even if it's only a small team. A part of a company that is better at retaining unicorns will outperform one that isn't. It's also possible in many cases to manage culture up or sideways. If you make things better for your team in whatever way you can—if you live the culture you want—you'll probably reap the benefits, and you may eventually change the company for the better.

> **From a culture perspective, what I'm looking for is people who are willing to flex the rules to find a better way to make the rules. Don't let the rules become something that hinders you. Willingness to break process, change process, challenge rules, and try things that don't work is one of the rules. That is both in terms of how we do things, and also what we do.**
>
> —Dana Cogswell, Executive Director, Targeted Marketing & Customer Lifecycle Management, AT&T

10 signs of bad company culture[1]

As a result of all our client experiences, we've become culture voyeurs. We're very interested in knowing if a potential client will fit or be a nightmare. As a result, we've identified a series of outward signs that a company has a good or bad culture. You can use these not only for agency/client relations, but also when searching for a job. No one of them, by itself, turns us off—and we're not saying that our offices don't have a few themselves. But if we see, say, five of them, we know we may have a problem on our hands. When you walk into an interview, look for them. You'll be glad you did.

1. THEY MAKE A BIG DEAL OUT OF THE PING-PONG TABLE. Having a Ping-Pong table is fine; bragging about one is not. Why? The corporate world has somehow equated owning one with having a fun-loving culture. If your potential employers emphasize theirs, it may be a sign they're checking off boxes rather than giving their employees what they really want.

2. THE PLACE IS A DUMP. Whenever we walk into an office, we look along sightlines. If we see boxes sitting in the aisles and chairs piled up in meeting rooms, we know no one cares about the place. And there is probably a good reason why.

3. ONLY THE LEADERS HAVE OFFICES. We're always leery of a place where everyone has a cube except for the bosses. That usually indicates a hierarchical structure in which management and employees are at odds.

4. NO ONE TALKS ABOUT CULTURE. Companies should try to sell you on their culture. If the person discussing a job or client relationship with you only wants to talk about your qualifications, ask yourself what she's not telling you about the work environment.

5. LEADERSHIP DEMONSTRATES BAD CULTURE. Culture always flows from the top. We may not have a chance to meet senior management, but we can probably track down a video of them. Our initial reaction often speaks volumes about how much we'll enjoy working with the company.

6. THEY TALK ABOUT EXCELLENCE. Every organization strives to succeed. That's a given. A company that emphasizes excellence may also hold its employees and vendors to unachievable standards. Rather than focusing on our work, we'll be worrying about meeting their expectations.

7. IT JUST SEEMS WEIRD. A happy workplace should hum. Some people should be up, moving around, and talking to one another. They should not seem bored or stressed. So take a look around and ask yourself if the average person seems happy or not.

8. THE COMPANY VALUES ARE POSTED ON THE WALL, BUT NO ONE SEEMS TO HAVE READ THEM. If values aren't lived, they're not worth having.

9. IT'S FIVE O'CLOCK, AND EVERYONE IS BURIED IN WORK. If you can, schedule any visit or interview late. Five o'clock gives you a great opportunity to see how a company manages the work-life balance. A few people working late are fine, but some should be heading home.

10. IF THEY ASK US, "DO YOU HAVE ANY QUESTIONS?," ASK THIS: "HOW MUCH TIME DO YOU SPEND WITH YOUR CO-WORKERS AFTER 5 P.M., AND DOING WHAT?" Good answers include having a beer and playing softball. Bad answers include anything to do with work, unless it happens only occasionally.

Obviously, you can turn all these around to find places with good culture. A humming, happy workplace with people laughing around 5 p.m., and a CEO who talks about how important culture is—all signs that a partnership or job with the company will be fine.

A UX DESIGNER

Let's see how culture can work, using an employee of ours named Justin. He is an unlikely digital person. Initially trained in public policy, he secured an internship in Washington DC after college. Next up was a move back to his home state where he took an assistant-level position at his state's Department of Transportation (DOT). This is normally the definition of a dead-end job, but for people like Justin, there are no dead-end jobs.

Once there, he noticed that the department's website needed help. It had no budget for it, of course, so Justin took it on himself to figure out how to make it better. He went to the library on nights and weekends, read books, and starting making improvements.

Then he realized something: his DOT was responsible for providing information on a large number of different things, including ferry schedules, mountain pass closings, traffic cameras, airport information, and travel alerts. But the website presented this information poorly. And if a user couldn't find it, what good was it?

Justin went back to his self-appointed school and started studying how people displayed information. Soon he found himself with a slightly different job: working with engineers and transportation experts to determine new ways to organize and explain what was going on in the state. He loved the work and developed his own methodology for doing it that was remarkably similar to the ones established over the years at companies like our own. The odd thing was, he didn't even know what he was doing had a name. He had simply created a role for himself at the Department of Transportation and filled it.

In other words, Justin had the perfect mentality for something as fluid and dynamic as digital. He naturally pushes himself out of his comfort zone—no need to encourage that. He learns well on his own and has a taste for doing so himself. He's a self-starter and likes to make things work better. In other words, he's a unicorn.

THE JOB CHAMELEON

Like all unicorns, Justin is also restless and curious about what's out there. He was learning a lot in transportation, but wondered if he could learn more somewhere else. So he began looking at job boards and soon found one of our ads. Reading it made him realize something—he was a UX designer.

Justin showed up for an interview and was soon hired at one of our offices. He wouldn't remain a UX designer long, however. One day, we put him in front of a client, and he did extremely well. Many people are conversationally lazy and always say the first thing that comes to their mind. Justin isn't like this. He always discards the initial idea and looks for something you might not know.

After a while, we pushed him out of his comfort zone again and put him in charge of a big piece of one of our accounts. Wait, you might say, that's not what he was trained to do. He's a designer— what does he know about managing a rowboat?

That's missing the point. As we said above, you can focus way too much on job titles in this business. That goes for managers as well as employees. The ideal unicorn does not know one subject; she knows how to learn many subjects. Justin could learn on the job, and we made sure he had plenty of help. We knew he wouldn't just become a good account director, he'd be a superb one. Why? He doesn't just know accounts. He also knows how to think like a designer. He can contribute creatively to any project, and when a problem comes up, he can explain it in a way the client can understand. In other words, by pushing unicorns out of their comfort zone, you sometimes get higher-performing hybrids that can be invaluable to your business.

Oh, and before we forget: Justin has moved on since then. He now heads up business development for our largest region. Who knows? Someday he'll probably run our satellite launching division— or perhaps the entire company.

THE IMPORTANCE OF RECHARGING

Marketing is a service industry with big launches and often crushing deadlines. Occasionally we have to work late at night and on the weekends. That's unavoidable in the short term, but a huge mistake if it becomes the norm.

Should we give employees a break simply because we're nice guys? Not really. We didn't always have this policy. We founded our first company in Seattle in the mid-1990s. Back then, we lived the start-up dream. We pulled incredible hours and slept under our desks. We built and painted our first conference room the night before a big client meeting. In general, we had the kind of lives you see celebrated in countless articles about Silicon Valley. And, yes, we eventually sold the company. So you'd think we'd be big advocates of that model for success.

Not so much. We were wrong. As counterintuitive as it sounds, 150 years of research have proved that if you want to increase productivity you should *reduce* hours worked per week to around 40.[2] Henry Ford did it to the surprise of his rivals—and reaped a more loyal, more productive workforce. Sheryl Sandberg, the COO at Facebook, shocked the world in 2012 when she revealed she goes home to her family every day at 5:30.[3] But if you can grow Facebook on 40 hours a week, you should be able to do pretty much anything in that time frame.

Digital marketing is a creative business. We're trying to inspire brilliant ideas. And those ideas will never come if you're exhausted, annoyed, tired, and sick of working on something. People burn out. They need breaks. They need to have time to take a walk on weekends, hang out with their families, and recharge. They need to not think about things so they can see them with fresh eyes when they return.

Does this really work? It has for us. In December 2012, for example, we had a client call up just before the holiday break and ask for an urgent response to a proposal. It was a big job that could have meant some decent revenue. But we couldn't do it. Our people had just finished up with their holiday deadlines, and they were tired. They wanted to spend time with their families.

So we told the client no. And we told them why. The good news is that they gave us a ten-day extension. Our people went and had a great holiday. When they got back, they were fully recharged and ready to kill it. Our competitors instead worked through the holidays and gave their people time off later. Guess who won? It wasn't them.

> **It is important to invest in marketers' education, getting them to sign up for the latest courses and stay current. If you stop investing in your teams, there's always a chance that the team will not be the right team.**
>
> *—Senior marketing manager at a global high-tech firm, as quoted in Forrester Consulting, "What CMOs Need to Make Digital Marketing Work," September 2014 (a commissioned study conducted by Forrester Consulting on behalf of POSSIBLE)*

THE ADVANTAGE OF DIVERSE TEAMS

Last point: outside of male modeling, few professions are more dominated by men than traditional advertising. According to Kat Gordon, founder of the 3% Conference, only 11% of the art directors at major agencies in design and advertising are female. One analysis of Super Bowl commercials found that 94% of their creative directors were male (93% were white).[4] Another internal analysis of advertising's biggest awards event (the Cannes Lions) showed that of delegates over the age of 28 at the conference, only 4% were female.[5]

This is a big problem. For one thing, women are much more important in the marketplace than men. In the United States, for example, they make or influence 85% of all purchasing decisions, and 78% of them research purchasing decisions online.[6] They also dominate social media by a great distance.

"Only 11% of the art directors at major agencies in design and advertising are female."

Yet we are not good at reaching them. An astonishing 91% of women feel that advertisers don't understand them.[7] Clearly, there is room for improvement, and that probably starts with a little rebalancing.

Besides, social scientists have spent much of the last decade intensely studying the value of diversity in teams. While the research is ongoing, a few interesting things have emerged that are relevant to the discussion.

TEAMS WITH DIVERSE GOALS RARELY SUCCEED. This is fairly simple. If you're not on the same page, your team will do poorly.

TEAMS WITH DIVERSE BACKGROUNDS SEEM TO BE MORE PRODUCTIVE. A racially and culturally diverse team will usually beat out a homogenous one.

DIVERSE TEAMS ARE PARTICULARLY GOOD AT CRE-ATIVE TASKS AND PROBLEM SOLVING. Which is, of course, what we're asking them to do in digital.[8]

All of this should make us ask, from a practical standpoint, why we're not pushing diversity more. It seems to work.

The 10 types of digital employees

When building culture, it's important to find the right people. And perhaps to be the right people. The following are some of the most important types, and how each of them can help change a culture for the better.

1. THE KVETCH. Every business has a group of people who love to hang around and point out what the company is doing wrong. Unfortunately, any smart person can figure out what's not working. It takes a special person to offer solutions and fix things. By sitting around whining about everything, kvetches rarely make anything better (including their job prospects).

> **Advice to kvetches:** Kvetches do well in areas like quality assurance, where fault-finding can be the job. Otherwise, you should find others like you and have lunch together, preferably away from everyone else. You'll enjoy it. But be wary. Complainers often torpedo their careers with their bad attitudes, and when that happens, they can turn into bitter employees that no one wants.

2. THE OPTIMIST. These are people who love working at a company and believe in its culture. If they uncover a problem, they take the initiative to find a solution. Think of the person in your office who makes coffee when the pot is empty, organizes a gourmet lunch group, and enthusiastically supports others when they have a good idea. That's your optimist.

"*My glass is half full.*"

Advice to optimists: Find great mentors to try to help your career along. Stay open to everyone's thoughts but don't pay attention when people go negative.

3. THE FENCE SITTER. Most people are fence sitters. Their behavior reflects the culture and the people around them. If they are near optimists, they become enthusiastic problem solvers; if a kvetch is complaining, they lend an ear. Fence sitters can do quite well in life. It's management's challenge to make the most out of them.

Advice to fence sitters: Find the optimists—they're going to help you the most in your career.

4. THE REALIST. Realists are truth tellers. They see things exactly as they are and tell anyone who will listen. Realists make great financial people, but they're not usually good in creative positions. The best realists are willing to take risks, even though they understand what the risks are.

Advice to realists: Timing is critical for you. While you may know the truth, you should pick your spots to speak up, especially when giving bad news.

5. THE BLOCKER. Blockers think they're realists, but they're not. They can always find a reason the company should not do something. Oddly enough, they do fairly well, because they tend to be cautious, not make mistakes, and not spend money. Management likes that. But eventually, they slow things down.

Advice to blockers: First of all, determine if you're a realist or a blocker. Be honest. Then learn to take on some risk. Not everything will always go badly.

6. THE "ME FIRST." Some people have big personal agendas that crowd out everything else. They are quick to blame others, boast about any accomplishment, and scheme to make management like them. Typically, they don't get ahead because they believe short-cuts matter more than actual work.

Advice to "me firsts": Realize your best path to success is to act like an optimist. Stop looking for the easy way up and work to make the company better.

7. THE MARTYR. Martyrs are always the first to come and last to leave. The work extra hard and believe that management will repay them for their sacrifice. Sometimes that happens, but usually martyrs get job security rather than promotions.

Advice to martyrs: Go home. You're killing yourself and destroying all of the creativity that would otherwise make you an optimistic problem solver. You'll get more done by working less.

8. THE FILIBUSTERER. A filibusterer talks more than acts. They fill up meetings with air, make objections to everything, and say things like, "Are we covering all the angles here?" Or "Why don't we think a little more outside the box?" The end result, however, is that nothing gets done.

"At the end of the day, big data necessitates high level gamification synergy with agile infographics and strategic thought leadership...."

Advice to filibusters: Set specific goals and targets for yourself. Rather than having a to-do list, set endpoints for things you want to achieve in a given time period. Then hold yourself to them.

9. THE SELF-LIMITER. Self-limiters are people who never feel good enough or important enough to speak up. They're often young and can be smart.

Advice to self-limiters: Most people grow out of being self-limiters as they get more comfortable in their careers. Some may need to get help with their confidence.

10. THE JOB-TITLE SNOB. This person likes a strict hierarchy between people at different levels of the company. We hate this. If we're going to a client meeting that's not all that important, we'd rather take some young person on our staff than one of our senior managers.

Advice to snobs: If you've climbed partway up the corporate ladder, be sure to involve young and junior people more in what you do. It'll be good for culture and great for them.

DOES IT WORK FOR YOU?

When it comes to culture, it's very important to build a much less hierarchical, open system where failure is OK, and learning is more important. To start thinking about culture, ask yourself these questions:

- Is our workplace happy?
- Are people working too hard?
- Is everyone's voice getting heard?
- Do we providing people with a sense of accomplishment?
- Are we holding them accountable at the same time?
- Are we diverse enough to ensure success?

ADDITIONAL THOUGHTS

If you can actually create a culture that fosters and creates the unicorn, you're doing a lot better than most companies in this space. From a cultural standpoint, you have to make it fun to come to work. You have to make a collaborative environment, and that's everything from designing the office space to making sure you have the right social events, etc. No easy answers, but it's incredibly important.

—BRIAN LESSER, Global CEO, Xaxis

I believe in and always try to promote a culture of creative *excellence and* tension. I like to break down the walls of silos or the ladders of hierarchy. A truly great idea can come from anyone, anywhere. We should not be too precious. I also often encounter teams wherein there is too much reverence for historical wisdom. There is indeed wisdom of experience, but we must also be conscious of shifts in context. It may have been a great idea at the time, but it may no longer apply to the current challenge. Of course, I also believe that great ideas endure, and their application may just need updating. Lastly, beware of false harmony. Authenticity towards each other entails fighting a good fight, as long as you are united in the pursuit of a shared goal: a powerful response to a single-minded, compelling brief.

—DEAN ARAGON, VP CX Brand and CEO, Shell Brands International AG

We believe in a culture of makers. There is a lot of conversation about having an entrepreneurial spirit, but that becomes meaningless if you can't execute on your ideas. To ensure we find the right cultural fit we ask candidates to participate in a creative challenge and present it to our team. This approach has helped us maintain our culture as we have grown.

—**ALICIA MCVEY,** Cofounder and Chief Creative Officer, Swift (a POSSIBLE agency)

I think culture determines everything. If you have a culture of fear, people are going to spend too much time focusing on the small details, and then they're going to miss out on the big opportunities. I think culture is the crux of the company performance.

—**CHRIS SCOGGINS,** CEO, National Rail Enquiries

A big part of retention is whether the work is interesting, intriguing, and dynamic—and also if the company is having success. Frankly, they're all probably equally weighted. You need interesting work, but you also need to make people think they're part of something that's going to succeed.

—**MIKE DODD,** Partner, Austin Ventures

I think that great teams are so much more than their parts. They always have a leader who a bold risk taker, but also knows that the team is stronger than any individual, even them. Then the individuals take personal responsibility for their work; know how to critique ideas rather than people; and use conflict, humor, and play to generate ideas. When you can do that in a fast, iterative environment, things can really happen.

—TONYA PECK, Chief Talent Officer, POSSIBLE

Even though the business world has co-opted the word "culture," I think it's important to step back and remember what that word means. For me, culture has two interdependent meanings that are both important for a healthy organization. First, there is the culture of a company, the shared values and ideals that hold people together as they navigate the continual change and evolution that companies inevitably experience. Second, there is contemporary culture itself—it is critical that companies find a way to connect with societal trends and changes. The potential for success happens when you bring those two things together. This way, your employees are experiencing—and creating—a company culture that feels true to what they care about in the rest of their lives. That in turn can only help a company that is trying to innovate and connect with customers in a relatable and relevant way. The corporate world has a lot to learn from culture.

—JON MCVEY, Chief Creative Officer, POSSIBLE

Respect, for your peers and clients, is key to building a great culture. If you feel respected at work, you're more likely to put yourself out there and challenge yourself. You're more likely to have open dialogues that lead to strong relationships, which in turn leads to a great agency culture. Without respect, it's hard to enjoy the typical agency perks (food, libations, Ping-Pong, etc.) that are so often associated with culture.

—**LIZ VALENTINE,** Cofounder and CEO, Swift (a POSSIBLE agency)

I am always looking and coaching my team to think about the next two jobs that they want to do, and how I can align the work I give them today to set them up for success for the next two jobs, not just the next job.

—**GRACE HO,** Managing Director, Marketing, SAP Asia Pacific Japan

At eBay, there's an annual Founder's Day where founders and CEOs of companies that have been acquired by eBay get together and talk about a range of topics geared around making eBay more successful. This is something that John Donahoe, the CEO, participates in all day. He brings in his staff. Many of the people on his direct staff were CEOs of companies they've acquired who moved up the ranks, and now have leadership positions in the company. He comes with a lot of credibility, to say, "We invest in you, we bought you for a reason. We want to see you have a lot of impact here."

—**MIKE FRIDGEN,** President & CEO, Decide.com (acquired by eBay)

Having a cross-departmental or cross-disciplinary view-point can be a risky and can leave people open to be taken advantage of. In the right organization, however, that person will be celebrated, because it's better for the business.

—CHRIS KERNS, Director of Analytics/Research, Spredfast, and author of *Trendology*

We need to welcome and embrace feedback from broad creative lenses. You might need a unicorn who has influence and control over the brand. But you need unicorns that are out there and allowed to explore. Because individuals all by themselves can't be all encompassing of what brands can be.

—PHYLLIS JACKSON, VP, North America, Consumer & Market Knowledge, P&G

"So what?" That's the single most important question to answer whenever we look to providing an idea or solution to our clients. It has to make business sense for the brands and more importantly it has to mean something to consumers. The right to speak and engage your consumers is paramount to this hyper connected world. One false move and you are looking at a barrage of negative sentiment to clean up. Therefore, there are increasingly more and more brands in Asia consolidating their marketing and digital teams into ONE. A team that builds brand experiences seamlessly. Change is definitely in the air.

—PAUL SOON, CEO Asia Pacific, POSSIBLE

"Possibility thinking" is something we're trying to add to our culture. It's about asking "what if" rather than [saying] "yeah, but." It can lead to very powerful, informed risk taking. If this is where we intend to be and what success looks like, let's think about what things have to be true to get there. Many times that's how innovation happens, and that's how breakthroughs happen. At the end of the day, we want our culture to be high velocity, because our market windows are significantly different than what they have historically been.

—**MCGREGOR AGAN,** Director of Marketing Corporate Affairs Group, Intel Corporation

Culture is the fuel of innovation. It's the fuel because it's about more than the environments in which we create. It is about how we hire, how we empower, and how we elevate our ideas. When you do this over and over and over to the point it becomes a habit, that's when innovation becomes the norm. Culture is about the team first and foremost. No one here does it alone. We succeed and fail together.

—**MIKE REEDER,** SVP, Brand Strategy & Insights, POSSIBLE

In business school we had a class on culture; I thought it was the dumbest class because it was just redundant. They just gave you one case study after the next about what's a good culture, what's a bad culture. I never gave it a lot of credibility. Then I had a couple of real jobs where I actually worked at companies that had good culture and bad culture. Omniture had a killer culture. It was an intangible. It's not in the words that you put on a wall, nor the paintings that you put on a wall, nor whether you've got nice office space or s**tty office space. All that does matter at some level, but culture is an intangible. Everybody goes to work, they work hard, they're having fun, and they're happy to be there. It builds upon itself. When a really talented, fun person to work for goes to a company, he or she attracts four or five people, and then they attract people, and so on. It's really hard to define. It's like porn. You know it when you see it.

—**MIKE DODD,** Partner, Austin Ventures

06
MEASURE WHAT MATTERS

POSSIBLE.com/principle6

INTRODUCTION

How do you know if you're making progress on your goals? You have to measure things that specifically ladder up to them. That's not always as simple a task as it seems. Today we have access to a huge amount of digital data—but much of it is one step removed from actual success: social media metrics, mobile usage statistics, and even media performance. Very often, easy measurements can mislead you into believing you're doing well (page views are up 100%) when you're not (but nonetheless sales have dropped 40%).

Instead we have to combine metrics or design new tools that allow us to measure more accurately the impact of what we're doing. That means embracing the difficult and sometimes inexact measurements that get to the heart of what works and doesn't.

> **Marketers have plenty of data available to them. But they are not yet able to turn data into insight. Many marketers lack the tools, know-how, and people skills to go beyond likes and click-throughs to align digital programs with business results.**
>
> —Forrester Consulting, "What CMOs Need to Make Digital Marketing Work," September 2014 (a commissioned study conducted by Forrester Consulting on behalf of POSSIBLE)

THE PERFECT WAY TO SAVE LIVES

The Bill & Melinda Gates Foundation offers an interesting perspective on measurement. It has a process it calls "outcome investing," which mandates that any grant (or investment) it makes must have clear goals and trackable metrics that are understood and agreed upon up front.[1] As their website explains:

From the outset of the grantmaking process, we work with partners to define the overall results we hope to achieve and the data needed to measure those results. . . . To give our partners flexibility in how they achieve results, we do not require them to report on all of their activities. Instead, we focus on purposefully measuring the most critical metrics of progress that support continued learning, adjustment, and alignment.[2]

"All lives have an equal value."

Sometimes their initiatives are easy to measure. In 2010, for example, the foundation made its largest grant ever: $10 billion to provide vaccines for children around the world. At the time of the announcement, Bill Gates noted that the program would save the lives of 7.6 million children in the next decade, mainly by preventing diseases like AIDS, tuberculosis, rotavirus, and pneumonia. That's about $130 per life, in case you're wondering.

"Vaccines are a miracle," explained Melinda Gates in a Facebook post. "With just a few doses, they protect children from deadly diseases for a lifetime. They are extremely cost effective, and they save lives. Vaccines led to the eradication of smallpox, and they are responsible for the amazing fact that polio cases have gone down by 99 percent in just 20 years."[3]

A vaccine's impact turns out to be easy to measure. You simply take the number of children you vaccinate and multiple it by the percentage of those who would otherwise die from a disease. If you have 10 million children, and 2% of them on average would die from rotavirus, that's 20,000 lives saved.

Not everything, of course, is as easy to quantify as this. The foundation also invests in things that are much harder to measure, such as research into better vaccines. Nonetheless, they don't abandon their approach. They come up with metrics for measuring murkier things such as the impact of a documentary film or the cost-effectiveness of a research project. For these more difficult measurements, they've adopted a sophisticated evaluation system using experts in the fields to determine if progress is satisfactory or changes in approach need to be made. And they also regularly evaluate that evaluation system.

> **Campaign results always have to be in view of the overall business results, and that gets lost quite often.**
>
> *—Denise Karkos, CMO, TD Ameritrade*

GOALS AND VANITY METRICS

Of course, as with everything, measuring what matters requires us to have strong goals and the criteria that support them. As we wrote in the first chapter of this book, goals need to be SMART and ladder up to business success. The metrics that we then use to evaluate them should really reflect success.

In particular, we want to avoid vanity metrics. They are readily available metrics, which by themselves do not mean anything. You can easily understand the problem of vanity metrics through a diet analogy. Let's say you're sick of feeling out of shape and want to eat better. So you go to a health website and see that the recommended caloric intake for a person of your age and weight is 2,000 per day. "Great," you say, "I can do that. After all, a Kit Kat chocolate bar has only 218 calories, and I love Kit Kats. So I'll go on a diet where I eat nine of them every day and be perfectly healthy."

Absurd, obviously. Nutrition is more than calories, just as marketing is more than single metrics. But you'd be surprised at the number of prominent brands that make just this mistake—and have been making it for years.

We have plenty of vanity metrics in digital—Twitter followers, for instance. App downloads. Page views. Such things do not necessarily indicate that you've had success. They merely indicate that you have attracted traffic. And if they are pursued for their own sake, they can lead you astray.

Recently, for example, a brand came to our agency with a problem. Over the years, they had embarked on an aggressive strategy to add Facebook fans. They were extremely successful and eventually built a large fan base.

Then they started asking questions about the fans. They soon noticed they couldn't find any correlation between their fans' activity and their sales. Their numbers had gone up, while their revenue had not. So we ran the numbers for them and learned that only a small percentage of their fans actually owned their products. In fact, a sizeable amount of them lived in parts of the world where their products weren't even available for sale. Those fans loved the content the brand was creating, but it wasn't really helping the business.

> **Marketers want to quantify the impact of their digital efforts, but too often they are measuring the wrong things. They have a long history of measuring ROI of traditional media, but lack commensurate best practices and benchmark data for digital marketing programs like social and mobile. To fill the void, marketing leaders count vanity metrics such as social media likes, but these metrics don't show what impact digital is having on business performance.**
>
> —*Forrester Consulting, "What CMOs Need to Make Digital Marketing Work," September 2014 (a commissioned study conducted by Forrester Consulting on behalf of POSSIBLE)*

The good news is that our client had moved a harmless metric. No one ever got shot for having a huge Facebook fan base, and they had learned a lot about creating good social content. Still, they needed to start making the property work harder for them. Once that became the goal, we devised a different set of metrics that worked much better.

How bad measurement hurts everyone

You might think that bad measurement only harms the measurer. Not so, according to Brian Lesser of Xaxis. He notes that when purchasing ads, marketers often want to pay less and get impressive click-through rates. That, in turn, discourages ad tech firms from carefully policing their systems—allowing botnets, ghost sites, and other fraudulent schemes into the mix.

"When all you care about is a click or an online conversion, you are inviting bad actors into the system. Those bad actors are running ads where nobody can see them or creating bots that click on ads and try to gain either view-through or click-through attribution," Lesser says.

In other words, caring about the wrong things is not just bad for you—it's bad for everyone.

IMPROVING SIMPLE MEASUREMENTS

To avoid making the mistake of measuring the wrong things, we have to be aware of three common biases: over-relying on available metrics, forgetting the long term, and paying too much attention to very recent activities. Let's look at how you can overcome them.

RELYING ON AVAILABLE METRICS

Advertisers have long purchased billboard space based on a simple metric: how many people drive by. The data itself is very easy to come by—simply multiply the estimated traffic by the number of days your billboard is up, and voila! You have successfully estimated eyeballs. In reality, though, this is a blunt measure. It doesn't look at how easy it is to see the billboard, what kinds of cars are driving by, who is in them, and whether they are susceptible to billboard advertising. You would need to deploy surveys and look at industry data to really find out the effect you were having.

For another example, let's imagine we wanted to measure the effect of a documentary on world hunger. We have a very easy measurement: number of views. We can count tickets and downloads, and might be tempted to use that as our definition of success. This won't work. Viewers are indicative of success, but the bigger question is whether that documentary was *also* successful at changing the viewers' opinions and behavior over time. They may see the movie and completely forget about it by the next day (or election). If so, it could be less successful than a movie that hits only a small audience but really inspires it to rally behind a cause.

Recently, we've seen a trend of so-called slacktivism, in which millions of people tweet a hashtag associated with a social cause. A notable early example was the Kony 2012 campaign, which urged people to tweet about a movie about war criminal Joseph Kony. The hope was to bring attention to the problem—his lack of prosecution. And it did bring attention. The movie garnered more than 100 million views, after celebrities around the world tweeted about it. The problem was that Twitter proved a poor way to catch someone who is completely off the grid. As of this writing, Kony is still at large.

In a business context, easily available measurements—such as Facebook fans and tweets—need to be paired with more difficult-to-obtain information, such as brand sentiment or revenue resulting from social. That's the only way we can get a full picture of what our activities mean.

BALANCING SHORT TERM
WITH LONG TERM

A few years ago, we worked with an apparel company to help the CMO optimize the brand's ecommerce performance. At the time, the brand's digital properties had a 2.5% conversion rate, but his bosses had decided to set his bonus based on improvements in that rate.

"We have to get to 3%," he said, naming a rate that would put him near the top of that category (at the time) in his industry.

That's a huge increase: 20%. So we got very aggressive with a testing program and eventually managed to move the needle all the way to 3%. However, we were worried that by doing this, we were making the site less interesting to those who weren't buying. So we undertook a different set of measurements. First, we used surveys to find out how many visitors to the site made a purchase elsewhere. That number turned out to much larger than those who bought on the site. People were clearly window shopping and then going to either a physical store or another online retailer to buy.

We then surveyed the visitors about the changes we had made and found they overwhelmingly disliked them. So even though 3% were buying on the site, 97% were frustrated by it. As a result, overall sales influenced by the site—a much larger percentage of total sales—slumped, even as our conversion rate rose. We were turning off a large number of customers to improve a metric that hurt our client's true bottom line. After we showed him the numbers, the CMO relented, and we went back to his old productive-but-not-exceptional website.

While we tend to think of short-term promotional activities as distinct from longer-term brand activities, both have consequences. You need to make sure you're balancing short-term success metrics with longer-term ones.

OVEREMPHASIZING RECENT ACTIVITIES

We can also put too much emphasis on what happened just before a conversion. You can't, for example, attribute sign-ups for test drives entirely to a post on Instagram. You have to do more than that.

To illustrate this point, we sometimes use the analogy of a great soccer forward who gets all the credit for her goals. As a result, an owner might overspend on her and neglect the salaries of the midfield and defense. Over time, fewer balls will get to the forward because the rest of the team is in a shambles, and all the money spent on the star player is wasted.

And so, whenever you look at a conversion, you should never attribute its success entirely to any one activity, and certainly not to the last click that occurred. Instead, you should try to get an idea of the various influences on the path to conversion and also what happened after.

At some level, we are victims of our own success in evangelizing the importance of measurement. Now, you can log in to any of a dozen tools that will provide, in excruciating detail, feedback on the most myopic of metrics. The real tragedy is that most of the metrics, while easy to obtain, have a peripheral impact at best on the measurements that really matter to a business—revenue, brand perception, loyalty, etc. We should be throwing away metrics that provide no value to all-up business goals other than the fact that they were easy to get in the tool.

Just because you can measure something doesn't mean you should. Our approach to measurement more often than not involves actually throwing away data that obscures or distracts from what's really important to a business.

—*Jason Carmel, Global SVP, Marketing Sciences, POSSIBLE*

MEASURING WITH DIRECTIONALITY

No measurement is perfect, but here's the secret: they don't need to be. For example, let's put you in charge of a restaurant. You have very few outlets for marketing, and all of them are pretty much terrible to measure. So you put up a billboard on a busy highway. Then you track two things. The first is your overall increase in customers. The second is a random survey you do with customers to find out what drove them to the restaurant. In the end, you won't have a perfect indication of how effective your ads were, but you will have some idea of whether you should up your investment in public space advertising.

With measurement, you don't need to know everything with absolute precision. Marketing does not take place in a university research lab. Noise is part of the business. Instead, you have to accept that even a partially hazy measurement usually beats no measurement at all—so long as it's measuring the right things. If your mother asks you the temperature outside and you don't have a thermometer, you can still stick your arm out the window and tell her if she should put on a jacket. Likewise, knowing something is better than nothing—and often adequate.

In technical terms, many measurements are *directional*. They are not 100% accurate, but they are still useful if you understand their weaknesses. They don't tell you the exact speed of the wind, but they tell you where it's going. With Does it Work?, you need to know roughly if things are working or not. The kind of measurements we suggest for hard things are not going to be perfect, but they are going to tell you useful information.

HOW TO MEASURE HARD THINGS

So how exactly do you measure hard things in digital? There are three basic techniques:

· Linking offline and online

· Measuring intent, awareness, and comprehension
· Understanding microconversions

Let's look at them in detail.

LINKING OFFLINE AND ONLINE

Imagine you're a big-box retailer that sells online and in store. Nowadays, you can do some interesting things with online and offline. For example, if you can get your customers to download your app, and if they enter the store with it on, a salesperson can know what sorts of things they've searched on and what they're likely to buy. That way, you can get excellent visibility into how well your online and mobile efforts are translating to brick-and-mortar success.

In other words, you've created a data link between online and offline activities. You can do similar things with loyalty programs and membership cards. Starbucks, for example, has an app that provides a good link between digital and the real world. By tracking the effects of app-based offers and promotions, the brand can easily find out what motivates its most loyal customers. Another obvious example is a points program for an airline or hotel—or a club card for a store.

You can also deploy what's known as a "trackback." This involves using information you have to make connections between unrelated data. For example, in the United States many records related to cars are public, and this data can be accessed relatively easily. From it we can learn who owns a particular car and where they live. So let's say you're an automaker and want to know if your mobile site is working. To do so, you can collect information on potential customers, such as their name and addresses. Six months later, you can check those names against the public database to see if they've registered a new vehicle made by your company. You can compare that information to what that person did on the mobile site, and get a pretty good idea of what's working or not.

MEASURING INTENT, AWARENESS, AND COMPREHENSION

A number of years ago, we had a telecom client who wanted us to help them sell more phones online. In the target market at the time, it was more common for customers to shop for phones in a store. Although we tried a number of things, we had only modest success with shifting customer behavior to buy the phones online—and not enough to justify more investment in the effort. But as often happens when things don't work, we did learn something that we could use to make the digital experience influence more purchases.

While few people purchased online, many visited the brand's site. So we started doing in-store surveys and learned a startling fact. If a person knew the name of the specific phone they wanted before they entered the store, they were four times more likely to buy one than someone who just asked about phones in general. We also learned there was a strong correlation between people who'd gone to the site and knew the names of the phones.

In other words, we were seeing evidence that the company's digital properties were driving awareness and intent. So we moved the focus of the site more toward introducing phones than driving purchases. We also shifted our success metrics to measure the site's effectiveness—and by extension, ROI—in a way none of us would have guessed going in.

What should you take away from this? You can always ask your customers questions. These surveys can occur online or offline—and even though such surveys are never 100% accurate, they can still give you a good indication of how well your marketing is working.

UNDERSTANDING MICROCONVERSIONS

Automotive manufacturers should all love those online tools that let you build a virtual car. Why? Because surveys have shown that people who use one are much more likely to buy a car than those who don't.

We call an activity like that a microconversion. It is a step that people take on the path to purchase, even though it is not a purchase itself. You can think of microconversions a bit like when you're trying to decide what to eat at a mall food court. If you walk in, that's a microconversion (it shows you're hungry). If you walk up to a particular restaurant, that's also one (it shows you're interested). Reading the restaurant's menu is a third. Accepting a sample offered by the cashier, a fourth. Finally, you buy some food—that's a real conversion. At every one of the microconversion stages, you show a greater intent to buy. Theoretically, you could always abandon ship at the last minute and go to the Applebee's down the road. But most likely you won't.

Another type of microconversion is known as a delayed conversion. This occurs when the customer signals strong intent, but will not be able to convert for a while in the future. For example, even when a person gets qualified for a loan to buy a home, he is not necessarily going to take that loan. In fact, the exact amount of the loan will depend on his finding a house he wants to buy, negotiating a successful agreement, getting approval on the price from a bank, and so on. So while he signals that he wants to buy a house, much can get in the way to keep him from actually doing so. And until that point the bank doesn't make any money from the consumer.

MEASURING LONG-TERM SUCCESS

Up until this point, we've mainly discussed short-term activities. If you're a brand advocate, you're probably wondering what this all has to do with you. So let's talk a little about brand value, how people typically measure it, and ways we think it can be improved.

Every year (and almost always on a yearly basis) major agencies and advertising holding companies release studies that assess the strength and value of global brands. They usually do this with a survey-based approach, compiling data from thousands or tens of thousands of consumers. They examine everything from brand recognition to brand sentiment. They also look at outside factors, especially financial ones. In the end, they settle on a value that they compare to others.

No matter how rigorous they are, all brand valuation studies rely on judgment calls. Someone somewhere has to decide how to weight the various data that comes in. For example, one metric they all use is "unaided brand recall." In other words, if we ask you for the names of ten smartphone companies, Apple and Samsung (in 2015) would probably be the first two you say. To determine the value of a brand, you have to come up with a number for that. Another question might measure the net promoter score (NPS), a customer loyalty metric that measures whether someone would recommend the brand to a friend. You have to assign a different number for that. In fact, you have a lot of measurements, but you are also making soft judgments about how much each matters.

Not surprisingly, such surveys vary widely in both their ranking and absolute values. Don't believe us? Let's look at two recent major global brand strength studies. Each was undertaken by a respected branding company over the same time period using a transparent methodology involving millions of questions asked around the world. Both validated their findings against sales and other financial data. Yet they came to startlingly different conclusions:

Survey 1		Survey 2	
1. Coca-Cola	$71,861 million	1. Apple	$153,285 million
2. IBM	$69,905 million	2. Google	$111,498 million
3. Microsoft	$59,087 million	3. IBM	$100,849 million
4. Google	$55,317 million	4. McDonald's	$81,016 million
5. GE	$42,808 million	5. Microsoft	$78,243 million
6. McDonald's	$35,593 million	6. Coca-Cola	$73,752 million
7. Intel	$35,217 million	7. AT&T	$69,916 million
8. Apple	$33,492 million	8. Marlboro	$67,522 million
9. Disney	$29,018 million	9. China Mobile	$57,326 million
10. HP	$28,479 million	10. GE	$50,318 million

In Survey 2, Apple is worth nearly five times more than in Survey 1. The tenth brand in Survey 2 is worth more than all but four of the brands in Survey 1. The number 7 brand in Survey 2 fails to make the top 100 brands in Survey 1. And no brand has the same rank in either survey. What does this tell us? That brand valuation is nonsense? Not really. It tells us that even small adjustments in methodologies can lead to large discrepancies in results.

Setting a value on a brand is a complex process. Each survey has a different set of methodologies. You could even them out by compiling the results of multiple surveys—but to do that, you'd also have to weight the surveys. Then, we're back at the same problem.

A larger question is whether a one-size-fits-all survey makes sense in the first place. Apple is nothing like Coke. IBM has little in common with Marlboro. What's valuable to the one may not matter at all to the other. In truth, surveys like this have more entertainment and marketing value than actual utility. They're fun to read, but you need to take them with a grain of salt.

BUILDING A BETTER MODEL

Big-brand studies have a few weaknesses that we'll need to correct to measure brand vitality in a useful way.

> **SPEED.** Big surveys typically take a long time to compile. For that reason, they're often only done on a yearly basis. This makes it difficult to understand anything more than the total effect of your efforts. It also makes it impossible for you to take action in the short term. By the time you uncover problems, they may become so entrenched you can't solve them.

> **RELEVANCE.** Many surveys stack brands up against one another in a free-for-all way. Instead, you should look at brand strength in the context of your competitors. If you're

solely monitoring your own brand's value, you could see some modest increases and think all is well. You may be missing the fact that while you're doing OK, your competitor's brand value is soaring, and it will soon be eating your lunch.

SPECIFICITY. Companies that have multiple products typically have different brand strength with different audiences. We see this with a company like Microsoft, which pundits have often declared dead because they judge it only by the product lines with which they are familiar. They miss that Microsoft has a rabid and vociferous following in other, less public areas, such as enterprise software and gaming. For many brands, overall brand strength matters less than knowing the strength of certain product lines.

ACTION. We need a methodology that enables us to take action, measure results, and move things forward. One reason we favor things like NPS is that they do provide actionable insights. They let us know whether people like or dislike our brand and why.

GETTING A SNAPSHOT

Let's start with a tool that's not a precise measurement of brand strength, but can quickly provide useful information on how your brand is faring: social sentiment analysis. It does two things. First, it looks at the volume of people talking about your brand. Then it looks at the content of the mentions and determines if they are positive or negative. By coupling these two together, you can detect rapid short-term shifts in customer attitudes toward your brand. If your cuddly puppy ad went viral, you should see a spike in both mentions and positive sentiment. If a rogue employee tweeted, "Our customers can suck it," likewise, you might see a slight downturn.

"DON'T TALK ABOUT ME."

For example, in 2014, we analyzed the data on NFL player Richard Sherman, who went on an epic, unsportsmanlike rant after the NFC Championship game. Sherman is a complex character—on the one hand an aggressive, dreadlocked, trash-talking football player; on the other hand a Stanford graduate, gifted speaker and writer, and passionate advocate of education. As the controversy unfolded, mentions of him spiked, while sentiment plunged. Then Sherman conducted several interviews, and when people saw that a thoughtful and smart person lay underneath the aggressive football player, their attitudes softened.

Sentiment Trend

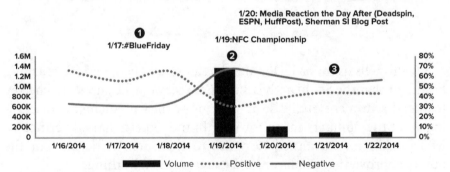

❶ On #BlueFriday and Saturday, Positive Sentiment for Richard Sherman social conversions was over 50%.

❷ Resulting from Sherman's "rant," Negative Sentiment increased by over 100% after the NFC Championship game.

❸ Since Sunday, after Sherman wrote on the Sports Illustrated blog and interviewed with CNN's Rachel Nichols, Positive Sentiment increased to 40%.

Social sentiment analysis can also catch similar trends for brands. One thing to note, however, is that social sentiment is not the same thing as brand strength, and you should weight and adjust it accordingly. McDonald's provides an excellent example of this. It has a very strong brand but relatively poor social sentiment. That's because the brand's fans are often silent on social media, while its detractors are loud and long-winded. The more salient point about McDonald's is that its brand sentiment hardly ever moves. For example, we tracked it during the run-up to the Sochi Olympics, when it was pummeled by gay-rights activists. Interestingly enough, although the brand's mentions increased, sentiment hardly budged.

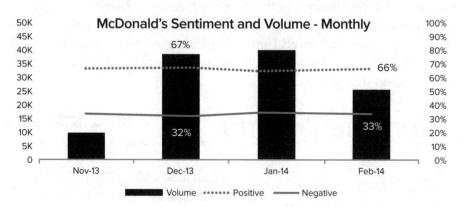

This tells us that McDonald's has a very resilient and far-reaching brand, or that the Sochi activists did not receive wide support. The key to social sentiment analysis, as with most measurements, is discerning what the numbers mean for you. Brand experts harshly criticized McDonald's for its muted response to the Sochi criticism, but the numbers prove that the brand did exactly the right thing.

GUIDELINES FOR LONG-TERM MEASUREMENT

Longer term, you'll need a process for understanding brand strength over time. Effective measurement can be different for disparate brands, and as a result, marketers have developed many systems for this task. We won't endorse any of them, but instead advise you to find a methodology that reflects your business. That said, there are a number of principles you need to follow in any brand valuation process.

UNDERSTAND YOUR GOALS. Brand value is not an absolute number. It reflects progress toward objectives. If you understand your business goals, you can start making intelligent decisions about what measurements matter. If overall brand recognition is important to you, weight it highly. If word-of-mouth recommendations drive your sales, then customer-advocates are a better measure of strength than name recognition.

BUILD AGREEMENT ON METHODOLOGY. We saw how widely the surveys above differed, which might lead you to think that brand strength analysis is nonsense. Actually that's not what the differences tell you. They tell you that there is no one-size-fits-all solution for brand value. Instead, you need to find a way to value your brand that makes sense to you and your industry. Then everyone in your organization needs to get on the same page and agree on the methodology.

USE BUT DON'T TRUST ABSOLUTE NUMBERS. Is Apple worth $76B or $143B? The answer doesn't matter. It only matters how you're doing relative to your last reading or your competitors. Apple can't sell its brand. That's not the point of brand valuation. You merely need to know whether your value is rising or falling relative to your competitors—and, more important, why.

INCLUDE YOUR COMPETITION. Always do brand valuation in the context of your competitors. You have to subject them to the same research and evaluation as yourself. That will give you an idea of your relative strength and drown out the noise created by the popularity (or not) of your industry.

GO FOR SPEED. Brand valuation is typically a slow process, taking up to a year. That simply won't work. Nowadays, digital tools allow you to check in on your brand much more frequently, allowing you make course corrections quickly if needed. Of course, speed may sacrifice some accuracy. You'll gain, however, the ability to act quicker on anything you find.

INCLUDE BRAND REACH. This is the number of people who know about your brand or product, and how big a conversation they're having. For example, we talked above about tests for aided and unaided recall, which can help you how many people know about your brand. You should pair that, however, with social sentiment analysis that shows you the volume and depth of your brand conversation. If everyone knows your name but no one is talking about you, that's a cause for concern. People are well aware of Cracker Jack. Very few of them talk about the brand.

DON'T FORGET BRAND SENTIMENT. Brand sentiment shows you what people think about your brand when they do know about it. This includes things like favorability and customer satisfaction. It also includes sentiment strength, or how likely people are to buy or recommend your brand.

CONTINUALLY REASSESS YOUR METHODOLOGY. Things change. If you start out as a challenger brand, you're going to be very concerned with how many people know your name. At that point, unaided brand recall is a big deal to you. As you move on, it may be less so. Just as the Gates Foundation continually evaluates its evaluation methodology, so you should also evaluate your brand vitality methodology. If something—either demographic or geographic—has changed with your customers, you'll need to change with it.

GOALS RULE

Of course, we have to end with a warning. Some brands take valuation too seriously. It is not an end in itself, and if you try too hard to move this number and ignore the rest of reality, you will get into trouble. Measuring what matters involves a balance. We measure short term and long term. We measure campaign success while keeping an eye on brand.

That means that business goals still rule our activities. If you have strong goals, you'll naturally seek out the difficult measurements that show progress against them. You can have 100,000-plus Facebook fans and still not impact sales. You can have 1,000,000 users of your service, but if none of them are paying attention to your ads, you don't have a business model. But with good goals, you won't be interested in those metrics. You'll be interested in seeing which fans convert to customers, and which ones help lift your brand perception.

Measuring such things requires forethought and ingenuity. It's not merely a science but also an art—one that can be as important to your business as any other creative idea.

DOES IT WORK FOR YOU?

Measuring what matters is vital to getting the most out of Does it Work? Here are a few questions to get you started thinking about how to measure the right things.

- What metrics are we using to gauge success?
- Can we tie them exactly to success, or are we taking a short-cut by looking at easy metrics like click-throughs, likes, and impressions?
- Are our metrics pulling us toward short-term thinking only?
- Are we oversimplifying things by focusing too much on what happens just before a conversion?
- When simple metrics are not available or don't ladder up to success, how comfortable are we in using directional metrics?
- Do we have tools and processes in place to measure long-term brand strength?
- Are we using short-term metrics like social sentiment to keep our fingers on the pulse of our brand?
- What's our ultimate measure of success, revenue or ROI?

ADDITIONAL THOUGHTS

For our own marketing at Google, we measure everything to constantly improve the individual user's experience. We use new web tools to do research, find out what works, measure results, and put them to use.

—**YONCA BRUNINI,** VP, Marketing, Google EMEA

With data scientists, it's about the mindset. Are they here to write research papers, or are they here to find creative ways to take their research and technology, and put it into production and good use? Not all data scientists are created equal to me. The ones that can quickly turn their work into product and marketing opportunities are worth more than a whole room full of researchers.

—**MIKE FRIDGEN,** President & CEO, Decide.com (acquired by eBay)

I think measuring the right things is critical. If somebody's looking for more trophies to put on the mantelpiece but those trophies don't actually come with sales, then the whole range of viral videos and excitement goes for nothing. At the end of the day, company management looks at margins and sales, and if margins and sales are not improving, you've got a problem.

—**TED CANNIS,** CEO FordSollers, Ford Motor Company

Marketers today have come a long way in their understanding of the importance of data, analytics, and testing. However, finding the two to five pieces of information that are going to help transform your business is still one of the hardest things for marketers to wrap their head around. You know your goals and you know your business. You need to think about what could transform your business, dig into those areas of data and focus on connecting them to your KPIs. Connecting your strategy to the data is what will help you leapfrog to the next level.

—**DMITRIA BURBY,** Global Director, Performance Marketing COE, POSSIBLE

Ultimately we all know that there are way too many KPIs out there . . . People get distracted and you end up with huge debates on things that actually are not important. Getting people focused on the very few metrics that matter is very challenging, but once you get everybody there—which usually has something to do with culture—it makes it all work.

—**PHYLLIS JACKSON,** VP, North America, Consumer & Market
  Knowledge, P&G

First of all, there is enough data to choke 1,000 buffaloes. You can really, really drown in data when you don't know what you are looking for. I don't believe in fishing expeditions, I believe in being very clear on what you are going to look for. Quite often, if not always, marketing (and its constituent parts) is the alchemy of post-rationalization.

—**DEAN ARAGON,** VP CX Brand and CEO, Shell Brands International AG

One of the biggest challenges for marketers today isn't having enough data, it's having too much, which leads to paralysis. Not knowing what to act on and what to put aside makes some people wait for the silver bullet which never comes. The best clients I've worked with have an intuition about what the data are telling them and can put themselves into a test-and-learn state of mind. They know it's not going to be perfect, but they can use what they have and work towards something better.

—**MICHAEL WATTS,** Associate Director of Performance Marketing,
  POSSIBLE

This concept of big data is all very fine, but we should only turn so many dials. We can't focus on everything. We have to figure out what is actually going to influence vital change and then work back from that.

—**RICHARD NUNN,** Brand & Web Director, Legal & General

Brand measurement often uses outdated approaches and is not meaningful in the digital age. A survey by Google and Sterling Brands in October 2013 found that only 50% of marketers consider their current brand metrics effective.

—**YONCA BRUNINI,** VP, Marketing, Google EMEA

There is so much data to sift through. The data should match what is reasonable, be tied to goals, and be actionable.

—**BRENT HIEGGELKE,** CMO, Urban Airship

Bigger companies need to start with truths that we accepted before data got big: they care about sales (short term) and brand health (long term) and cost-efficiencies in media. Everything that is new ought to show how it relates, correlates, or replaces the systems and KPIs that did that before—otherwise they run the risk of being seen as cool but not fundamental.

—**NICK NYHAN,** CEO, WPP Data Alliance & Chief Digital Officer, Kantar, a WPP Company

This may sound overly simplistic, but I have learned that it is easy to make things complicated but extremely hard to make things simple.

—**JUSTIN COOKE,** CEO, UK, POSSIBLE

We are measuring too many things. We are doing too many things. Whatever the flavor of the month is, whatever gets us "excited," we try and use without much regard for factual analysis of the outcome.

—**AVINASH KAUSHIK,** Marketing Evangelist, Google & Market Motive, and author of *Web Analytics 2.0*

07
WHAT IT'S WORTH

POSSIBLE.com/principle7

INTRODUCTION

In a perfect world, we'd all have an infinite amount of money to spend on things such as innovation, marketing, and connecting with customers. Instead, we're faced with budgets and hard choices on how to spend them. Marketers may have hundreds of ideas but the resources to do only a fraction of them. So which ones do we choose? How do we know we're making the smartest decisions?

The answer is a process known as relative-value modeling. It involves figuring out the potential impact of activities before we do them. Of course, these values are not absolute—after all, you can never predict what will happen with perfect accuracy. Instead, they should be derived the same way and should be accurate relative to one another. That way, you can make informed choices about the things you'd like to do for your brand.

> The questions we ask are—which I always ask—"I know I can drive a new sale, and that's worth X. But how much is it worth to get someone to sign up for online account management?" That helps us determine how much resources to put into it, how to prioritize that against other messages and other objectives . . . I think it's absolutely critical to do that and to get out of the land of "This is a big strategic priority" into one that says, "This is worth $75 every time you succeed." That's what we need to get to and that's what all marketers need to get.
>
> —Dana Cogswell, Executive Director, Targeted Marketing & Customer Lifecycle Management, AT&T

A TALE OF TWO CONVERSATIONS

In marketing, many of the commonly used metrics are one step removed from actual revenue. We may know that 300,000 people saw our commercial, but not have a good idea of impact. We imagine 1,000 Facebook fans must be worth something, but how much is hard to say. Since digital is still relatively new, this has put it at a disadvantage. People have been doing TV ads for a long time. That makes such ads an easier sell, than say, a brand presence on Instagram or a video on YouTube. In an uncertain world, we go with what's familiar.

So let's imagine a conversation between a digital CMO and CEO about this very topic.

CONVERSATION 1

"Hello, Bob," says the CMO, walking into the CEO's office. "I was thinking we should probably shift additional resources from TV to our mobile efforts next fiscal year. We think it'll make a positive impact on our customers and brand perception."

The boss turns to her. "You know what I want it to have an impact on? Sales. We're down 4% this quarter, and the board is not happy. We don't sell anything on mobile, so we'll stick with what we know. We just need better commercials."

"I think you should look at this long term," the CMO says. "It's all about building our capabilities over time. If we don't strengthen our skills now, we're going to fall behind."

The CEO sighs. "The board doesn't care about capabilities. It cares about making money this quarter and this year. I'm afraid we're just going to concentrate on what has worked in the past. If our numbers improve maybe we can think about it later."

You won't win this argument or many similar ones. As you move up the ranks of corporate management, sooner or later, you'll find that only one thing will help you make your point: knowing what something is worth. It might start at the director level, or maybe the C-suite—you never know. But eventually money talks, and hashtags walk. To make a difference, you're going to have to make digital speak the language of financial impact.

So let's imagine a different approach.

CONVERSATION 2

The digital CMO again breezes into the office. "Hello, Bob, nice tie."

"Thanks."

"Look, I'm going through my budget, and feel we should prioritize developing our capabilities in mobile next year."

"Why?"

"We've analyzed our customer base and found that our mobile efforts are driving 43% higher purchase rates among customers who engage with us on that platform."

"Wow, but why are sales down 4%?"

"Our purchase demographics are increasingly shifting toward mobile. Our key customers now spend 40% of their media time on their phones. And that number is rising. So if we're trying to hit them with marketing primarily in other channels and not on mobile, we'll miss them. As you know, the best 5% of our customers account for 20% of our revenue. Based on our research, they're also the people most likely to get involved with us on mobile devices."

"But still, sales are still down. It's clearly not making that much of an impact."

"You're right, but we have to look at the scale. While we're seeing good things from the mobile users we do have, we don't have that many. Less than 0.5% of our customers are engaging with us on the platform. So while mobile is not having a significant impact on revenue, the potential is there. If we can get usage up to 3, 4%—which is normal for the industry—we could easily get your 4% drop back."

The CEO leans back and closes his eyes. "What's this going to cost?" he asks.

"We could do it without any budget impact. If we could shift 1 to 3% of our budget away from TV, we believe we could drive three times as many sales over the next two months as we could just letting that money stay where it is. That could also help our TV efforts since we know that more and more people are spending time on their mobile devices while watching TV."

"Are you sure?"

"I'm not sure, but I'm confident. In fact, you can incentivize my team. If we fail to move these numbers, you can hold us accountable and take the budget back for TV out of whatever is remaining from mine."

In the end, that CEO would probably relent and agree to the changes.

> **In terms of the balance between marketing and finance, you can't have one without the other. If a marketing strategy is moving the business forward, you've now got your CMO and your CFO totally aligned, which is great because now your management team is focused in the same direction. If they're pulling in opposite directions, then something's off. . . . If finance doesn't understand the value of the marketing, then they're not understanding how that's impacting their top line. That's a problem. Similarly, if marketing can't understand how we've got to deliver budgets to grow the business, that's a problem. It's a partnership.**
>
> —*Diane Holland, Global Chief Financial Officer, POSSIBLE*

HOW RELATIVE-VALUE MODELING HELPS

This conversation reflects many of the reasons we should try to determine the relative value of opportunities. Let's look at them in a little more detail:

UNDERSTANDING POTENTIAL IMPACT. You can think of relative-value modeling as setting Does it Work? criteria prior to deciding on an action. In other words, it's a scenario-based estimation of what you think is most likely to happen if you do something. Over time, your estimates will get better as you gain a better understanding of what matters most to your customers or prospects.

ELIMINATING WHAT'S NOT WORKING. You can find activities that don't seem to be driving sales near term or long term. Stopping them will enable the brand to focus and capitalize on things that matter more.

REMOVING PERSONAL BIAS. Your CEO may like hobnobbing with celebrities, but if it's not driving sales, that's all you need to know. Good modeling can help remove subjective bias from decisions and put an end to pet projects. Everything is objective when you use the lens of revenue.

IMPROVING ACCOUNTABILITY. Everyone talks about accountability, but with relative-value modeling, you can deliver it and demand it. Some leading-edge brands have already begun to hold staff and vendors to their estimates. Coke, for example, has tied campaign performance to agency compensation.[1] Though scary to some, this actually is a positive development, so long as the compensation model is reasonable, agreed upon, and takes external factors into account.

Relative-value modeling is designed to focus on what's really important to a business. While it may seem like that risks putting too much emphasis on short-term revenue metrics at the expense of longer-term brand value, awareness, and customer experience, it shouldn't. Instead, a good model should be holistic and incorporate all of these essential elements into the mix, as well as recognize that they also drive revenue.

PRINCIPLES OF RELATIVE-VALUE MODELING

Relative-value models can be sophisticated, but the principles are not. The first principle is that you're really only looking at two things: increasing revenue or reducing costs. Most of our efforts in marketing, of course, are focused on increasing revenue rather than cost reduction. In fact, we can use relative-value models to justify increased investment in campaigns or other activities.

The second principle is that user behaviors fall into two categories: direct and indirect. Direct behaviors are entirely visible to us and lead to conversions fairly quickly. They are also very rare in digital, outside of ecommerce. The reason is that the purchase funnel is not what it once was. We used to think of moving seamlessly though the stages of awareness, consideration, purchase, and loyalty. Digital has upended that model. The consideration phase alone now occurs on a much wider range of platforms. We hear about a product from social media, we check out what people are saying on Amazon, we go to a brick-and-mortar store to look at it, we read professional reviews—all long before actually buying anything. In fact, we have to acknowledge four truths about today's customers:

1. There are people who interact with your digital properties and convert (buy, call, become leads).
2. There are people who interact with your digital properties and do not convert, but buy your stuff elsewhere (other websites or brick-and-mortar stores).
3. There are those who stop by and never convert.
4. There those who never interact with your digital properties but nonetheless buy your stuff.

In other words, no one said that it was easy to model the value of our digital efforts.

MEASURING INDIRECTLY

Luckily, "difficult" does not mean "impossible." Let's say that you have a company that makes computers. You know that a certain number of customers are visiting your site. You know some of them buy there, while some head over to Amazon and buy there. A few more will buy at retail stores. Because of this complexity you might think you can't know the real value of your digital channels. But with a little help, you can quickly get a rough idea.

Google Think, for example, provides data on consideration. Let's say that its studies suggest that for your industry or product type, roughly 47% of the sales you digitally influence actually happen on your own properties; 35% or so will occur on other sites; while 18% will occur in brick-and-mortar stores.

In this case, you know that your digital properties account for 800 sales every month. Based on that, you can roughly assume thanks to Google that this represents only 47% of the total sales you digitally influenced. The total number of sales you influenced is 1,702. Of those, 18%—or 306—took place in retail stores; 596 on other sites. Your digital ROI may look poor if you look only at your digital sales. However, it is actually twice as high if you include a reasonable estimate of how your digital properties influence spend in other channels.

Obviously, this is an extremely quick-and-dirty way to understand relative value, but it's a good starting point. In a real exercise, we would have to determine additional facts, not the least of which is how far your digital influence varies from Google's industry standard.

Almost always, "value" is a relative term. The most useful method for determining the value of an action is to compare its worth to related actions.

—Nick Leggett, Associate Director of Marketing Sciences, POSSIBLE

THE THEORY OF RELATIVITY

But even with the noise of applying industry statistics to your business, you don't always need absolute value to derive substantial benefit from your models. You need relative value that your organization agrees on. You only need to know if one thing is worth more than another.

Relativity is easy to understand. Imagine, for example, you want to know if a particular bear is faster than a particular dog. You could set them both down and see if the bear has the dog for lunch. But the authorities would frown on that. Instead, you opt for a more humane method: a radar gun. Unfortunately, when you arrive at the testing site, you realize that your radar gun is off by a few miles per hour, but you can't tell how much. Do you abandon the test? Of course not. You don't care what the actual speed is; you simply want to know which one is faster.

Similarly, we don't need to know if a Facebook fan is absolutely worth $20 or $24. That can vary depending on the source of statistics you are using for your model. What's important is knowing the relative value of a Twitter follower to a Facebook fan. If, by using the same methodologies, we determine that the Twitter follower is worth $18, we know all we need to know. In a very real sense, with this type of modeling, you can be wrong—so long as you are *consistently* wrong.

LIFETIME VALUE

Another important truth about relative-value modeling is that customers don't merely convert—some convert and convert again. A soft drink customer is not worth $1 to a brand. If the brand can make the customer a lifetime buyer, they can be worth $1 per day instead.

For a more sophisticated example, let's say you're a B2B company and you want to launch a campaign on LinkedIn. The new effort will cost you around $100,000—most of it due to hiring outside consultants. You then run some projections based on market growth and find that you will generate 388 new leads. Of those, 10% will become actual customers.

Let's also assume those leads will result in ROI of 165% this year. Unfortunately, your executive management has required that all projects of $100,000 or more must show at least an ROI of at least 185%. But you don't really have a 165% ROI if you take a long-term view. You've also bonded with some people on LinkedIn and locked in some customers. The former may become clients, and some of the latter will purchase upgrades. In fact, you estimate that over the next five years, you'll achieve 275% ROI from the original investment. Not too bad—and in terms management is going to understand.

From this, it might seem that relative-value modeling is more art than science, and there's some truth to that. It can be incredibly hard to understand what effect a fleeting visit on your Facebook page means to your overall success. But that doesn't mean you shouldn't try.

> Our company has three slogans, which although they are not original, really stand for what I believe makes a success: (1) Just do it, (2) Make a difference, (3) Make it happen. Basically, I want my staff to get on with things without any excuses as it is their job to make things happen. Equally I am aware that not every decision that is made will lead to a successful conclusion, but at least it is a decision. I find there is nothing worse than a person who thinks simply "coming to work" is their job.
>
> —Paul J. Kerr, CEO, Small Luxury Hotels of the World

ACCOUNTING FOR CHAOS AND EXTERNAL FACTORS

Relative modeling is never perfect, and that's OK. Markets are too chaotic to predict absolute value. To understand why, let's look at an ice cream store that had a model that predicted a $1,000 increase in sales due to a particular promotion in June. The store runs the promotion, but instead year-over-year sales drop.

Was the model wrong? No, it was right. But your business, it turns out, doesn't just depend on advertising. It also depends on the weather. Many more people buy ice cream when it's hot than when it's cold. And that year, it rained all June.

All models are different because they need to take into account a variety of unique factors. These include seasonality, brand quirkiness, geography, product availability, competition, and an ever-evolving consumer landscape. The best models learn from these idiosyncrasies and incorporate them into the system. The ice cream vendor should probably integrate weather data into his model to make sure he's not throwing out a good model that was torpedoed by a factor beyond its control.

Some prefer to deal with the murkiness of the estimations by using ranking and scoring systems for relative value models rather than dollars. We don't advise this, because dollars are what people understand. If you have a system that doesn't use them, it won't seem as real to you. That said, you have to realize that dollars may not be perfectly correct. In fact, in creating relative-value models, you will include assumptions and educated guesses. That's fine. In most cases you're simply creating a model that everyone can agree on and that helps you evaluate your options.

SOCIAL RELATIVE-VALUE MODELS

Relative-value models, like measurement itself, involve a creative process that demands out-of-the-box thinking. They can be quite different in different situations. To show how you can start to model, let's look at one of the most difficult problems in relative-value modeling today: determining the value of social media.

We'll start with a silly example we call the Charlie Sheen Twitter Relative-Value Model. At the height of his notoriety in 2011, the *Huffington Post* revealed that Sheen had received $50,000 for a single tweet about a brand. At the time, Sheen had 10 million followers. If we divide the cost by the number of followers, we can find out how much brands were paying for an impression, that's adspeak for a tweet in each of the followers' feeds. The number is $.005 (10,000,000 / $50,000 = $0.005). We'll leave out retweets for the sake of simplicity.

So imagine your brand has 1,000 followers. By using the Charlie Sheen Relative-Value Model, you can price out each of your tweets as roughly $5 in free advertising (1,000 × $ 0.005 = $5).

AD RATES AND RELATIVE VALUE

Of course, this is ridiculous. Sheen was going through a well-publicized meltdown at the time, and while this isn't an issue with our model per se, it did make his followers pay more attention to his tweets than they do to those of other celebrities. That gave him a tweet premium. For example, Kim Kardashian, who has 20 million people following her, was once reported to get only $10,000 per tweet. That puts her at $.0005 per impression, or one-tenth of Sheen's 2011 rate.

"*Winning?*"

In fact, a 2013 HuffPost survey showed that the amount a celeb gets per tweet varies immensely. At the time, teen mom/adult entertainer Farrah Abraham was getting around $.0004 per impression. Former heavyweight champion Mike Tyson clocked in at more than twice that at $.00086 per impression. Jersey Shore alum Snooki, believe it or not, had one of the higher rates, at $.001. (Are we alone in detecting a certain pattern in the types of celebrities the HuffPost selects for its surveys?)[2]

When looking at the value of your brand's social media channel, you could play the "Is your brand more like Leann Rimes or Justin Bieber?" game. But you'll probably want to come up with a more stable and workable model.

Using real advertising rates makes more sense, not least because tweets and native ads appear very similar. *Adweek* recently reported that Twitter ads cost $3.50 per thousand impressions (this is known as CPM, or cost per mille), which yields a rate of $.0035 per impression. That's 3.5 times what Snooki gets, and that's probably a reasonable markup. Why? You can target ads based on keywords. As a result, the ad model gives you a higher-quality audience than Snooki's, and we mean that in more ways than the obvious one. Snooki's fans are not targeted based on content.

COST VS. VALUE

Still, this is not very good. The problem is that cost is not value. Charlie Sheen may cost $50,000 for a tweet, but what value does he deliver? When we try to understand the value of an activity, we often default to cost because it's easy. Instead, we have to look at what something is really worth.

Put simply, Charlie Sheen does not deliver value for most brands, and for a number of reasons:

ASSOCIATION. A celebrity known primarily for epic comic timing and public meltdowns is not good for most brands.

TARGETING. The people following Charlie Sheen are probably not in most brands' most desired demographics.

AUTHENTICITY. Few brands could say that he is a natural fit for them.

As a result, Charlie would likely not deliver much value—and at a cost that's far too high.

HOW TO MODEL THE RELATIVE VALUE OF FACEBOOK

We can make a better model. To see how, let's turn to Facebook and try to figure out how much a post is worth to a brand. If your knee-jerk reaction is "absolutely nothing," well, that's not exactly right. To show why, let's say you have a car company. Automotive companies work well for relative value models, because their products cost a lot of money, and they have a lot of fans.*

First, let's look at how many fans you have. In this case, we'll give you a whopping 10 million of them. Next, how many of the people who become your fans are in the purchasing demographic? We don't want to count people who don't live where your cars are sold, for example, or those who are too young to drive. Luckily, we can get this number from Facebook Insights, which provides a lot of great data. In your case, it'll be 20%.

Next, we want to know how many of them will be influenced to think about purchasing by seeing a post. We also learned from surveys that only 4% of them felt more inclined to purchase a car after seeing a post. Unfortunately, another survey revealed that only 3% of those people then visited a dealer. From dealer stats, we also knew that only 10% of the people who visit actually purchase a car.

---

*We built a more complex version of this model for an automotive brand, though we've changed the values substantially.

Confused? Hopefully this chart will help:

If you do all the math, you'll get, as you'd expect, a low number. It's 10% of 3% of 4% of 20% of your likes, meaning that any given Facebook post has a .002% sales influence. And here's the bad news: even that's giving it too much credit. Why? Attribution. Other things influence purchases too. Let's say a person sees a post, then clicks on the car brand's Facebook page, and then heads over to the website and signs up for a test drive. In that case, the post does not deserve 100% of the credit for the purchase. Instead, the action has been influenced by the Facebook page, the website, and presumably the sales guy.

For this reason, we have to reduce it again. To do this we use additional research and survey to come up with an attribution. In this case, let's say the number is around 30%. So what's a post worth? We model that using profit from a car purchase (please note, we're keeping this simple by assuming every person who likes your brand sees your post, which is not true):

There's finally some good news. Remember that the posts work as ads, but since they are on your owned channel, you didn't have to pay for that exposure out of pocket. So we can tack on some additional value of cost savings that you would have otherwise spent to reach those same people. Our calculation here is similar to the one for Twitter ads in the previous post—we find out the ad rates for Facebook and multiply it by the number of impressions we had.

To make it simple, we'll use an ad rate of $2 CPM, or $2 for every 1,000 impressions, which is fairly current. That gives us 10,000,000 × $2 / 1,000, or $20,000. Now your Facebook posts are worth $180,000 + $20,000, or $200,000 each.

This number may be a little high. The model assumes that all its followers will view the post (or that all of the followers are real people, for that matter). Obviously, that isn't the case. Many people may fail to log in to Facebook the day you post it. In addition, Facebook is currently shifting the way posts appear, particularly from brands. For example, users are much more likely to see posts from people and brands they interact with on a regular basis. So depending on the current state of those algorithms, we will likely need to reduce the cost savings again.

Still, the number is not crazy. It would normally cost you a lot of money to reach 10 million fans of your brand.

Besides, these numbers are not primarily about real value. Instead, you should think of them as relative to one another. It is important to make sure they are valued in a consistent way that everyone in your organization agrees is correct. That way, you can use them to understand how to prioritize activities, where to focus, and what's working well and not. They're also great for measuring performance over time, allowing you to see how you're doing this year compared to last.

> This sounds odd coming from a data guy, but it's OK to be a little bit wrong in our modeling as long as we are consistently wrong across all channels. Our goal for understanding digital value is a quest for relative value, not absolute value. We mostly don't care that a Facebook follower is worth $12. But we care a great deal that a Twitter follower, processed through the same model, is worth two times that Facebook follower.
>
> —*Jason Carmel, Global SVP, Marketing Sciences, POSSIBLE*

SETTING PRIORITIES

Let's imagine that tomorrow you come up with a brilliant idea that could really help your brand. When would you get to it? Probably after you've done all of the things you're currently planning on doing. That's just how most planning goes. New ideas automatically go to the back of the queue, no matter how impactful they have the potential to be.

Instead, we advise something known as dynamic prioritization. It involves using relative-value modeling to determine the potential impact of activities, and especially that of smaller improvements we make to our digital properties. We put each potential project into our model and then order them according to effort they require and the potential outcome. That makes it easy to choose between projects and allocate resources effectively.

You have to regularly reprioritize projects as well. Sometimes you'll find that an idea that was your number five priority may, because of developments in the marketplace, shoot up to number one. And sometimes, an idea that started at number three stays at number three while new projects that promise even more revenue jump the queue.

HOW TO GET STARTED

Relative-value models may be one of the most difficult aspects of Does it Work? to implement. They require you to be creative about how you use data, and they require your organization to agree on its numbers. In addition, they often bring you into conflict with pet projects and big egos.

As a result, it may be best to start with an easy relative-value model first. We often, for example, start by modeling the tests we run to improve digital performance (a topic we discuss at length in the next chapter). That way, we can prove the value of modeling before moving on to much more complex things, like social media.

Additional examples of relative-value models

Let's look at some examples of relative-value models to see how they can work.

CUSTOMER SERVICE

Customer service is one of the easier things to model. It typically comes with a very high price tag that's simple to quantify. According to call center analysts Contact Babel, for example, the mean average in the United States in 2013 was $7.76 per call. And 19% of all calls cost more than $12.[3] Customer service interactions on Twitter and e-mail are far less expensive, and those that occur on an automated website cost, well, next to nothing. It's very easy to see which one you want to prioritize and how much you'll save by shifting customer behavior from troubleshooting on a phone to using online documentation.

SALES

Sales are trickier in the real world. In order to understand digital's impact on them, you have a number of things to consider. First, there's your top line revenue: how many dollars you get. Next, you need to look at the cost of those dollars. If it's cheaper for you to sell offline, that's something you want to know. If online is cheaper, that may be a place to encourage sales with free shipping or coupons. In addition, your focus should never be on top line revenue alone. You also have to step back and look at the overall impact on profit.

Finally, you need to think long term. What is the relationship as a whole worth, not simply the sale you get today? If you close a deal for enterprise software, the lifetime is worth far more than the initial impact. A car purchase, on the other hand, is worth less since loyalty to auto brands has fallen significantly in the last few decades. It all depends.

LEAD GENERATION

Lead generation can be complicated. In retrospect, it's easy to say that if you convert 10% of all leads into customers and each customer is worth $100, then each lead new lead you generate is worth $10. But it gets tricky because all leads are not created equal. If you hand out free iPads, you'll get all the leads you can handle. But far fewer will convert, since most are just there for the free stuff. In fact, they may tie up sales-people who could otherwise be dealing with real potential customers, which could depress your sales.

Lead generation activities have to focus on obtaining quality leads that increase revenue and profit.

PAID MEDIA

Ads are not the easiest thing to model, because their impact on sales is often indirect. An ad that gets lots of attention or reaches a lot of people may still not be effective (we started this book with a discussion of an ad that got tens of millions of views but had a questionable impact on the metrics it was trying to move). A few additional things complicate the picture:

- Sales driven by an ad online can occur offline.
- The sale can be delayed.
- Attribution is a huge problem if a brand runs multiple ads across multiple channels at the same time.

As a result, we have to employ additional research or clever tracking to see what kind of effectiveness ads have.

DOES IT WORK FOR YOU?

Relative-value modeling is a core Does it Work? tool. It enables you to understand the potential impact of digital initiatives and have some rational basis for choosing where to spend your money. Some thoughts to get you started.

- Do we quantify the value of different behaviors or actions?
- Do we have activities we're doing that we suspect are worthless?
- Are personal agendas part of how we choose projects?
- Do we have any way of measuring the impact of more complicated things like social media engagement?
- Would I be willing to be held accountable for my efforts? Do others in your organization feel the same way?

ADDITIONAL THOUGHTS

The concept of monetization may be new to some people but . . . with all the things that we invest in we have to think about the business outcome and monetized value to the company. It's important to have a simple, clear measure that is consistent over time. We can't change the measurement every 12 months, because then all the great work we have done to set the foundation won't get translated into impact.

—**GRACE HO,** Managing Director, Marketing, SAP Asia Pacific Japan

We struggle to prioritize in our lives, whether that is in business or personal affairs. Imagine having a calculator that could tell you the relative value of reading a book to your child versus playing catch with them. They are both important, but if you knew one was more valuable to the success and long-term well-being of your son or daughter, your focus might change. Leveraging the tools we have in marketing we can make informed decisions about where to focus our time.

—**DMITRIA BURBY,** Global Director, Performance Marketing COE, POSSIBLE

How do we leverage core capabilities that we know are going to drive revenue, while filtering out the noise to continue to invest in innovative capabilities that may not be proven or are going to show benefits a bit further down the line but will enhance our customer experience?

—**SCOTT A. LUX,** VP eCommerce & Multi Channel, Diesel

A lot of times, marketers rely on gut feel, and to some extent on, "Oh, it's always been that and therefore, we've seen the result, and therefore, we should continue doing this." So we invest our marketing dollars in order to drive an outcome that we think will happen, as opposed to really looking at the data and proof points we have accumulated over a period of time to back up our decision making.

—**GRACE HO,** Managing Director, Marketing, SAP Asia Pacific Japan

All marketing is supposed to translate to sales. Unfortunately, that's not always the case, and they need to have a little faith to proceed. Fortunately with the types of data available today (behavioral, attitudinal, and market research) you can put these together and formulate simple models that tell you a lot more about the data than just clicks and visits alone. They aren't perfect, but as long as they are used through several marketing cycles, they can be relied on to bolster that faith and give better information about what's working, what's not, and what to prioritize.

—**MICHAEL WATTS,** Associate Director of Performance Marketing, POSSIBLE

There are a lot of skeptics who deny that social media is effective because it is so hard to measure its impact on ROI. The problem is that they are true believers too, and there's no more reason to agree with them than with those who blindly believe in the value of an Instagram post. We should never mistake knee-jerk skepticism for intelligence. We simply need to measure better.

—**JOE SHEPTER,** Freelance Marketing/Advertising Writer and Strategic Consultant

As a CFO, I know people in my role want real numbers if we can get them. We're not as tone-deaf to the softer aspects of a business as some think, but I'm happier if we can put things in financial terms and look at them through a KPI lens. It makes it much easier to justify spending and investment on them.

—GUS WEIGEL, Chief Financial Officer, Americas, POSSIBLE

Today's customers are not just buyers of products but also potential advocates. This requires marketers to move away from a funnel-centric look of their marketing channels and shift towards a model that spans across the entire customer lifecycle.

—ALI BEHNAM, Cofounder, Tealium Inc.

08
NEVER STOP IMPROVING

● POSSIBLE.com/principle8

INTRODUCTION

Over the years, digital marketers have developed some idea of what works and doesn't. But when it comes to the details, as we'll see, they're not very good. And details matter. We don't know exactly what message will resonate most. We can't know in advance the optimal layout for a mobile app. We don't know if something that works on Wednesday will work even better on Saturday. In the most crucial areas, when we are trying to motivate customers, we aren't entirely sure. In those cases, anything we launch is simply a hypothesis, which we should test.

Luckily, digital allows us to do just that. We can try out two things and determine which one performs better. We can easily put up three different versions of a page and test them. We can also take an existing property and introduce modifications to try to improve performance. Over time, even small changes can have a huge impact not only on the user experience, but also on our bottom lines. Professionals call this process optimization, and it's a big part of making things work better.

> Striving for "continual innovation, not instant perfection" is one of Google's eight principles of innovation. Our iterative process often teaches us invaluable lessons. Watching users "in the wild" as they use our products is the best way to find out what works; then we can act on that feedback. It's much better to learn these things early and be able to respond than to go too far down the wrong path.
>
> *—Yonca Brunini, VP, Marketing, Google EMEA*

SO YOU THINK YOU CAN PREDICT

On a regular basis, our agency goes through an exercise called a Does it Work? throwdown. It is a great way to teach people that they know less about digital than they think.

Our throwdowns all revolve around real tests we're performing for our clients. We start with an original version of a digital property and let everyone know how well it works. Then we create three or four alternative versions intended to improve the performance against specified goals. We show the options to our team and our clients and invite everyone to predict which one will win and by how much.

Since anyone in the company can participate, we've been able to see how good a broad range of people actually are at identifying what will perform the best. You might think that senior staff and highly seasoned UX designers perform better than average. If so, you'd be wrong. Not only do highly experienced people fail to beat the average, they do worse.

In fact, we've compiled our findings about predictions into a general set of observations:

1. No one is consistently right.
2. The majority of people are usually wrong.

3. If you want to pick a winning guesser, you're better off with an executive assistant than the executive for whom he or she works.
4. *In fact, the more experience and seniority you have, the less likely you are to be right.*

These results hold for both our clients and ourselves and have been consistent over time. That said, we don't want to exaggerate the point. It's not that senior people are never right and only interns win. But as a general set of rules, it works.

> **The best-case scenario launch will squeeze 60% of the potential value of an opportunity. If you want to realize the remaining 40%, be prepared to engage in smart, prioritized optimization after launch.**
>
> *—Jason Carmel, Global SVP, Marketing Sciences, POSSIBLE*

TESTING AND SUBJECTIVE INTERFERENCE

In Chapter 3, we looked at a process by which creative decisions are sometimes made. It goes something like this:

1. Creative people or strategists come up with a large number of ideas.
2. Managers of that team then select two to three ideas to show to either clients or decision makers. These options usually are more conservative.
3. A senior manager decides which one to use.

If you think about it, this process pretty much guarantees mediocrity—at best. In the first place, you have a senior person without an intimate understanding of the problem making decisions about the solution. He or she does not even see the more daring options. Based on what our throwdowns show, this person may also not be the best qualified to make the decision

So who should make the decision? We'd suggest the customer. Rather than see your decision-making process as an inverted pyramid driven by managerial decisions, it's better to try a variety of options and see which one works best. You should of course include the ones you think will work. That's fine. But you should also cover your bases by creating hypotheses and testing them.

Test basics

For those of you who need a review, testing is quite simple. It requires one of three different types of tests—and the traffic needed to bring them to statistical significance. Here they are:

SPLIT TESTING

Split testing is the simplest of all: you pit one new option against a control (typically, the thing that's already there). For example, let's say you run a chicken restaurant and wanted to know which headline on a paid media ad gets a greater response. You divide your ads in two. Half of the people see the original headline "Nobody beats our wings," and the other half sees "Flap on by and give our wings a try." You run the test, and when you get a statistically significant number of results, you go with the one that works better.

A/B/N TESTING

A/B/n is exactly the same as split testing, except that you add additional versions. Instead of two options, you could test many according to any number of different hypotheses. (Will something edgy work: "You'll suck because our wing sauce doesn't." Maybe something value oriented: "Wing More. Pay Less." How about a nutritional push: "Hot Wings. Not

212 | DOES IT WORK?

Fat Wings.") A/B/n testing can increase your testing efficiency, but only when you have enough traffic to complete the test in a reasonable amount of time.

MULTIVARIATE TESTING
Multivariate testing involves changing more than one element in a system at the same time. For example, let's say you wanted to test different combinations of headline, background color, and image. If you had two versions of each, you'd end up with six different combinations to try. A multivariate test, of course, demands that you have a lot of traffic to reach statistical significance.

WHAT TO TEST

We've already seen how companies like Google have enough data to test down to an incredible level of detail, including shades of blue and pixel-widths of boxes. Google's wealth of data has helped it create digital services that are remarkably intuitive and work extremely well. However, most digital marketers won't have this luxury. They have only a number of areas where they can test and get actionable results. If you're in this situation, you may want to focus on a few key areas:

HEADLINES. Headlines of all kinds can have a huge impact on read and open rates. They are usually a first choice for any optimization program.

CALLS TO ACTION. "Learn more," "read more," "buy," "go," "take me there," an arrow vs. a message—calls to action are one of the most tested areas in digital. We advise testing everything from size to color.

SIZE OF PROMOTIONS. The size of any element can drastically change performance. With size, however, you want to make sure you understand the positive impact of increasing the size of one element versus the negative impact it may have on other elements.

IMAGERY. There is a reason digital properties often have smiling faces on them in certain parts of the world and none in others. It simply depends on what motivates users.

LAYOUT. In Japan, digital properties are often cluttered; in Sweden, spare. Layout can have a big impact on performance, and that will vary around the world.

PUSH MESSAGING. Push messages are a natural area to test. They offer a very intimate way to connect with your customers, but you have to be very careful you don't end up annoying them. Tests on small parts of your audience can be invaluable to fine-tune messaging prior to a large-scale rollout.

PAID MEDIA. Putting ads out there? You should be creating multiple versions of each and testing them. Why? Any normal media buy involves a significant number of placements, so testing is usually possible. In addition, most media services assume you're going to test, and they provide tools to help you. If you're not trying out multiple variants, you're not doing your job.

LANDING PAGES. Too often, campaigns are seen as locked-off efforts, where you launch and cross your fingers. It shouldn't be this way. Anytime you have a campaign driving traffic to a digital property, you should have a plan and budget in place to test and improve it.

E-MAIL SUBJECT LINES. Most e-mail marketing tools make it very easy for you to test. A slight word change in a subject line, for example, can greatly affect open rate.

TESTING BEYOND CREATIVE

So far, most of the examples we've used have talked about creative changes: messages, layouts, and image placements. Unfortunately, many organizations think this is the only way to improve. This is a mistake.

To understand why, let's look at an analog example. Large variety retailers typically keep umbrellas on wheeled racks at the back of the store. The reason is that when it rains, they can quickly move the rack to the front, where customers are more likely to see it. It's easy to understand why. If the racks were fixed in place, you could only keep umbrellas in one place. And so, you would probably see a slight uptick in umbrella sales if you always kept them in the front, but that would likely cause your overall front-of-store performance to decline. However, if you place them in the front only on rainy days, you will sell a lot more without hurting your sales otherwise.

"Raincheck."

Most of the time, opportunities like these are brand- and product-specific. Rain has only a slight effect on how many candy bars and toasters a store might sell, but a big one on jackets and umbrellas. In the digital world, we see similar things. For example, people are more likely to use career-related social networks like LinkedIn during the workday, and family-and-friend related ones like Pinterest and Instagram in the evening. They are all social networks, but their visitors skew based on the time of day.

That's why when you're trying to improve digital performance, you should definitely consider the following:

WEEKDAY VS. WEEKEND. People do not behave the same way on a hurried workday as they do on a relaxing weekend. We've found, for example, that shorter content works better on a weekday, and longer content on a weekend.

EVENING VS. WORKDAY. Time differences, as we've said, matter a lot—and it's not just on social networks. People are more likely, for example, to pop on to Amazon.com in nonworking hours. They're more likely to use laptops during working hours and mobile devices later. You should customize your experiences to take advantage of these changes.

TIME OF YEAR. Paying attention to time of year can save or make you a lot of money. For example, almost no one works during August in Scandinavia or the first week of the year in Russia. In many Western countries, the run up to Valentine's Day is great for flowers and chocolate. In China, November 11 is National E-commerce Day, during which consumers purchase more than on any single day of the year. Time of year also affects everything from movie downloads and mobile game play (more in winter) to kayak sales (more in spring). So it's definitely something you should examine.

GEOGRAPHY. As we've mentioned before, performance can change from culture to culture around the world. You may want to test different versions for different locations.

TARGETING. Targeting allows us to treat different segments of customers in different ways. This is a big topic, so we'll take time to discuss it in detail in the next chapter.

For EMEA, it is important [that] we are always testing a few things in every country but not testing the same things. We want to be efficient and learning from each other, but not copying each other, as things perform differently.

—*Yonca Brunini, VP, Marketing, Google EMEA*

Mark Twain was wrong

An old saying, attributed to Mark Twain, says that there are three kinds of lies: lies, damned lies, and statistics.* He has a point, but it's worth expanding on: statistics don't lie—people do. And when it comes to marketing, the people they most often deceive are themselves.

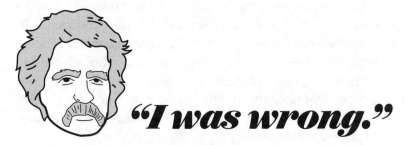 **"I was wrong."**

Everyone likes to interpret things in their favor and see patterns where there aren't any. If you watch any basketball game, for example, it will certainly seem to you that a particular player is on a hot streak (and the announcer will likely reinforce this view). But a behavioral science team at Cornell tested this notion by looking at player statistics over time. They found that a player who shoots a basket 65% of the time has a 65% chance of making any given shot. A "hot hand" is largely a statistical aberration that will smooth out over time.[1]

---

*The true source of the quote is unknown. Twain attributes it to the British politician and novelist Benjamin Disraeli, who almost certainly did not say it.

We make similar mistakes in marketing. It's easy to think things are going one way or the other, but merely because Option A has gotten the first five responses doesn't mean it will win over time. Tests have to be tests, not foregone conclusions. We had a test once in which Option A was winning 75% of the time over Option B halfway through. Most people would think that that spread is so wide that we didn't need to continue the test. Not true. In the next half of the test, B came roaring back, and we reached a null result. Lesson? You have to have the discipline to see tests through to the bitter statistical end.

TESTING PROGRAM BASICS

So you'd like to test. Over the years, we've reviewed many testing programs and found that most had significant areas where they could improve. Typically they were too timid, testing too few things or things that would not yield a meaningful result. Or they tested too rarely. One or two tests every few months does not a testing program make. Testing is one of the few places in marketing where you know that you can make improvements—so a lot of testing is recommended. A better performing in-store push notification system will yield higher sales. A more intelligently timed social media ad buy will give you more traffic. It's that simple.

That's why we typically advise setting aside 5 to 15% of any project budget for postlaunch optimization and running six or seven tests at a time. In addition, we advise a few more things:

TAKE RISKS. You can't take a conservative approach to testing. Without risk, you won't have any reward. Test big things and take chances.

RESPECT HOW STATISTICS WORK. Make sure everyone understands that tests take time and you need to build consensus around test duration. That said, some tests may not make sense, because they will take too long to be actionable.

START WITH CREATIVE. If you have no optimization program, at least optimize your properties for copy and imagery. You'd be surprised at the big improvements you can make in a short period of time.

EMBRACE ADDITIONAL OPTIMIZATION. Don't stop at the obvious. Try to think if there are other factors affecting your audience and how you can take advantage of them. In fact, it is a good idea to plan a series of tests rather than building them out individually so that you can iteratively evolve toward more meaningful test subjects.

MAKE OPTIMIZATION A PROGRAM, NOT A PROJECT. Many people look at optimization as a phase of a project—or a way to fix a known problem. Instead, you should make it an ongoing, long-term strategy to shape your understanding of your customers and serve them better. Don't think of one test. Think of a dozen, prioritize them, and then adjust them as you learn from each result.

Our final advice is to have fun with testing. Does it Work? throwdowns are great for culture. They turn optimization into a game where everyone in your organization can compete on a level playing field. As a result, they'll not only have a good time, they'll also start to understand the value and importance of your testing program.

WHEN TESTING FAILS TO MAKE IMPROVEMENTS

Did you ever have one of those friends (or maybe parents) who insisted on fixing some old vehicle or appliance to the point where it no longer made any economic sense? This can also happen with any digital property. As the culture and sophistication of users change, you may find yourself with a property that doesn't need improvement so much as a rebuild. Banging on it just won't make sense.

How can you tell if something has gone stale? A lot of times, your instincts will be sufficient to inspire that hard look. If you think a property is dated and boring, it probably is. Still, just as with your friend in love with his piece of junk, many people in your organization (not to mention your customers) may have fallen in love with the old ways and not want to change. If so, here are some more scientific indications that you need to rebuild:

- You badly lag industry benchmarks for performance. If this is true, your property may have fundamental flaws.
- Your users post numerous bad reviews or make social media complaints. This will also, incidentally, happen when you make any change, but persistent negativity could be a sign that drastic change is necessary. In particular, you should watch things like app reviews. If once good reviews start trending bad, you may need to make updates.
- You're seeing performance declines across the board. This is a sign that user expectations have shifted away from where you are.
- No tests you run seem to cause any significant improvement. In this case, you're either not being bold enough with your tests, or your property needs a upgrade.
- You see radical changes in behavioral data—a massive surge in tablet usage, for example, for a digital property might signify that a new strategy is needed for digital that goes beyond simple optimization.
- Your usage numbers overall are decreasing while competitors' are increasing. This can happen for reasons unrelated to your digital properties, but it can also be a sign you need to evolve.

Put simply, you never want to make testing a straightjacket for creative or strategic thinking. It can help you improve performance, but it should not be your sole source of insight. You still have to do the hard work of staying on top of trends and making sure your digital properties are fresh and current, and reflect contemporary expectations. You can improve any bad property through testing, but you should also ask yourself every so often if it's too bad to salvage.

> **Brands are continually investing more in ongoing optimization. However, even the brands that are doing this the best in the industry struggle to identify when it's time to bring in a new big idea versus iterate on the details. Having a clear understanding of the ROI on tests over time helps to identify the time to mix things up a bit and try a new big idea.**
>
> —*Dmitria Burby, Global Director, Performance Marketing COE, POSSIBLE*

A CULTURE OF OPTIMIZATION

Marketing departments and agencies often get pushed one way and another by personalities who think they know right from wrong. Building a culture of optimization requires you to accept that no one is right all the time. In fact most of us, even the so-called experts, cannot predict user behavior very effectively. That's why it's important to build a culture of improvement, filled with people who accept their own weaknesses and want a process that leads to things that work. Let's look at a few characteristics of such a culture:

IT LIKES GOOD QUESTIONS JUST AS MUCH AS GOOD ANSWERS. Most marketing organizations today incentivize people for coming up with brilliant solutions. But they also need to find people who know how to ask interesting questions as well.

IDEAS COME FROM EVERYWHERE. Everyone in your company can have an idea of how to make things work better. When we're improving digital properties, we have to incorporate many viewpoints.

IT UNDERSTANDS NOTHING IS PERFECT. Drop the egos. With a good testing culture, you have to be able to be wrong a lot of the time. That's a big reason why we advocate Does it Work? throwdowns. They keep everyone in check.

IT NEVER FINISHES ASKING QUESTIONS. Does it Work? requires you to constantly think of new things you don't know and then test them to find the answer.

IT ACCEPTS FAILURE. Sometimes it's just as important to know what doesn't work as what does. If a test fails to provide the lift you want, don't despair. If you set up the test properly, and the control wins, that should teach you what not to do in the future. Drill down to see if there's something you can learn.

IT SHARES. A good testing program makes its findings available to everyone. Creative people especially like to know what works so they can incorporate it into their next campaign or marketing idea.

> If there's a test, and we learn something on our logged in site, why wouldn't we take that learning and apply it to our other sites? There's a tonality there we can probably steal. Then, why not talk to the digital advertising team? Or even the television team? If you find some winning concepts or messages, why can't they be translatable? It can be hard to get an organization's head around this idea because people like to do their thing and then move on.
>
> —*Denise Karkos, CMO, TD Ameritrade*

FINAL POINT: IT'S PEOPLE, NOT TOOLS

A lot of times when we talk to clients, they say they lack the tools to do testing. Sometimes they're right. But usually when we look at the technology they have, we discover, lo and behold, that it has testing tools on board. The truth is that a good, insightful optimization program with a mediocre tool is a hundred times better than a bad one with the latest and greatest. Instead of worrying about technology, you should focus on building the skills you need to run an effective program.

As Forrester Consulting noted in the study we commissioned, "Investing in customer insights and analytical tools is a baseline requirement. But these tools are nothing without the right teams to turn data insight into measurable actions."

In other words, get a reasonable tool—or check the ones you already have—and start testing now. You'll be glad you did.

DOES IT WORK FOR YOU?

In the next chapter, we dig deeper into testing and see how we can target different parts of our audience with messaging just for them. In the meantime, remember that continuous improvement is one of the biggest missed opportunities in digital today. It is one of the few places where you can almost guarantee better outcomes while learning about your audience.

Some things to think about:

· Is there anything about your digital properties that you think is broken?

· Was there ever something you've always wanted to try on the home page but couldn't get full approval? Could you incorporate it into a test?

· Are you testing at all?

· Are you budgeting for improving campaigns after they launch?

· Is optimization an ongoing program, or simply a thing you do once in a while?

· Is your organization OK with failed tests?

· Are you making this an element of your culture or the responsibility of a smaller part of your organization?

· Do you think your organization is ready for Does it Work? throwdowns?

ADDITIONAL THOUGHTS

Create a process and a mindset that allows for creating communications plans that are flexible enough to adapt to real-time market and consumer changes. Begin to shift the focus from rigid one-and-done annual plans to more adaptive planning that flexes to accommodate new opportunities as they arise.

—FORRESTER CONSULTING, "What CMOs Need to Make Digital Marketing Work," September 2014 (a commissioned study conducted by Forrester Consulting on behalf of POSSIBLE)

For our own marketing, we measure everything to constantly improve the individual user's experience. We use the new tools offered by the web to do research, find out what works, measure results, and put them to use.

—YONCA BRUNINI, VP, Marketing, Google EMEA

Even the best planned execution can have unexpected challenges and opportunities when actual customers interact with it. If we are too busy to see those interactions and take advantage of iterative evolution post launch, then we risk losing a lot of potential value.

—JASON CARMEL, Global SVP, Marketing Sciences, POSSIBLE

When you learn as you iterate and keep your eye on your business goal, that's where you have informed risk and can make a difference to your business.

—MCGREGOR AGAN, Director of Marketing Corporate Affairs Group, Intel Corporation

I think that the test-and-learn methodology is probably the most important contribution of legacy direct marketers in the modern era of digital marketing. Most direct marketers have in their blood an awareness that great marketing is inspired, but also tested. You need to be really good at finding out what works quickly and doing more of it, and stop doing things that don't work.

—**DANA COGSWELL,** Executive Director, Targeted Marketing & Customer Lifecycle Management, AT&T

All too often, a brand will become unsatisfied with the performance of an existing digital property or campaign. They decide to rebuild from the ground up, theorizing that it is beyond repair and not worth the effort to try to fine-tune. The danger in this line of thinking, of course, is that there is no guarantee the new one will be any better than the old. Worse yet, loads of cash was spent without learning why it didn't work in the first place. Perhaps the old one wasn't broken, but rather the audience was all wrong. Or new competitors entered the market. Or the weather changed. You can insert your unidentified variable here.

—**BRAD GAGNE,** Regional Director of Marketing Sciences, POSSIBLE

We need an attitude of continuous improvement. You do your first campaign. You get a $5 CPM. You work on it and get it down to three and then two. Unless you can really do that, you're just going to find the medium quite ineffective. I think most marketers that find it ineffective do so not because it is truly ineffective. You need a hypothesis-driven approach. You have a hypothesis, and you test it. That's how many predictions work, and I think many people would say that digital marketing works in the same way.

—**MARK READ,** CEO, WPP Digital

Your culture has to allow for lots of experimentation. You have to expect some things to work and some things not. And if every time something doesn't work, you don't shoot the people, because then they obviously aren't going to want to experiment.

—PHYLLIS JACKSON, VP, North America, Consumer & Market Knowledge, P&G

Digital marketing inherited a focus on milestones from traditional marketing. Once the magazine launched or the TV spot aired, there was very little you could do to change it, so your time was best served moving quickly onto the next opportunity. But that analogy breaks for digital. A "launch" is a completely fabricated event. In actuality, we now have an always evolving platform, and our ability to continuously improve things after they are out in the world is one of the biggest advantages of digital marketing.

—JASON CARMEL, Global SVP, Marketing Sciences, POSSIBLE

Any piece of work you put into the digital ecosystem is as close to perfect as it ever will be for a singular moment— when it launches. From there, the best thing you can do for your ego, and your bottom line, is to understand its performance and continue to optimize it in real time.

—HALINA LUKOSKIE, Sr. Digital Analyst, POSSIBLE

We try to hold back some of our budget for ongoing improvement at LGEN. We reserve a certain amount of budget at the outset of a program to test what is going to work best in terms of content. We then use those learnings to our ongoing programs. We are constantly learning in this way.

—RICHARD NUNN, Brand & Web Director, Legal & General

Consumer behaviors in digital are constantly changing. Our best clients build marketing strategies to innovate, test, and then scale. Our job is to predict where digital is heading, figure out a safe way for our brands to experiment, and then drive scale to recapture the investment.

—**JIM CHESNUTT,** UK, Managing Director, POSSIBLE

One way to measure great organizations is not just by what they do, but also about what they don't do. Great organizations know that by focusing on only a few initiatives, they can get the best results. This is also true with digital campaigns. Organizations that focus their efforts on few initiatives and continue to improve them ultimately are more successful than those spreading their resources thin.

—**ALI BEHNAM,** Cofounder, Tealium Inc.

Brands dedicated to mastering the evolving digital landscape need to make two commitments: seek opportunity in innovation and invest in iteration. Too many great opportunities are dismissed prematurely by brands because of modest initial results.

—**THOMAS STELTER,** VP, Emerging Solutions, Americas, POSSIBLE

Perfection is never achieved; it is only striven for. Don't lose the vision. Keep iterating, tweaking, and improving.

—**BEN REUBENSTEIN,** President, POSSIBLE Mobile

09
ONE SIZE
FITS NO ONE

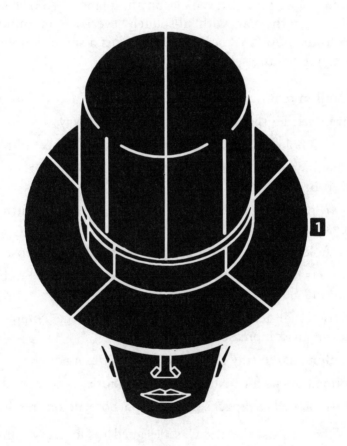

INTRODUCTION

In 2001, one of the most bizarre vehicles ever conceived rolled off the GM assembly line in Ramos Arizpe, Mexico. Intended to signal a bold design renaissance, the Pontiac Aztec bore the tagline "Quite possibly the most versatile vehicle on the planet." And it certainly was. GM built the car with absolutely everyone in mind—from Grandpa to the NASCAR scene. Below is just a small sampling of its mind-boggling feature set:

· A built-in removable console cooler
· Cargo netting that could be configured 22 ways
· A cargo hold that could carry a four-by-eight sheet of plywood
· Hyperaggressive styling—angry enough to be Walter White's car in *Breaking Bad*
· A two-piece tailgate with butt-shaped contours for sitting while tailgating
· Cup holders built into the tailgate for the same purpose
· Two sets of stereo controls so you could operate the radio while drinking a beer on the tailgate
· An optional tent/inflatable mattress package complete with built-in air compressor
· A pullout cargo tray that could hold 400 pounds
· Optional racks for bikes, skis, snowboards, canoes, and more
· Seat-mounted backpacks (for what purpose, no one really knows)

In other words, the car was designed to do every conceivable thing anyone would want it to do. If you were an outdoorsy type, you could use it as a camper. Like to go to the game? Nothing like having a built-in cooler and a killer stereo setup for tailgating. Mom on the go? There are more ways to get your shopping bags in order than you could possibly imagine. Handyman? Load 'er up with Sheetrock and decking. Bad back? Check out the killer slide-out cargo tray. You'll never have to lean over again.

"I'll sell my Aztec for $100, no, $50."

Yet no one bought one. Expecting to sell 75,000 of them every year, GM never topped 30,000. The reason is pretty simple: people don't want a car made for everyone. They want one that's made for them. One size fits no one.

I don't believe in "always on." I believe in "always relevant." There is so much stuff that brands put out on the web which merely show they are present. But, unless it truly speaks to you and what you consider worth engaging with, why would you care?

—Dean Aragon, VP CX Brand and CEO Shell Brands International AG

COMMONSENSE MARKETING

"One Size" is not rocket science, or even model rocket science. It's plain common sense. We all know that we respond better to what's more relevant to us. In today's more personalized age, we expect brands to know a little about us and treat us in a novel and surprising way. And it doesn't have to be much. At the time we're writing,

Kroger has the longest unbroken string of quarterly revenue increases. One reason is that they've gone well beyond the usual one-size-fits-all supermarket circular. Instead, they look at their rewards card data to see what their customers buy, and then send them coupons for their most common items.

Besides, providing the same experience to everyone leads to two big problems.

BLAND MESSAGING

Let's say you're a chef and you have to prepare a banquet. The only problem is that you can only serve one dish, and everyone has to be able to eat it. Well, you'd like to make everyone lobster Newburg, but you know that some people won't like the fact that their dinner was crawling around a few minutes earlier. So crawly crustaceans are off the menu.

Then you realize meat of any kind won't work, because some of your guests may be vegetarians. For that matter, someone could be a vegan, so no dairy or milk either. Of course, everyone seems to have a gluten allergy these days, so that takes bread and pizza out of consideration. And what if they're on a low-carb diet? That means you can't have refined rice, tomatoes, or potatoes. Pretty soon you're down to the point where the only thing you can make is a salad that everyone will hate.

Imagine if you could serve two dishes or three—or better yet, a whole menu of them targeted to different tastes. In that case, you could easily serve everyone something they absolutely loved. Marketing is quite similar. The more generically you target the message, the less impact it will have.

INADVERTENT TARGETING

Of course, most brands don't make that mistake. They make a different one: creating a somewhat targeted message and directing it at everyone. We can see the problem with an ad that appeared several years ago.

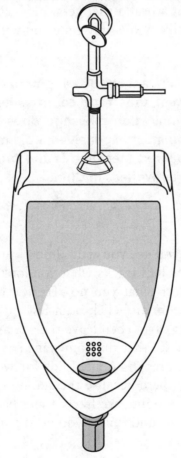

targeted advertising fail

In it, an insurance company offered bargain rates for women drivers. Only problem? The ad appeared over a men's urinal. While some men doubtless may want to alert their girlfriends or wives to the policies, most are unlikely to respond well.

A certain degree of One Size targeting makes sense. Handbag designer Michael Kors doesn't have a huge teenybopper market to address, so his marketing can target more upscale clients and leave them behind. But within Kors's audience, there will naturally be subgroups that will find different types of bags and price points.

One example of a brand that gets this is REI. Visit the homepage, and that is very likely the only time you will see it that way.

> Given China's unbalanced development between coastal east and inland west, urban and country, mega city and small town, one communication message does not reach everyone. As one of the most expensive media markets, targeting audience with tailored message is the only way to deliver efficiency and effectiveness in China.
>
> —*Elaine Ng, Operations Director, Asia Pacific, POSSIBLE*

The next time you go, you will almost certainly see something different. The reason? REI tracks what you look at and then customizes its pages to reflect what you do. Try the following to see how it works: go to REI.com and click on a few pieces of women's wear and put some in your cart. Then leave the site and return a few minutes later. You'll now see that the homepage has been reskinned with softer tones, and features discounted ads for women's clothing. The clothing is obviously there because the site now thinks you're in the market for it. The discounts are likely there because the site knows you didn't buy last time and thinks you need a nudge.

In other words, REI leaves the Aztec in the shade (or show-room). The company has used a few small insights based on customer activity to generate pages that respond to you.

DIGITAL IS SIMPLY GREAT FOR TARGETING

Some brands can go very deep into One Size thinking. Amazon, for example, knows what you've bought, and their properties suggest additional products based on that. If you like Japanese manga, they'll find it for you. And you're probably happy with them doing that and will buy more comic books as a result.

Most brands don't have the traffic, data, or product mix to pull off this level of personalization. That's perfectly OK, and it shouldn't force you into one-size-fits-all thinking. Even the most lightly trafficked digital properties still have ways they can shift experiences to be better for different groups of people. The reason? Digital was born for this stuff.

Without much effort at all, digital technology can give you a lot of insight about your audience. As your customers browse through your digital properties, they're constantly telling you the things about themselves. We can divide these insights into two broad categories: behaviors and profile.

BEHAVIORS

Behaviors usually track whatever you've done on a digital property—everything from what you've looked at to what you've bought. A very partial list of these includes:

- **PREVIOUS VISITS.** Have you been there before?
- **ACTIVITY.** What exactly are you looking at?
- **PREVIOUS PURCHASES.** What have you bought?

- **MULTIPLE PURCHASES.** If you're a loyal customer, maybe you can become an advocate.
- **CAMPAIGN.** Are you coming from a promotion or campaign? If so, you can be targeted based on that.
- **REFERRAL.** Perhaps you're coming because a friend has mentioned you in a social feed. If so, you can be targeted based on the context and content of that mention.

PROFILES

Typically, profile information comprises either demographics (age, sex, and income, for example) or psychographics (a fancy way of saying things like interests and what you tend to do). It can be just about anything, so long as it's relevant to a brand. Some examples include:

- Gender
- Interest in golf
- Location
- Number of times you've made a purchase in a brand's brick-and-mortar store (you can get this from a loyalty card)
- Number of beach vacations you take each year
- Industry conventions you attend
- Education level
- Weather in your area today and yesterday

Above all, profile information tends to be brand specific. Different brands care about different things for different reasons. Airlines are interested in how you travel, restaurants in how you eat. Getting their agenda to match yours is the whole point of targeting.

TARGETING TYPES OF CUSTOMERS

Essentially, the goal of One Size Fits None is to isolate meaningful segments of your customers. Segments are, of course, nothing new in marketing. They're simply groupings of likeminded customers. You've probably heard people talk about men 18–25, female skiers over 50, male gay travelers, or affluent retired golfers. All these groups have specific traits that allow you to target them with much more relevant information and offers.

Typically, segmentation analysis involves a lot of expensive research. Marketers undertake extensive surveys that divide their audiences into groups and uncover the key messages that will motivate them most. With digital, you can do better. You can construct great segments simply by combining behavioral and profile data together.

Here's how it works:

WHAT WE KNOW	POTENTIAL SEGMENT	HOW WE KNOW THAT
Lives in Santa Barbara, CA, searching on a travel site for flights to Vail, CO, during winter	Affluent skier/outdoorsman	Santa Barbara is a fairly wealthy location; Vail is an expensive ski resort.
Has never visited before, checking in from a zip code that has been having heavy rain	First-time shopper, open to discounts on protective clothing	People tend to make purchases to guard against recent events. Generator sales, for example, spike after power outages.
On a golf site, referred to by an ad for golf instruction video	Avid amateur golfer, middle income at least; probably open for gear purchase	Person responded to a golf ad for instruction.
Rural area, searching on the site of a nonlocal brick-and-mortar store	Avid e-commerce shopper, interested in free shipping	Person lives in an area that does not allow him/her to visit a store.

> **Salad consumption in Detroit is less on windy days. The hypothesis around this is that windy days and picnics aren't really the best because your stuff's blowing all over the place. All those different things that people don't really think about, like how we can actually use the weather conditions, can help brands be there for consumers before those decisions are being made.**
>
> —*Curt Hecht, Chief Global Revenue Officer, The Weather Company*

PERSONAS

So you've built some segments. Now what? Good question, because the problem with segments is simple: they are not always relatable. That makes tactics difficult. If we say "affluent skier," what do we exactly mean? Most creatives don't have a reference point for this. As we've seen before, creative people typically don't do well with numbers or categories (and it's not just creative people; no one does). So as we're trying to build separate experiences for different segments, we need to start thinking about them much more as simple ideas and real people, rather than categories.

That's why we advised (in Chapter 2, "A Collective Vision") that you create personas, or realistic stories about people that capture the essence of the data.

Once you have personas, you can use them to provide the creative push to customize your customers' experience. This can be as simple as changing a headline or as complicated as redesigning an entire site or app. Whatever you do, you should be prepared to test against the benchmark of your existing properties and check for lift. Typically, as we'll see in the next section, your performance will improve substantially.

SMALL CHANGES DELIVER
BIG REWARDS

Even making small and obvious changes can have a huge impact on your performance. To see how, let's look at two examples—one from a financial company and another from an appliance company. Note, these examples simplify real-world engagements in which we helped to boost profits by making subtle changes in digital properties.

FINANCIAL WEBSITE

A financial company wanted to see if it could find out a way to increase sign-ups for its online stock trading service. We came up with the hypothesis that noncustomers who came to its digital properties for the first time would have different motivations from other noncustomers who had been there before. The reasoning is fairly obvious. The first group might not be shopping around and could respond to a financial incentive. The second was likely shopping around and would have a better understanding of their options. We found through tests that this was correct. First-time visitors tended to respond well to money-off offers—free cash can be a good motivator to a casual purchaser. The returning customers didn't care about a few extra dollars. They had been looking at other sites and were primed to think about the cost and value of trades over time. Instead of cash, we offered them free trades. Voila, we had a big increase there too.

APPLIANCE MANUFACTURER

The appliance manufacturer was somewhat unique in that it only had a handful of models. That allowed us to do something highly effective with returning visitors. Most people, we believed, were only interested in one of the company's products. If they came and looked at a washing machine, they would not come back and look at a toaster. So we created a unique home page touting each model with its own messaging and imagery. If you came to the site and looked at a dishwasher, the next time you returned, the home page would be mostly about that dishwasher. The results were dramatic. Their engagement numbers shot up by 200% and buying actions increased by 125%.*

In other words, small changes can have big results—and you don't necessarily need sophisticated data to make them happen. You merely need to be smart about how to divide up your audience.

> **People don't want the cookie-cutter messaging. They don't want the same thing. The reason they're doing this is that they want an individual experience. We are getting to the point where a broadcast mentality is just fundamentally incongruent with the consumer's expectations.**
>
> —Brent Hieggelke, CMO, Urban Airship

WHY BRANDS FAIL TO TARGET

If you're not targeting today, don't beat yourself up. You have some very prestigious company. If you're primed to look for this kind of thing, you'll notice missed opportunities everywhere. Off the top of our heads, the names include major banks, car companies, huge retailers, and well-known restaurant chains. Go to an online store and search on bicycles, and you'll be surprised how few times a bike shows up in a prominent position the next time you visit.

Brands typically fail to target for two reasons: strategic failure and technological failure.

---

*The company did not sell its products directly online. So "buying actions" would be things that showed an intent to purchase, such as using the retailer locator tool.

STRATEGIC FAILURE

Strategic failure occurs when marketing priorities take precedence over customer needs. Customers do not always respond well to blanket messaging. Sometimes they want one kind of message; other times they're looking for another. However, many marketers forget this and push their own agendas instead. For example, if a product manager sees Product Category X as the future of the company, she won't want to promote Product Category Y, even if a customer has shown interest in it.

This failure can also happen when a marketer misunderstands the significance of a metric. For example, online sunglass retailers know that home try-ons are a great indicator of a person's intent to buy. However, you'll notice that many of them throw ads for a free try-on at you, even if you've already ordered their product and know your size. This blindness occurs because they're looking at a single metric and not interpreting it in the context of the total customer journey.

TECHNOLOGICAL FAILURE

Even if they have the strategic vision, many brands lack the technology to create varied experiences. To do so, you need a pretty good content management system or optimization technology. Are they cheap? The good ones, no. But they are worth every penny if you have the people and processes to take advantage of them.

PRINCIPLES OF ONE SIZE FITS NO ONE

So you'll want to get started with One Size Fits No One. Congratulations, you won't regret it. But there are a few things you'll want to know first.

LEAD WITH BUSINESS GOALS. This step should have stopped surprising you by now. Begin with clear goals so that you know what outcomes you want to generate.

LEARN WHAT CUSTOMERS WANT TO HEAR. One Size Fits No One requires a customer-centric viewpoint. This means that you should be less interested in what you want to tell people, and more interested in tailoring your communications to their expectations. You don't have to abandon all marketing strategy and leave the site experience solely up to the user's desires, but you should incorporate their mindset into your thinking. Sometimes they may want to hear something different from what the big dog wants to tell them. If your company wants to be known as the best slipper-sock maker in the world, congratulations, you have a goal. That said, if a customer comes and searches on sandals, they may already own a drawer full of slipper socks.

WORK WITH THE DATA YOU HAVE. It'd be great to have a Google-sized mass of data, but most brands don't. Still, you can work with almost any scrap of information. Every marketer will have different opportunities. Some will only be able to act on basic things, such as previous and next visits. Others will have access to detailed information about users. You should never use a lack of detailed data as an excuse for inaction.

FORM HYPOTHESES ABOUT CUSTOMERS AND DEVISE DIFFERENT EXPERIENCES FOR THEM. For more on testing basics, please see the previous chapter.

MAKE SURE THE MESSAGE FITS THE MEDIUM. As you target different groups with messages, you may be tempted to overdo it. If you know, for example, that Group A responds to a particular message well, you may want to plaster it everywhere for them. Instead, you need to remember that their experience is going to be poor if you oversell. For this, you need to trust your smart creative people and have a little restraint.

TEST AND BE TRANSPARENT ABOUT RESULTS. The reason we ask Does it Work? is because sometimes it doesn't. Only good testing discipline will deliver the long-term success you want.

LEARN. As you work to make better experiences, take the data you gather to learn more about your visitors. You can use the data to uncover other relevant segments or ways to target them. Then apply this information as broadly as you can to other digital properties.

SHARE. Let everyone in your organization know what you've learned about your customers.

THE PERILS OF LAZY TARGETING

Google AdWords is a terrific product that gives almost anyone access to targeted advertising. The way it works is that you choose to advertise on particular keywords that people enter into the Google search engine (you can also have your ads show up on blogs with specific content). For example, if a person searches on "sprinklers," a hardware store can place an ad featuring lawn care products. If Google finds a food blog with a biscuit recipe, it can display an ad there for your patented biscuit cutter.

That said, brands over time have gotten this hilariously wrong—mainly because they failed to understand the mindset of people making searches and the kinds of content they might be looking for. For example, eBay sells everything under the sun, so its Indian marketing team came up with very clever idea. If a person searched on a keyword, the headline of the ad would be that keyword. If you clicked on the ad, you searched the auction site on that and saw results based on that. Sounds brilliant at first. If someone searched on "jackhammers," the ad's headline would be "jackhammers," and clicking it would take you to a search result page on eBay filled with jackhammers. Perfect. Except—what if you search on something you normally don't buy?

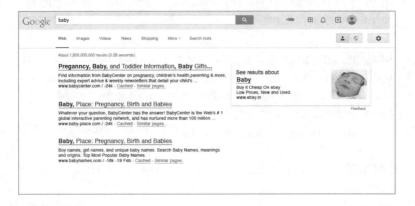

In fact, if you searched on "baby," eBay offered to sell you one—either new or used. This would not, we imagine, have been terribly effective. And you don't even need to search to have things go horribly wrong. You just need to have the wrong keyword.

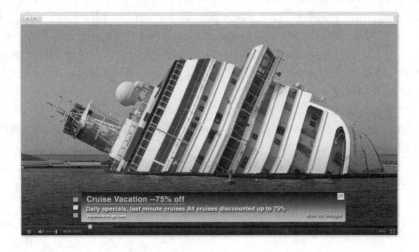

Shortly after the Costa Concordia cruise ship went down, videos of it appeared all over the Internet. Some featured overlaid ads that offered discount rates on cruises! In other words, pay attention.

THE PRIVACY PARADOX

A much-less-amusing problem occurs when marketers overstep their boundaries. Digital behavior can reveal an enormous and sometimes troubling amount of information about a person. For example, think for a moment of the books you search for on Amazon. Somebody studying that information might know that you have a child with discipline problems, an embarrassing medical condition, or a dire financial outlook. Even more disturbing, marketers can match patterns with certain life conditions. You don't even need to search on something—we can tell from the way you navigate a site that you fall into a particular category.

This came to light most notably when Target started targeting newly pregnant women. The reason they did so is simple: pregnant women, for whatever reason, tend to be very loyal customers to the first provider of their baby gear. Of course, targeting such women is nowhere as complicated or involved as most newspaper articles made it seem. You simply have to find a woman who suddenly starts searching on maternity wear and infant products. You would probably need to test your algorithm a bit to isolate women shopping for someone else's baby shower—but this wouldn't be too hard.

Unfortunately, once it had worked through this problem, Target chose an overly obvious targeting method: it sent each expectant mother a printed booklet with ads for maternity clothes and diapers. When a man got one for his teenage daughter, he grew understandably upset and complained to the store. Of course, she turned out to be pregnant. That's creepy.

Interestingly enough, the pressure to use data to target specific segments, however, does not only come from marketers trying to make a buck. It also comes from consumers demanding better and more responsive experiences. Companies like Apple use their data very effectively to anticipate customer needs—and deliver experiences that can seem like magic. As consumers, we expect that level of responsiveness, and it often only comes with extensive data collection.

We call this the privacy paradox. On the one hand, consumers want us to understand them better. On the other hand, they want their private information to remain exactly that. We can't resolve this question for you. Brands will have to navigate for the foreseeable future, and the rules will likely change over time. At some point, consumers—not marketers—will set the guidelines for what's an appropriate trade-off.

Even so, there are already a few ground rules we can establish.

AVOID PERSONAL TOPICS. We all have personal information that we'd rather keep private. In most cases, you should not ask personal, private questions of your data. If you're caught doing so, the damage to your brand could outweigh any benefit.

MASK TARGETING. Even if you're not doing something as creepy as Target, it's a good idea to sometimes mask it a bit so as not to make people uncomfortable. Make sure you include random, untargeted content along with the targeted materials. Sometimes saying less can be more impactful than saying everything you may know.

USE TARGET-NEUTRAL LANGUAGE. Ads and promotions should appear natural. Try not to say, "we noticed you were doing X, would you like to do Y." Simply present the ad for Y.

Ultimately, it's up to you, but if you have any question as to whether something would be appropriate or not, err on the side of caution.

TARGETING IN THE PHYSICAL WORLD

Targeting gives us the ability to learn a lot about our customers. But don't forget that what you learn online does not have to stay online—and that technology can give you insight even when people aren't actively using it. As location-based services and wearable technology advance, we'll have greater insight into what the people in our physical locations need and expect.

For example, let's say you're a frequent flier, logging more than 400,000 miles per year. Airlines love you—in fact, you're a platinum member of three different carriers. You also have downloaded all their apps, and because you travel so often, you tend to leave them on all the time.

That enables the airlines to do all sorts of things to tailor their experience to you. They know when you arrive at the airport, when you're waiting for your luggage too long, and even where you like to stay. That could allow them to bundle together hotel packages that make sense for frequent business fliers.

More important, they know when you don't fly with them. Airline A can track where you fly when you don't book with them. They may learn that you prefer another carrier on certain routes because it has a direct flight and Airline A doesn't. Or that you prefer another carrier on a route Airline A has. In that case, they may want to look at the timing of flights or costs.

In any case, Airline A can look at their segments, uncover demand, and figure out ways to serve you better. They just have to start somewhere.

DOES IT WORK FOR YOU?

One Size Fits No One is a simple idea: make things better for people based on what you know. It can require sophisticated technology or just plain common sense. However you do it, it should increase the responsiveness of your digital properties and feed into consumer expectations of smarter, better experiences. Here are some questions to start thinking about:

- Does our organization treat all of our customers and prospects the same?
- Do we worry that we need sophisticated segmentation data to treat people differently?
- Do we use readily available digital information to segment customers?
- Do we have any hypotheses about how we can divide up our customers using readily available digital tools?
- Am I concerned about going over the line and targeting customers with overly personal information?
- How can we use digital segments in other areas?
- When creating content for our digital channels, are we focusing on creating the one version that will "work for everyone" or different versions for different audiences?

ADDITIONAL THOUGHTS

The trend of moving to personas versus traditional segmentation has helped because you can bring a composite of experienced drivers that usually will break down traditional age, socioeconomic concerns, etc. We think about the personas of those that are going to be early drivers for our business, the early movers and the early majority. In B2B, our biggest challenge has been to speak to a persona in terms of emotion and experience that makes them want to have that product inside of their end products. If you can start creating a connection at a more emotional or experiential level, in large part, you can actually have more pull on the market than a traditional segmentation approach.

—**MCGREGOR AGAN,** Director of Marketing Corporate Affairs Group, Intel Corporation

Tailoring a digital experience is a lot like planning a date. It's likely you have an idea of what your date's personality is like, what their likes and dislikes are. You try to think of things that you both will enjoy doing. The same goes for digital—you have to think about your partner, or consumer, and build an experience that makes them feel special, unique, and understood.

—**HALINA LUKOSKIE,** Sr. Digital Analyst, POSSIBLE

Marketers have said, "Right person, right time, and right message" for decades, but it's really meaningful now because you actually can do that. We are all enabled. The question is, how do we catch up and build the resources—and the infrastructure—to create this personal message?

—**DENISE KARKOS,** CMO, TD Ameritrade

If you look at the early days of digital, it was relatively easy. It was Google or Facebook, or similar services. Now there is a myriad of different digital groupings because, as individuals, we buy into a different basket of things, depending upon our level of needs. Keeping up with all of those things—understanding audience and how that changes with different weeks and different gender mixes, and matching those to what you need in a specific campaign—is different than it used to be. Often, now, we're looking for the group that is highly social and the heavy users of our products in the early stages, so that they help us boost the social channels and are telling their friends. That's different for every product, so finding the right, most efficient way of doing that has made what was a media planning role much more complex. It's now all about getting to audience. There are just more channels—that's important.

—**ANDREW CONNELL,** CMO, Western Europe, Devices Business, Huawei Technologies

Being able to talk to your customers in a personalized, one-to-one way is one of the holy grails of marketing. As close as we can get to this vision of brands talking directly to people, the more authentic and relevant the brand message becomes to the customer, and the more opportunity we have to understand how we can grow the business and best serve customers.

—**ANDERS ROSENQUIST,** Phd, Director of Emerging Media, Strategist, POSSIBLE

The other thing that we're seeing is that for moms, weather is probably the first marketing impression of their day. They wake up, they get out of bed, and they used to turn on the *Today Show* to start things out. Now what we're seeing is that they're grabbing their iPhone, seeing what the weather is, and it's like, "All right, let's get the family in line." They're going to play outside today. Do they need a jacket in the morning? They don't. Are shorts going to be appropriate at noon? Can they wear long pants in the morning? I think for a mom it's extraordinarily personal for them and everything that they need to do.

—**CURT HECHT,** Chief Global Revenue Officer, The Weather Company

It's usually more effective to target based on mindset rather than demographic segment. A 28-year-old mother of two and a 67-year-old nun behave in remarkably similar ways when they get a toothache. Data people who can ask the really relevant questions and dig into the underlying motivations of people at specific points in time are invaluable.

—**JOE SHEPTER,** Freelance Marketing/Advertising Writer and Strategic Consultant

I believe that we still continue to be in the world of one-size-fits-all thinking. It's because a part of it is that it is actually hard to have an enormous amount of content, promotions, images, and text and call to actions. Most people who work inside companies profoundly underestimate how hard it is for a company to create content.

—**AVINASH KAUSHIK,** Marketing Evangelist, Google & Market Motive, and author of *Web Analytics 2.0*

Loyalty killed marketing. To place in context, Apple has never done better in terms of sales and brand affinity simply by providing the best consistent connected experiences. The way that they launch global campaigns is seamless and not tiresome. And if a brand is serious about building a long term commitment to the consumers, then experiences before campaigns. Loyalty before marketing. Marketers are embracing marketing technology now to empower themselves to better perform real-time. The secret sauce is then to find an agency partner that is committed to building the best experiences and content to stitch everything together.

—**PAUL SOON,** CEO Asia Pacific, POSSIBLE

Much of Swift's work is published on our clients' social channels. It's not uncommon for us to publish two to three variations of a social post targeting two to three different groups of people. We work with our clients' media agencies to determine success and failure of the creative against the target and optimize for the future.

—**LIZ VALENTINE,** Cofounder & CEO, Swift (a POSSIBLE agency)

There are great tools available now to personalize based on segmentation rules. It is more often the case that the marketing decision makers are overwhelmed with data points and options, [rather] than that they lack the tools to deliver on the personalization promise. I think the best rule of thumb is start simple, keep a close eye on the success metrics, and make adjustments to tune each case.

—ADAM WOLF, Chief Technology Officer, Americas, POSSIBLE

The future of digital marketing is to segment users using a unified view of customers across channels, and targeting those segments or personas with a consistent or cohesive message. Organizations engaging in a unified marketing approach will be the ones winning the marketing battle.

—ALI BEHNAM, Cofounder, Tealium Inc.

10
FRAMEWORK FOR INNOVATION

DON'T BE FIDDLER DICK

Imagine you're a recently minted travel agent in 1996. You love your profession, you love helping people, and you think you'll be putting them in spacious hotel rooms and cramped plane seats forever. But within five years, travel sites like Orbitz and Expedia have taken away your job and transformed your industry.

Stories like these put us into panic mode. What if our field is the next to be wiped off the map? What unseen danger is stalking my business? What can I do about disruptive change? If you're concerned things are moving too fast for you to handle, let us introduce you to a man whose thriving enterprise was upended not in five years—but on a single day.

His name was Fiddler Dick. At one point, he was the innovative leader of a gang of pickpockets who worked London train stations. Early in his career, he had noticed something interesting. As a train arrived, the people getting off tended to be distracted: they looked for loved ones, they picked up luggage, and they jostled through the crowd. All of this hustle and bustle made it easy to relieve them of their cash and jewelry.

Dick also noticed something else: while the thieves worked the crowd, *the train was getting ready to depart.* It made the perfect getaway vehicle. All you had to do was steal a few things and stroll on board. Because information in those days could not travel faster than a train, you would be long and safely gone before your victims realized they'd been robbed—or the authorities could do anything about it.

The scheme worked beautifully until August 24, 1844. On that day, a policeman used a new invention, the telegraph, to wire a description of Dick and an associate ahead to the next station. The astonished thief was caught and sentenced to 10 years in a penal colony.

Dick offers an extreme example of the dangers of a lack of innovation. While he had been brilliantly inventive early in his career, he grew lazy and happy. Disruptive change came, and that was the end of him.

> Too often ideas live and die in a conference room, never getting the chance to be tested. True innovation requires trying things in the real world. Try often, learn from the successes and, more importantly, from the failures.
>
> —Ben Reubenstein, President, POSSIBLE Mobile

WHY DICK LOST EVERYTHING

It's easy to cast Dick as a stupid man, blind to developments that now seem obvious. This is unfair. In spite of his choice of profession, he clearly wasn't a fool. He was quite respected (or notorious) in his trade for his skill and success. His funny name tells us he had a strong brand in certain circles and had taken the time to learn the violin. And to be fair, we all have our blind spots.

Still, Dick lacked two things that might have helped him: an innovation process and luck. We'll see that it was the latter, not the former, that was probably more decisive in his case. Here's why.

DICK WAS INNOVATIVE, ONCE. His initial railroad pickpocket scheme showed a mastery of the communications and transportation technology of the time. Unfortunately, like most criminals, he was a little lazy. Once he found something that worked, he stuck with it and did not innovate further. He assumed that what worked today would work tomorrow.

HE WASN'T CURIOUS. Dick didn't bother to develop an innovation radar. He stuck to his trade and didn't concern himself with things outside his field. As he watched workmen putting poles in the ground and stringing wires along them, he should have asked a few questions. If so, he might have realized that his business model had viability issues.

HE DIDN'T PAY CLOSE ATTENTION TO OTHER INNOVATIONS. If something fundamental changes, you'll want to recognize it as quickly as possible. After Dick's arrest, for example, the other pickpockets in town reacted swiftly to the news. London papers reported that they were quite afraid, and most stopped stealing for a while until they understood the implications of the new technology. Of course, criminals tend to be highly sensitive to new developments in their fields. You should follow their example.

CONSTANT INNOVATION IS KEY. The London pickpockets failed in another respect, however. They were unprepared for change, and so had to lay low for a considerable time until they could figure out the new landscape—which doubtless hurt their bottom lines. But imagine if they had a culture of innovation. Thieves who were continually looking for new ways to pilfer pocketbooks would have transitioned seamlessly to the post-telegraph era. Instead, they were used to doing things a certain way, and when disruptive change hit, they went hungry.

USUALLY, YOU CAN ADAPT. Most peoples' skill sets are transferable. The telegraph didn't put a stop to railroad station pickpocketing, but it did cause its practitioners to rethink the risks underlying their business model. Eventually, they either diversified into other verticals, such as shoplifting and armed robbery, or found new ways to ply their trade.

Last point: Dick was also unlucky. Only a very small number of pickpockets were tripped up by the novelty of the telegraph (though it proved a useful crime-fighting tool overall). If Dick had woken up that morning with a bad flu, someone else would have been caught, and he would have had another shot at innovation.

DEFINING INNOVATION

You can find plenty of definitions of innovation. A dictionary will say it's something new. A book on innovation will occasionally tease out fifteen different types of innovation, each with its own definition and needs. For Does it Work? purposes, let's keep things simple: *An innovation is something new and better that helps us achieve a business goal.* Let's break this down.

NEW. This should be obvious. You have to come up with something that isn't around. This does not necessarily mean that no has ever done it before (in fact, you'll always be hard-pressed to find truly new things). However, it should be new to your organization and the way you do business.

BETTER. Innovation means looking at existing problems and fixing them. You can improve your customer experience, reduce costs, or extend your audience. You could also improve your customers' lives, which they'll like.

HELPS ACHIEVE BUSINESS GOALS. Like everything in Does it Work?, we don't set out to innovate without thinking it through. There is no room for innovation for innovation's sake. All innovations must ladder up to near- and long-term business goals and success metrics. We can create a terrific new campaign idea, but if it's merely pretty or reaches the wrong demographic, the innovation is pointless.

To make a big impact, you have to start with revolutionary, not evolutionary, thinking. To create a culture that supports this type of thinking, it's critical that businesses reward the right things and support and celebrate failure because we learn by taking risks.

—*Yonca Brunini, VP, Marketing, Google EMEA*

WHERE TO INNOVATE

Henry Ford is often credited with saying that if he had asked customers what they wanted, they've have said, "a faster horse." Whether he actually said this doesn't matter; the point is clear. He followed his own ideas of what was needed and created the Model T, a car that was so affordable that it opened up an entirely new market. Since then, this quote has crystalized a debate around whether innovators should listen to what customers say or not. We'd, of course, say both. You need incremental improvements, especially in digital properties. Otherwise, they become stale. But you should also swing for the fences sometimes. Look beyond what your customers tell you and start thinking about what you could do that they would like, irrespective of whether they know about it or not. After all, you're the technology experts, not them.

So where to start innovating? You have to uncover your customers' problems and look for solutions that fix them. To get started, ask yourself some of the following questions:

WHAT'S WORKING? You can ask this inside your industry—or better yet, outside. It's not important to pay attention to every single innovation that hits a blog somewhere, but you should make sure you're paying attention to the big ones, the things that are really taking off. They will be places you may want to focus.

WHAT'S NOT? No company's marketing processes are perfect. So ask yourself what kinds of problems you are having. The big ones will jump right out. You're not engaging with your customers between purchases. You are struggling to differentiate a superior product in the retail space. Your customers have an unmet need they don't even realize. Attack those problems and you're well on your way to innovation.

WHAT PROBLEMS ARE WE HAVING? You can ask this question both internally to your organization and externally to your customers. Problems that need solutions are ripe areas for sustainable innovation.

WHAT RISKS OR POTENTIAL RISKS ARE WE FACING? You should consider if anything systemic or coming in the marketplace is threatening your business. That's a clear area for innovation.

WHAT ARE MY COMPETITORS DOING? Here you should take an honest look at their efforts. Is there anything you want to copy, emulate, or improve?

When exploring each of these questions, you should be filtering the results by areas where you can make a difference in your customers' lives. You shouldn't, for example, ask whether you can make a splash on a new social property. You should ask whether you can do so in a way that deepens and improves your relationship to your customers. An innovation is simply not useful or even desirable if it does not provide value.

You also have to have innovation that goes beyond just what the user wants, because there are things that you think of that the user can't imagine.

—*Lars Madsen, Business Strategy & Development Director, Canon Europe*

DIW STEPS TO INNOVATION

So what does a good innovation process look like in a Does it Work? context?

DEFINE SUCCESS. As we said before, you need to understand what you're trying to accomplish with innovation, and what success looks like. And needless to say, "being innovative" cannot be a success metric.

SET A REGULAR BUDGET. You have to be able to plan for innovation, so you'll need to set a stable budget that exists on an ongoing basis. The good news is that it doesn't have to be a huge amount. Coke sets aside 10% of its marketing budget for innovation. Which is to say that 90% of its budget goes to things the company is reasonably certain will work.

DON'T PUT ALL YOUR EGGS IN ONE BASKET. You should think of innovation more as a portfolio strategy. Trying a handful of high-risk projects makes it more likely you'll succeed with a few. Venture capitalists tend to do this, backing 20 or so different start-ups, but only expecting about one in ten to amount to anything.

CREATE A SAFE ENVIRONMENT. We need to allow for failure and for people to have the space and lack of interference needed to produce magic. You have to make sure everyone knows that they'll be judged by a good smart effort rather than success or failure.

ALIGN CULTURE. One of the big mistakes innovators make is not allowing for the culture of their organizations. You shouldn't innovate so far out of the box that your company will be unable to use the resulting innovation or your customers will be able to understand it. You need to make sure that what you create aligns with your organization and audience.

ASK, "DOES IT WORK?" It's a powerful thing to come up with a new idea. We build narratives around them and imagine their success to be overwhelming. As a result, many people cling to innovations much longer than they ought to, just as venture capitalists will stick with an innovative company long after its success appears highly doubtful.

With innovation and Does it Work?, you not only have to stipulate ahead of time what success looks like—you also have to measure and be transparent in your evaluation of whether it's working or not. If it doesn't work, take heart. As we saw before, even the most innovative companies don't have a particularly good track record with innovation.

Final point: one-off innovation rarely works. Instead, you have to be prepared to iterate on your innovation and make it better. We'll discuss this in detail below.

> **Fear is one of the biggest barriers for innovation. We are risk adverse sometimes because failing could get us fired or could cost a lot of money to the company. I think the only way to break this barrier is to not put all of the eggs in one basket. We need to manage risks, and we need to try to minimize risks. That is the function of the marketing team. All of us are professionals, so at the end, we need to empower our marketing teams to take risks and to know how to handle the situation. For me, that is the culture. What's very important in companies is how we can start feeding this culture and how we can start empowering people.**
>
> —Guido Rosales, Europe Group Integrated Marketing Director, The Coca-Cola Company

RISK MANAGEMENT

You might not think of a film studio as an innovative or risky business, but it is actually one of the most so. The economist Arthur De Vany (better known as one of the fathers of the Paleo diet) and W. David Walls have created statistical models that demonstrate the extreme unpredictability of the outcome of a movie opening.[1] The dynamics are similar to those found in viral videos and other high-impact campaigns. Not surprisingly, film studios have developed a sophisticated portfolio system for managing risk. The yearly budget is divided into multiple funds, each with a pool of resources. Each fund invests in several feature films. Overall, roughly 20% of the films will fail and lose money, 60% will break even, and 20% will make a lot of money. By managing extreme risk in this way, larger studios thrive, while independent studios tend to flame out with their first big failure.

"20% of films will fail and lose money, 60% will break even, and 20% will make a lot of money."

All innovation efforts carry risk. The Boston Consulting Group does an annual survey on the subject and usually ranks Google in its top three, if not first. The reason is obvious: it has produced many successful innovations. But the company has also had a number of notable failures, among them Google Wave, Google Buzz, Google Dodgeball, and Google Knol. So when we look at innovative successes, it's important to consider the context in which they occur—one in which failure is expected and accepted. Google is a great innovator because it's also good at failing.

"Make money, I will."

The important thing is to understand risk and failure, and put them into your own context. To do this, we define risk in three different ways:

RISK. Risk occurs whenever you try to do anything new. Whenever you innovate or set aside a practice group for innovation, you have to be comfortable with the idea that it may produce nothing or that what it produces may fail. The important thing from a Does it Work? standpoint is to ensure that you understand your failure and learn from it. Google Wave may have failed, but it allowed the company to explore an innovative way of looking at communications. That provided its teams with insights that likely influenced the much more successful Google Docs product.

GREATER RISK. Doing too much. This occurs when you're doing too much innovation and trying to do too many things at once without tying them to the future success of your business. Your appetite for risk needs to be controlled by the exigencies of your budget and the realities of your brand. Coke devotes 10% to truly innovative marketing every year. Of course, you may only be able to do less. But don't bite off more than you can handle.

GREATEST RISK. Not innovating at all. If you're sitting on your hands in a field that's moving, well, you could end up like Fiddler Dick.

WHAT TO DO WHEN YOU SUCCEED

Done right, innovation often leads to something that used to be unusual in marketing: an actual product. Nowadays, it's inexpensive and relatively easy, for example, to make something and put it in an app store. You might think this is a great idea—and it is. But apps are not intended merely to surprise and delight your customers. Rather, they exist to help build deeper and more intimate relationships with them. Done right, they can make your brand more valuable to the customers who matter most to you. Unfortunately, that only happens if you're prepared to sustain the innovation.

We call this the "bug-fix paradox." We did a brief study on it in early 2014 that looked at a snapshot of fast-food apps. We divided them into two groups. The first had made recent or frequent updates. The latter had launched a version months in the past and then mainly performed bug fixes. We then compared the apps' all-time ratings to those of their most recent update. That could tell us whether people liked them more or less after the most recent improvements.

The recent and innovative apps, of course, usually had ratings that had improved over time. The bug fixers' ratings all fell. This seems counterintuitive. A less buggy app should still beat out a buggier one, shouldn't it?

We can trace the problem to two causes: the environment effect and external competition. Both are new and unique to the digital space.

THE ENVIRONMENT EFFECT

Brands traditionally marketed against one another in their own category. In other words, Burger King tried very hard to make a better sandwich and more appealing ads than McDonald's. It did not try to be as whimsical as Bud Light or as tough as Ford trucks. By a similar logic, when one of the chains' marketing departments releases an app, the others should simply release a better one.

Unfortunately, this simply doesn't work anymore. Nowadays, consumer expectations are shaped by the whole product, technology, and marketing landscape. Google, Apple, Netflix, Facebook, and Amazon set the pace for what a digital experience should be—not Subway or Dunkin' Donuts. This is something we call the environment effect. With it, your rivals do not set the bar for the experience you create; instead you must meet your audience's expectations for smart, seamless, useful experience. This issue is particularly acute for companies that target millennials, as they come with highly digital expectations out of the gate.

Probably no product company has understood this better than Nest. Before its arrival, thermostat companies competed solely with one another. Nest instead built an appliance for an environment shaped by peoples' experiences with digital services. It was intelligent and connected, saved money, and made peoples' lives easier.

Some brands get this too. The Five Guys app, for example, has a feature that lets you reorder your last order. That's the kind of smart capability that dovetails nicely with customer expectations. In other words, whenever marketers build a product, it has to meet the high standards of a digitally savvy populace. You can't just help people find a restaurant; they want something more.

EXTERNAL COMPETITION

The second worry you have is that your product, service, or unique differentiator will run up against real-world competitors committed to doing the very thing you are. When creating the FuelBand, for example, Nike ran into FitBit and Jawbone. Both of those companies lived and died by their fitness products. It's all they did. That can be tough to beat, even for a strong brand like Nike.

Competition can be hard to avoid and even anticipate. A good example of the competitive environment is the US-based brand Sea Tow. The company is a category killer in the business of towing stranded boaters. Working much like the American Automobile Association or the ARC Europe, it allows you pay for a yearly membership for a low rate. Then, if your boat breaks down on the high seas, Sea Tow comes to the rescue for free. This can be a compelling deal, as a single tow from an independent provider can cost thousands of dollars.

Sea Tow leaped into the digital age with an app perfectly related to its brand. It gives boaters useful information when they're on the water: wave and weather conditions, tides, and even a GPS. And if you need help, it syncs up with Sea Tow's rescue service to dispatch a boat to your exact location.

It sounds great—until you realize that there are hundreds of apps out there that do many of the same things better. There are weather apps that give up-to-the-minute wind advisories, apps that log all your expenses on a boat, chart apps for the entire world, distress beacon apps, dozens of weather apps, and so on. Sea Tow has an advantage over the others in that it doesn't need to make money from its app. But its competitors are working hard to maintain a qualitative edge.

So while Sea Tow has done a great job of extending its brand, it has also clashed with a hungry class of developers who do nothing but sea-based apps. To stay relevant, it has to be just as agile and aggressive as they are. And that can be tough for a brand whose real focus lies elsewhere.

ITERATIVE INNOVATION PROCESSES

Obviously, there is no one-size-fits-all innovation process, but a sketch might be useful to show the contrast with typical marketing processes. Here are some typical phases in product development:

1. OPPORTUNITY DEFINITION. First, you define the design brief and the problem you're trying to solve. There are a number of ways to do this. We usually combine brainstorming with in-depth research into what's working, what competitors are doing, and what consumers are missing in the marketplace.

2. USER JOURNEYS. Following the design brief, you define the different ways in which you want people to interact with the product and what the outcome should be. What do you want people to do and feel? What are the touchpoints that will be required? What are the functional and technical requirements?

3. CONCEPT DEVELOPMENT. In this phase, you hone user journeys into hypothetical concepts that may serve as solutions. You can then evaluate them using a range of tools from prototypes to focus groups and user studies.

4. DESIGN AND BUILD. We believe strongly in a two-pronged approach to designing and building. First, we have an iterative design and prototyping phase in which we define the concrete vision for the experience. We follow this with an Agile development process that iteratively builds toward the product vision.

5. MARKETING PLANNING. As important as the interaction design of the experience is, it won't work if people don't know about the product. And we're not just talking about publicity and name recognition. One large problem digital marketers face is that they're bringing an unfamiliar interface to their consumers. Obviously, you should follow best practices for design, but marketing is a good way to ensure that you're not releasing something completely unfamiliar to your users.

6. BETA TESTING. You have to ensure that the experience is completely honed and refined before it goes out the door. Beta testing is a great way to have real users test your product in a live environment. Be sure to get both qualitative as well as quantitative feedback from them and make any changes you can.

7. LAUNCH. Remember to bring a bottle of champagne. It's tradition.

8. OPTIMIZATION. Collect data and other research (e.g., A/B testing) to determine what's working and what's not so that you can make iterative improvements to the experience.

9. EVOLUTION PLANNING. The final step is to plan for what's next. Every experience is part of a larger landscape of products and technologies, so it's important to end every project by looking forward and anticipating how the experience will need to evolve. Many marketers launch a product with the idea that they will "see how it goes," and then improve it later if it takes off. Instead, you should budget for three additional iterations of a product. Test, listen, see what's working and what's not, and improve.

COMMITMENT AND INNOVATION

You might think that with such an unfamiliar process, it would be difficult for brands to have success with these kinds of products and services. Nothing could be further from the truth. The path to success is actually fairly simple: you have to stop thinking like an advertiser and start thinking like a product designer and manager. If you want to be a big part of your customers' lives—and there's every reason to attempt it—you have to commit to building things they're going to love.

So what kind of commitment?

TIMELINE. Timelines are much longer. This doesn't mean that you necessarily take a long time to make updates and changes (Tesla famously reworked its onboard software seven times in the first two years after launching its product). It means that you're in it for the long haul with a steadier effort rather than a big push.

STABLE BUDGETING AND PROCESSES. Needless to say, a longer timeline means that you need to have a more regularized budget and a continuous effort to maintain or improve the experience.

STAFFING. The biggest difference for marketers may be in the approach to outside talent. Traditionally, agencies have relied on the expertise of external vendors or freelance creatives for specialties that they lack. For example, they might work with production companies to produce video, photographers to shoot stills, and technology vendors to provide campaign-specific solutions. With marketing as a product, this all changes. You need continuity. You have to bring all relevant areas of expertise in-house—at the very least at a leadership level—in order to ensure a tightly integrated, nimble, and effective team.

ORGANIZATION. The people who work on product-focused development also differ from what you might traditionally find at an agency or marketing department. Here are some of the highlights of what's different from traditional organizations.

1. **CREATIVE.** The creative team needs to have strong user experience and interaction design.

2. **STRATEGY.** Strategists need to incorporate user research. Their role is as much about forming empathetic insight into people's needs vis-à-vis the brand as it is dissecting the competitive landscape.

3. **TECHNOLOGY.** The team has to do more than simply select vendors; it takes a leadership role to ensure that the platforms being developed can be sustained by the organization that will be managing the product.

4. **PROJECT MANAGEMENT.** The team takes an active role in shaping the user experience.

TRUST AND PATIENCE. Marketers are used to launching a project and seeing how it does before doing more of the same. Innovation efforts won't necessarily succeed at first. Technology often launches with bugs; content can take time to get right. That's why you need to have a long-term plan to make improvements and updates, and the tenacity to stick by your ideas to make them work.

CUSTOMER CENTRICITY. From user-centered design to sensitivity to shifts in desires and needs, you have to stay ahead of what customers want.

MARKETING. Interestingly enough, you need to promote these properties, just as you might a product or service. We'll have more to say on this in a bit.

> I like being in an environment where I want you to swing big. I want you to embarrass yourself every once in a while. I want you to swing so hard that you fall down at the plate, because every once in a while you're going to hit a towering home run—and that's what I'm here for.
>
> —Josh James, Founder & CEO, Domo

GOING BEYOND CAMPAIGNS

In marketing, innovation can occur both in a campaign and outside of one. But some of the best innovations aren't necessarily the flashiest. Every once in a while, you identify something that can live for a while or an idea that can be repeated again and again. Marketers should always have these kinds of innovation on their radar, because they're the best kind.

What are we talking about? A few years ago, our analysts made a discovery that enabled us to offer an entirely new service for targeting ads to people on travel sites. It's called, for lack of a better name, WYAWYG optimization (Where You Are and Where You're Going).*

Our client had tasked us with improving response rates on digital properties. This involved everything from selling customers additional services to improving their experience by tailoring resources to them. To do this, we tried a number of things: changing layouts, messages, colors, and so on. We also looked at things such as loyalty and geography. If you came from an affluent zip code, for example,

---

*You can pronounce this "why a wig," or simply not pronounce it at all.

we might serve a four-star hotel promotion when you booked a flight. If you came from a middle-class one, three stars might be more your speed.

Then our scientists suggested looking at where people were booking from and where they were going at the same time. Once they came up with the idea, it made intuitive sense.

For example, let's say a person books a flight in December to Tampa, Florida. In December, Tampa is one of the warmer places in the United States; it's not uncommon to have great beach days. It's also relatively inexpensive, which makes it a popular tourist destination. So if people are booking a ticket from a colder location, chances are, they're coming for vacation. You'll do well serving them up promotions for seaside hotels, fishing tours, and so on.

But what if they're not from a cold place? Let's say they're booking from Corpus Christi, which lies on the Gulf Coast of Texas and has roughly the same weather as Tampa. Those customers are not interested in beaches. They're either visiting family or attending a business convention—and probably the latter. That gives you a different set of options for serving their needs. By targeting promotions content with a notion of cold vs. hot, you will see a lift in response rates every time.

We found that similar WYAWYG concepts worked in many circumstances. If you're doing a map search on restaurants from a location 500 miles away, it's fairly likely you'll be visiting that place. So in addition to serving ads for what you're seeking, we might look at promotions for travel-related services. We've found that without knowing anything else about our users, we could make reasonable guesses about their intentions. Over time, that enabled our clients to improve the customer experience (and make more money, too).

As unsexy as it is, WYAWYG is a great innovation. Why?

> **IT'S TRANSFERABLE.** We can use it on almost any client, especially those in travel and hospitality. Even though the exact triggers may differ, WYAWYG principles will almost always help brands in that space.

IT'S REPEATABLE. WYAWYG works the same in every context. We can use it again and again for different brands with similar results.

IT MAKES A MEASURABLE IMPROVEMENT. The benefits reaped by WYAWYG outweigh the costs.* In fact, we can very roughly predict the amount of sales lift a brand will get with this kind of optimization.

IT DRIVES LONG-TERM BUSINESS SUCCESS. Any travel-related brand that uses WYAWYG will serve its customers better. Their promotions will target customers more effectively and provide them with things they're interested in, not distractions. That helps improve the brand relationship and customer experience—while driving increased revenue.

A BRIDGE TOO FAR

All that said, with invention, you can easily go too far. It's difficult to make people accept an entirely new paradigm. To make inventions work, you'll need to innovate around understood norms. Apple did this quite smartly. It introduced users to its interface concepts through a series of product releases: iPod, iPhone, and then iPad. Each built on the others, so that while the products were revolutionary, users understood them quite well.

For a counterexample, we can look at one of the most touted innovations of the last 20 years: the Segway PT. Invented by Dean Kamen, it was launched with incredible hype. Noted venture capitalist John Doerr said it could be bigger than the Internet. Steve Jobs declared that it could be potentially more important than the PC (he reportedly later said that the design "sucked").

---

*Up until a point. We've also found that trying to get too granular with this technique eventually diminishes the returns.

However, the product struggled immediately. Aside from the fact that Jobs was probably right—riders do look a little odd—the Segway had a bigger problem: nothing preceded it. It simply appeared—a wholly new way to transport yourself. Its name even indicates a transition to something entirely new. But by definition, that meant that the existing world was not ready for it. There was no infrastructure to support it, and nothing quite like it. Workplaces didn't have any place to store them. And there were no public charging stations available.

As a result, no one knew quite what to do with them. We can see this most obviously from the legal framework that has been built around the vehicles. In Austria, a Segway is legally a bicycle. In Denmark and Norway, it's a moped. In Germany, you need a permit to ride one on a sidewalk. In the Netherlands, you can only ride one on a sidewalk if you have heart disease. In Mexico, you can ride them anywhere. In Great Britain and most parts of Australia, you can't ride them anywhere except on private property. Regulation in the United States, however, takes the cake. Every town can make its own rules, and many of them do. Segways can be permitted on roads in a city and forbidden in its suburbs. Then again, thanks to the Americans with Disabilities Act, handicapped people are allowed to use them anywhere, but only on sidewalks.

Of course, Segways were not a complete failure. People eventually found uses for them. They're great for tour groups, for example. Law enforcement and security companies use so many of them that Segway makes a special model just for them. And as we write, the company has made a move into robotics, turning the technology into a platform for development, especially for military uses. In the end, Segway proved successful. To do so, however, it had to struggle and adapt an extremely innovative product to uses that made sense for it.

Is innovation only about technology?

What is innovation to most people? The graphic below gives us an idea. It details a comparison of searches on three different terms: *marketing innovation, business innovation,* and *technology innovation,* over the last 10 years. In 2006 at left, you can see there was a wide divergence between the ideas of businesses innovation and technology innovation. Over the last five years, however, the two have completely converged. They now move almost in lockstep.

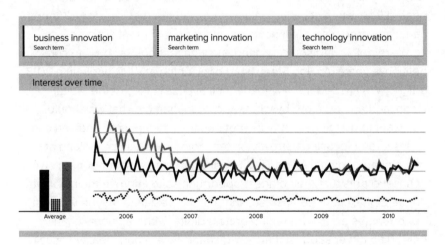

This tells us something interesting: technology has come to be seen as the core innovation strategy for businesses. This may seem natural; after all, technology is where we see the greatest advances today. But it is also far from the only way companies can innovate. For example, they can improve customer service, manage employees better, employ creative retailing strategies, simplify (or complicate) supply chains, expand how they market—and the list goes on. Technological innovation, by itself, is not the only innovation strategy.

In fact, even many supposed tech companies became successful without being particularly technologically savvy. Zappos offers probably the best example. We think of it as an innovative online pioneer, but in the beginning, its technology was dead simple. Owner Nick Swinmurn started the business by taking pictures of shoes at local retailers and then posting them to a website. If a customer placed an order, he would physically retrieve the shoes from the store and ship them. Even then, this was hardly the apex of technology.

The true innovation for the company came with customer service. At the time, people saw a great risk in buying shoes and clothing online. They couldn't try them on, and it cost money to return something, if it didn't fit. So Zappos (known as Shoesite.com then) did its research and found that people know their shoe sizes fairly well and are far less likely to return footwear than any other piece of apparel. So the company offered free return shipping on any item, and the rest is history. Zappos had uncovered a simple innovation and rode it to great success.*

We're not saying you can't innovate with technology, but the competition is fierce. As Jon Steel, head of planning at WPP, wrote in a 2013 article, "We are seduced by the technical possibilities of the digital world, and are led more by what we can do than by what we should."[2] You want to do things that work, not because they're cool and you can.

Instead of focusing narrowly on technology, we advise looking at the entire picture to gain an edge. Whenever we start an engagement, we counsel clients that their biggest opportunities to improve their ROI may not be digital channels. Instead, some of the best (and maybe the best) opportunities exist in better integrating digital with traditional channels. We'd never suggest that new technology is a bad idea; we usually advise exploring it in the service of other ideas.

---

*From its humble beginnings, Zappos rose to become the #1 online shoe retailer. It was sold for $1.2 billion in 2009 to Amazon.com.

DOES IT WORK FOR YOU?

These days, everyone is clamoring for innovation. Does it Work? approaches the task with a reasonable, straightforward ask. All we're trying to do is market better and help our business reach its goals. So, a few things to think about:

- Do we have a budget specifically for marketing innovation?
- Do we know what success for our innovation program would look like?
- Is our organization OK with failure?
- Can we create a safe space for innovation?
- Are we planning for innovation on an ongoing basis?
- Do we have a way to manage risk, or are all our eggs in one basket?
- Once we come up with something new, do we have a process for ensuring its continued success?
- Are we looking beyond campaigns for ideas that will work?

ADDITIONAL THOUGHTS

The truly great companies are the ones that pay close attention to how consumers are using their products and then feed that information back in to make sure the next product is even better.

—**ANDREW CONNELL,** CMO, Western Europe, Devices Business, Huawei Technologies

I might be a little bit of a contrarian. I don't believe that you can say, "Today is the day to innovate." In fact, . . . what we find and what I have seen is that you, in a sense, do something and you discover it as an innovation. Very often we don't set out and say, "This is a new innovative approach." It's almost like, catch yourself doing something great versus command yourself to do something great.

—**MCGREGOR AGAN,** Director of Marketing Corporate Affairs Group, Intel Corporation

My personal view is that true leadership must drive innovation, especially in large organizations. Unfortunately, organizations in general tend to fall down on new ideas or tend to do the same thing. Innovation requires a push to learn more, do more, and try more.

—**TED CANNIS,** CEO FordSollers, Ford Motor Company

The beauty of innovation is that it's trial and error. As soon as you move ahead, you can learn from the things that you did well and the things that you did poorly. You need to understand why you failed and then avoid making the same mistake in future.

—**GUIDO ROSALES,** Europe Group Integrated Marketing Director, The Coca-Cola Company

When I think about innovation, I always think about the West Coast offense in football. It's a system. And any team that wants to run this system needs to bring in very specific players with differing skill sets than other offensive systems. We call them unicorns around here. But for them to be successful and drive real innovation, we have to have a system. It should guide every decision we make and inform every piece of code, art, copy, and data point we create. A system—with the right skills operating it and properly defined goals—will almost always lead to innovation (or the end zone).

—MIKE REEDER, SVP, Brand Strategy & Insights, POSSIBLE

When you take risks, they need to be informed risks. There must be a hypothesis behind what you're doing so that you learn from it.

—MARK READ, CEO, WPP Digital

I think too many large corporations are still too much stuck in the committee way of innovation, and then, it becomes a much more internal group that decides what actually gets out there.

—LARS MADSEN, Business Strategy & Development Director, Canon Europe

For me, a brilliant idea is when you see it, and you wonder why no one thought of it six months, 2 years, or 10 years ago.

—JEAN-PHILIPPE MAHEU, Managing Director, Global Brand & Agency Strategy, Twitter

Innovation is a cultural and operational commitment to establishing practical guardrails that are malleable enough to encourage creative exploration. The perception, processes, and definition of innovation certainly vary; however, the commitment to these guardrails creates a framework where innovation becomes practice.

—**THOMAS STELTER,** VP, Emerging Solutions, Americas, POSSIBLE

A .250 batting average can be really good when you're doing a lot of innovation. Innovation must incorporate a willingness to take risks and a willingness to try things that probably won't succeed. Because in the end, if you try 10 things, and you find two or three winners, that's a good success rate.

—**DANA COGSWELL,** Executive Director, Targeted Marketing & Customer Lifecycle Management, AT&T

When you take a small team and point them at an opportunity or problem without constraints, I think they're more likely to come up with something interesting.

—**SAM DECKER,** Chairman, Clearhead and Entrepreneur, Investor, and Board Member

With mobile, so much of what's happening right now is innovative just because it's never been done before. There's no playbook for a lot of the things that are happening, especially when you think about apps.

—**BRENT HIEGGELKE,** CMO, Urban Airship

The most important component for innovation is a mind-set: being open to disruption. It is easy to declare a desire to innovate; it is quite a different thing to create the conditions in which true innovation can take place. This requires putting aside the status quo—and all ways in which an organization is dependent on the status quo—in order to be open to new solutions. . . . The counterbalance of this openness needs to be the appreciation that innovation for innovation's sake is a meaningless distraction. Innovation should not be judged on its degree of newness; rather, it should be judged on the degree to which it solves a problem in a new, better, and essential way; by its inherent value, not just its comparative novelty.

—JASON BRUSH, Executive Creative Director, POSSIBLE

11
CONCLUSION AND NEXT STEPS

A LOOK BACK

We began this book with a discussion of the most awarded campaign in advertising history, *Dumb Ways to Die*. To many, our critique may seem like sour grapes, but we think it highlights a major challenge for our industry: the need to move from merely celebrating the things we love toward embracing great work that also makes a difference.

Every year in our industry, campaigns from the recent past compete for what are called "effectiveness" awards. In most cases, the success metrics are self-reported. There are no challenges to them, nor any investigation of the claims. Not surprisingly, in 2014 *Dumb Ways to Die* tore a bright path through these contests. It won four golds at the Asian Marketing Effectiveness Awards, and on June 17, 2014, was shortlisted again at Cannes.

The timing could not have been worse. A few days earlier, a 17-year-old boy had broken into the rear carriage of a Metro train with his younger brother and a few friends. To show off, he decided to stick his head out of an open window. He struck a signal pole and later died at a nearby hospital. The memorial, which happened one day before the shortlist was announced, was heartbreaking.[1]

A few weeks after that, a popular Melbourne street artist known as Sinch stripped off his clothes and climbed on top of a Metro train in an apparent publicity stunt. As horrified passersby looked on, Sinch accidentally touched some of the equipment linking the train to the overhead power lines. He immediately went into convulsions and died.

Melbourne wasn't done. A week after Sinch's death, a slickly produced video appeared online. It featured a so-called Spiderman group performing stunts that involved jumping on and off the outside of Metro trains. To date, it has received more than 120,000 views on YouTube and thousands of likes. In the wake of all this, a bemused official called for an increase in penalties for such activities. Apparently unaware of *Dumb Ways to Die*, he also called for a public service announcement![2]

Like most public transportation systems, Metro Trains is very safe for its regular passengers. But Melbourne teens have a well-earned reputation for reckless behavior around trains. Every year, police arrest more than a hundred for crimes like train surfing and coupler riding, a local invention that involves clinging to the back of a moving train.

Dumb Ways to Die seems to have done nothing to curb this activity. In fact, coupler riding has become so popular that some are calling it a craze. So let's be honest with ourselves. The video, song, and app were wonderful pieces of content that probably didn't do much good. That's OK. Not everything does. But instead of praising it for effectiveness, we should be considering why it had such a limited impact. We might start by asking young people in Melbourne what they think of it.

If we are to be taken seriously as an industry, we have to stop asking what we love and start paying attention to what's great and also works. We have to be clear and transparent about our objectives before we launch a campaign. We have to define success up front. We have to measure the right things and be honest about the outcome, even if it's not what we'd hoped. We have to learn from our mistakes (yes, we all make them) and strive to make a meaningful difference for brands, young people, or whomever we're trying to affect.

Sometimes that difference may be a few percentage points of revenue, an increase in buying-related actions, or a bump in brand perception. Much more rarely, we're going to be called upon to save lives. When that happens, we have to have the tools and the mindset to move the metrics that matter. We have to care about what works.

DON'T MISS THE POINT

That said, you can make a big mistake with Does it Work? Shortly before finishing this book, we held a meeting to try to come up with a title for it. After hearing our analysis of *Dumb Ways to Die*, one of the participants suggested that we call it, "Does Your Marketing Work: Calling Bulls**t on Advertisers." She seemed to think Does it

Work? is anti-advertising, anti-Cannes, and anti–everything else. It is a way to feel superior to an entire industry. That misses the point entirely.

We cherry-picked *Dumb Ways to Die*. It's an odd campaign with an unusual objective. It says nothing about the industry as a whole and certainly nothing about Cannes and other awards. In fact, our research showed that Cannes juries are pretty good at finding effective projects. They may not always choose the best, but that's fine. Rewarding campaigns solely based on performance would be a joyless task. And criticizing anyone for honoring *Dumb Ways to Die* at this point would be asking too much. The video came from a good place, had good intentions, and reached a huge audience. If it had been created to strengthen a major brand, it would have been a smash success. Unfortunately, it had a different set of success metrics, and Does it Work? requires us to be honest about that.

Data should not be a way to beat people up or overturn widely held assumptions. Rather, Does it Work? recognizes that data can help our industry understand the impact of its activities better than ever before. It can help us avoid certain mistakes and identify real opportunities. It can enable us to recognize success and learn from failure. It augments our knowledge; it does not replace our instincts.

We live in a remarkable time for marketers. Today, consumers want so much more from us. They want us to inform and entertain, but they also want us to share their values and aspirations. They want us to help change perceptions and support them as they change the world. Campaigns like Dove's "Real Beauty" are making women feel beautiful, even if they don't look like the women on the covers of magazines. Nike's "Find Your Greatness" celebrates ordinary people who decide to commit to a new life of health and fitness. Brands such as Coke are bringing people together with wonderful ideas like vending machines that make friends collaborate to get a beverage. When marketing has a mandate for positive change, it becomes something we all want to do.

Does it Work? celebrates this direction. It's a companion and a helper, a way of growing and learning to be more effective at what we do. If brands are going to do important work, they should do it well. Too many people today think of data as limiting or as something that tells us what we don't want to hear. But data is only useful if an intelligent and creative person is asking it good questions. It's only valuable if it's pushing things forward and making us better and our consumers happier. It does not serve the cynical and disdainful. It serves the optimistic and helpful. It serves those who care about making things work better than they already do.

A COMMITMENT TO CREATIVE IDEAS

As we said at the beginning, Does it Work? is a strategy for creative people. Its purpose is to harness new tools and capabilities to ensure that organizations develop the best ideas they can. Although many of the principles seem afield from this, they're not. In different ways, they serve the ultimate goal of making us better at our main task. Let's review how each principle can do this:

BUSINESS GOALS ARE EVERYTHING. Without goals, you can't know what metrics your creative ideas are trying to move. You're not advertising, you're simply creating content. Our role as marketers is not merely to entertain, we have to entertain with purpose. Business goals lead the way.

A COLLECTIVE VISION. Today, a great idea can come from anywhere: project management, user experience, copywriters, even receptionists new to the company. By making everyone understand objectives and work together toward them, we can knock down silos and achieve a more horizontal environment that unlocks our organization's true potential.

DATA INSPIRES CREATIVITY. With the help of data, creatives can actually become better. The catch is that data must be translated into clear insights that can inspire them to work more effectively.

FINDING UNICORNS. Unicorns make everything better. Whether creative themselves or good creative cheerleaders, they keep things positive and the conversation flowing.

CULTURE PREDICTS SUCCESS AND FAILURE. Culture also predicts whether you have an environment that enables creativity to thrive or keeps people locked up and afraid to take chances. A good culture shares information, listens to every idea, and selects the best one—no matter where it originated.

MEASURE WHAT MATTERS. Measurement is about honesty. It's about understanding what works and doesn't. If we measure what matters, we understand whether our creativity is having the effect we want. Are our brilliant ideas really as brilliant as we think? By measuring correctly, we can know, and we can improve.

WHAT IT'S WORTH. Digital marketers are in the business of helping businesses make money. We need to focus all of our creative energy on the things that matter most. That requires us to use relative-value modeling to understand where to put our energy, even if we're not precisely sure of the exact impact.

NEVER STOP IMPROVING. You no longer have to throw bold ideas in the garbage because you're afraid they won't work. Instead, you can test multiple versions of an idea and stick with the one that wins. In addition, you can always improve on a good idea and make it great.

ONE SIZE FITS NO ONE. Targeting specific groups requires a different kind of creativity: asking the right questions of data. Soon, every creative idea will include a creative understanding of our audience.

FRAMEWORK FOR INNOVATION. This one is simple. You need to create a framework where smart people can come up with creative ideas and help them grow.

IMPLEMENTING "DOES IT WORK?"

It's easy to write a book painting an abstract picture of a business strategy and insist that everyone follow the rules blindly. This is a mistake. The task of changing an organization from its current state to one that embraces all aspects of Does it Work? is huge. It's something you work at, but never complete.

At least there's some good news: you don't have to do everything at once. You may find it easier (or more logical) to implement some aspects than others. You may not make relative models for all social activities today or for a long time. You may not find a single unicorn next year—or have the budget to hire a mule, for that matter. But you may be able to shore up your goals with meaningful metrics. You may be able to align against a collective vision. You may be able to shift resources to allow for postlaunch optimization.

So as a final point, let's look at how you can implement these principles and in what order. Above all, we should remember that Does it Work? is a philosophy more than a blueprint. It's up to you to decide how far to go with it.

BUSINESS GOALS ARE EVERYTHING

Business goals are nonnegotiable. If you don't have goals and the criteria that support them, you have no way to know if you've succeeded or failed. It's that simple.

That said, you can start out slow. If a business has goals (and most do these days), they may not have metrics to support them. That could be your first step. Next, you can start giving some projects goals and using the results to learn and grow. The good news is that goals are both fun and easy. The important thing is to start setting them. Ask yourself, "What are the Does it Work? criteria for this initiative?"

A COLLECTIVE VISION

Alignment comes not far behind. Goals are not terribly useful if no one knows what they are or has any reason to work toward them. You certainly need to align both employees and agencies with clear incentives to make a difference.

Alignment can also help with silos, but this is a bigger task. It requires not merely an understanding of shared goals, but an understanding of shared touchpoints. For that, you're going to need to create touchpoint maps and commit to an ongoing process of self-examination.

DATA INSPIRES CREATIVITY

Very few organizations today use data to inspire creativity, and this is a shame. As long as data remains an evaluation tool, creative people are unlikely to embrace it. They need to see it in action before understanding how it can help them.

With this, we recommend starting small. Select a few projects that bring data and creativity together. Gain experience and success, and then slowly roll it out into the rest of your organization.

FINDING UNICORNS

Finding unicorns is a slow, ongoing process. Most companies do not turn over their workforce overnight, though some really bad ones come quite close. That said, you should start building a digital workforce as soon as you can, developing new talent and keep digital top of mind in both retention and acquisition efforts. As you add new employees, you can slowly start building a team of unicorns.

CULTURE PREDICTS SUCCESS AND FAILURE

It's critical to ensure you're providing a climate that works for unicorns. This will mean striving toward a low-key, egalitarian atmosphere that fosters a sense of achievement. Unicorns like different challenges, and you'll need to make sure they have the chance and the processes in place to let them learn and grow.

You also need to give all your staff a sense of achievement, of doing things that make a difference. That will develop naturally as you implement more of Does it Work? The data-driven processes that measure, test, and refine your properties will deliver a clear understanding of what works and what outcomes have occurred over time.

MEASURE WHAT MATTERS

How soon can an organization get rid of click-through and conversion metrics and start focusing on the real metrics driving its business? It depends. Measuring what matters requires both organizational discipline and specialized skills.

First, you have to find creative data people, those who know how get beyond the usual measurement and understand what drives business. You also have to get your creative staff used to the idea that they will be measured. And you have to get everyone accustomed to the idea that not everything will always go well. The important thing is to learn from mistakes and keep moving toward your goals.

WHAT IT'S WORTH

We first wrote about the core concepts behind relative-value modeling in *Actionable Web Analytics* back in 2007. When we reviewed the book in preparation for writing this one, we realized something: no one was doing it then, and almost no one is doing it now.

Relative-value modeling is tough. Not because it's hard to model things, but because it goes straight at the center of how most organization operate. It requires you to agree upon a methodology for understanding what things are worth. Many of these activities will be difficult to price out, and skeptics will have plenty of weapons to use to support their pet projects.

That said, we can't overstate the rewards of a modeled approach. Simply knowing what won't work or doesn't work can free up resources for things that do work or might work. Relative-value modeling gives you that insight. It allows an organization to think dispassionately and practically about its choices and activities. We've seen simple modeling activities save brands huge amounts of time, money, and effort.

Sometimes, the harder things in life are worth it.

NEVER STOP IMPROVING

Optimization is an easy one on paper. You simply set aside funds for a program to improve your digital properties. Acquire a testing tool and go to work. Done.

Here's the rub: brands that start to optimize initially see a big lift. That's great because it will convince others in your organization of the value of your program. Unfortunately, it will also set expectations too high. While you will always see benefits, you'll tend to hit the low-hanging fruit first. After that, your results will be meaningful but less dramatic. Enthusiasm may wane.

This is a mistake. You need to make optimization an established practice and commit to it indefinitely. As digital disruption continues, new opportunities will always arise, and they will require you to have sharp optimization skills. And with steady, incremental improvement of existing properties, you'll benefit financially and learn more about what works for your customers.

ONE SIZE FITS NO ONE

The good news with One Size Fits No One is that it can grow naturally out of your optimization program. Once you have established a testing program for page elements, it is not much different to test out different versions for different audiences.

Still, like anything in Does it Work?, One Size Fits No One is about finding the smart people you need and creating a disciplined organization that can accept what it learns. You have to ask creative questions if you want outsized results.

Many companies hold back from targeting because they feel they don't have sophisticated enough marketing data. Remember that segments can be anything. Even very simple targeting, such as changing the experience if a person has visited a site or not, can yield significant results.

FRAMEWORK FOR INNOVATION

Chances are, your organization is probably working on innovation. The trick is to apply Does it Work? principles to the practice. In other words, say goodbye to innovation for innovation's sake. Instead, you need to develop practices with clear goals and methodologies for evaluating success. You also need to ensure that any innovation effort supports what your business is trying to achieve.

This is not always as easy as it sounds. The marketplace is awash in competing theories of innovation, which may seem more sexy than the practical approach we suggest. Still, if your organization is working in general toward Does it Work? principles, innovation will naturally support goals.

A "DOES IT WORK?" WORLD

Today, we have a real opportunity to understand the effectiveness of our digital marketing efforts. No, it won't be easy to get there. Some measurements are difficult to make. Some are uncertain or relative.

And many will tell us exactly what we don't want to hear. But if we're willing to embrace them, they all can help us understand what we're doing and what we're achieving. They can support bold directions and visionary thinking. They can take marketing out of a world of guts and gurus—and into one where we know what we're doing and can forge truly creative ideas that work.

Does it Work? may not come easily or naturally to some people and organizations. But if you're trying to make the change to a more creative and data-informed world, we hope these 10 principles can help guide the way and provide the arguments and support you need to move things forward. There's a world of data out there that can help make good creative great and great creative as effective as it can be.

All we have to do is start asking: *Does it work?*

To continue the conversation, please visit www.DoesItWorkBook.com or www.POSSIBLE.com/DoesItWork, or comment using the hashtag #DoesItWorkBook on Twitter.

WHAT CMOS NEED TO MAKE DIGITAL MARKETING WORK

A Forrester Consulting
Thought Leadership Paper
Commissioned by POSSIBLE

SEPTEMBER 2014

In 2014, POSSIBLE commissioned Forrester Consulting to investigate how (or if) global CMOs were trying to make sure that their digital marketing works. Forrester interviewed 30 CMOs from around the globe, analyzed their answers, and produced the following study.

ABOUT FORRESTER CONSULTING

Forrester Consulting provides independent and objective research-based consulting to help leaders succeed in their organizations. Ranging in scope from a short strategy session to custom projects, Forrester's Consulting services connect you directly with research analysts who apply expert insight to your specific business challenges. For more information, visit forrester.com/consulting.

Executive Summary

In the age of the customer, an era in which the only source of competitive advantage is to be customer-obsessed, digital is disrupting every business and marketing function. As the world becomes less predictable, it creates new opportunities for savvy chief marketing officers (CMOs) to see the potential of digital, but they struggle to turn digital from a tactical silo into a measurable, business-driving strategy. These CMOs are hampered by cumbersome, historic processes; the traditional marketing mindset of their teams; and difficulty in effectively leveraging data to link marketing programs to business outcomes. CMOs must create a new digitally savvy organizational mindset that is accountable, adaptable, and focused on making digital marketing work.

In April 2014, POSSIBLE commissioned Forrester Consulting to understand how CMOs are quantifying the benefits of their digital marketing efforts and what resources, processes, and technologies they are investing in to capitalize on the wealth of potential intelligence and opportunities that the digital age provides. Forrester conducted in-depth interviews with 25 CMOs and marketing leadership professionals in the US, Europe, and China. These interviewees shared with us their strategies, successes, and hurdles for making digital marketing work.

KEY FINDINGS

Forrester's study yielded these key findings on the state of digital marketing effectiveness:

> **Digital marketing is now essential, but maturity is polarized.** Digital marketing has reached a tipping point, becoming an expected component of any marketing strategy. But marketers are in different stages of digital maturity. Those who are more mature have a post-digital mindset whereby digital is integrated and measured as part of their business. Digital newcomers are more tactical and reactive, trying to hold on to the roller coaster ride of digital change.

> **Many marketers don't know if their digital marketing efforts are working.** Marketers have plenty of data available to them. But they are not yet able to turn data into insight. Many marketers lack the tools, know-how, and people skills to go beyond likes and click-throughs to align digital programs with business results.

> **Agency partners are critical, but they are not held accountable for results.** Agencies remain a critical partner for marketing leaders. But in a world where CMOs are increasingly expected to deliver revenue results, most of these marketing leaders— particularly in the US and Europe—are reluctant to hold their agencies equally answerable. Chinese marketers take a more businesslike approach, setting clear incentives for their agencies to deliver revenue goals.

CMOs Struggle To Demonstrate That Their Digital Marketing Is Working

Digital has become a C-suite-led priority as it disrupts their customers and their business, but many firms are not equipped to realize digital's potential. Forty-one percent of business executives believe their business has already been disrupted by digital technology, and 52% expect their business will be disrupted in the next 12 months (see Figure 1).[1] Seventy-four percent of business executives say their company has a digital strategy, but only 15% believe that their company has the skills and capabilities to execute on that strategy.[2] As a result, digital leadership has risen up the ranks to become a CMO responsibility; 20% of CMOs or marketing SVPs now set the digital vision and strategy for their firm.[3] Chief marketing officers are pivoting from digital execution to optimizing digital performance, but measuring success remains elusive. Today we see that:

› **Digital has evolved from side project to core strategy.** Marketers are focused not just on doing digital, but on doing digital well. And they are increasing spend to support it. Over half of business-to-consumer (B2C) marketers will increase spend on digital marketing in 2014, 46% would spend more if they had additional funding, and 63% are shifting spend from traditional vehicles to fund digital (see Figure 2).[4] Consumer packaged goods giants are leading the way; a multinational confectionary, food, and beverage conglomerate plans to invest 50% of its advertising dollars in digital by 2016.[5]

"Three to five years ago, 80% of marketing funds were going toward more traditional ways of marketing. Digital was just a lever. . . . Now it has shifted to 80% digitally led, 20% more traditional."
—*eCommerce manager at US retailer*

› **But digital measurement is focused on counting likes, not quantifying business results.** Marketers want to quantify the impact of their digital efforts, but too often they are measuring the wrong things. They have a long history of measuring ROI of traditional media, but lack commensurate best practices and benchmark data for digital marketing programs like social and mobile. To fill the void, marketing leaders count vanity metrics such as social media likes, but these metrics don't show what impact digital is having on business performance.

"Trying to get metrics isn't easy. We need new ways to measure."
—*Marketing and product development manager at global telecommunication firm*

› **Digital skills are scarce.** Marketing leaders tell us that they are often handicapped with legacy teams that grew up in the world of traditional marketing. Some marketers are rapidly expanding their teams to staff the new digital channels, securing budget to bring on more specialized digital skills and hiring people who are more digitally savvy. But many marketers who do not have new headcount budget must make do with what they have.

"I'd like to say that my staffing changes, but it does not."
—*Market director at US healthcare organization*

FORRESTER®

FIGURE 1

Business Leaders Are Not Ready For Digital

41%	Agree that their business has already been massively or moderately disrupted by digital technology
52%	Expect their business to be massively or moderately disrupted by digital technology in the next 12 months
74%	Say their firms have a digital strategy
15%	Believe their company has the necessary people and skills to execute on that digital strategy

Base: 1,254 executives in companies with 250 or more employees

Source: Forrester/Russell Reynolds 2014 Digital Business Online Survey, Forrester Research, Inc.

FIGURE 2

Marketers Shift Dollars To Digital Marketing

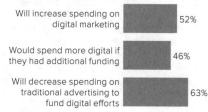

Will increase spending on digital marketing — 52%

Would spend more digital if they had additional funding — 46%

Will decrease spending on traditional advertising to fund digital efforts — 63%

Base: 52 B2C marketing leaders

Source: "B2C Marketers Must Turn Fragmented Marketing Budgets Into Business Budgets," Forrester Research, Inc., December 12, 2013

DIGITAL MATURITY DEFINES ATTITUDES TOWARD PROCESS AND MEASUREMENT

Digital marketing has created an exponential change in marketing. Marketers describe this change as "revolutionary," "rapid," "a whole new world," and "the Wild West." In this rapidly changing new world, our study shows that marketers are split into two camps:

> **Sophisticated digital marketers exercise marketing discipline.** Mature firms have sophisticated processes, tools, and measurement such as marketing mix modeling or CRM. These firms have clear long-term and short-term business objectives and key performance indicators (KPIs) as part of the business or marketing planning process. And they apply these same disciplines to digital.

> "As a company we have a 2020 vision for the future, a three-year strategy and road map. We look at marketing priorities to align long term with the day- to-day priorities to keep going in that direction."
> —*Senior manager online marketing at global telecommunication firm*

> **Immature digital marketers are often tactical and reactive.** With limited budgets, knowledge, and data, less mature marketers take a more tactical and reactive approach to planning, marketing, and measurement, especially when it comes to new digital channels. To stay abreast of channel changes, these marketers self- educate through syndicated research and media industry trend reporting. But all too often these smaller firms with smaller budgets frequently switch tactics to react to fast-moving competitive actions and customer needs. Constantly in reactive mode, they will fail to create a strategic digital vision for their brand.

> "We have limited resources and budgets. Our biggest challenge is to work on long-term strategic plans when faced with often unplanned short-term tactics."
> —*Global marketing communications manager at large European CPG firm*

FINANCIAL PERFORMANCE EXPECTATIONS DIFFER BY REGION

Marketers' primary objectives are to build brand awareness and drive top-line sales growth; driving revenue is paramount. Most marketers in our study measure success based on revenue generation metrics such as sales or pipeline leads. A separate survey supports this finding, with 54% of CMOs aligning marketing goals with revenue targets (see Figure 3). But macroeconomic and cultural factors also create regional differences across the US, Europe, and China:

› **Revenue growth is a common goal for all marketers.** Most marketers work toward the same set of high-level company revenue goals as their peers, and some are incented by formal bonus structures tied to annual performance reviews. But for many CMOs, individual contribution to these results is loosely measured, especially in the US and Europe. In contrast, China has clearly defined alignment between company and performance goals. Chinese leaders reward employees with monetary rewards, honorary rewards, holidays, and training. A sign of a tight job market is that many European and US respondents view a job well done—and retained—as their reward.

"Ultimately, it is about driving sales."
—*Advertising director at US financial services organization*

"Growth, measured in performance. It is how the CEO leads every discussion."
—*Director of channel marketing at US telecommunications firm*

"We definitely share common goals with colleagues in other departments. Our ultimate goal is to expand and strengthen our corporation. The goals of the corporation are closely related to the goals of each employee."
—*Marketing director at Chinese high-tech firm*

"The marketing department and sales department are interlinked. Our common goal is to increase the company's sales and profits."
—*Marketing director at Chinese retailer*

› US and European marketers seek to optimize spend. In Europe and the US, revenue is the goal and ROI is a tool to assess which elements of the marketing mix are working. The lingering European recession continues to cast a pall over marketers' ability to plan for the future. European marketers are fiscally cautious and short-term focused. Some are unable to plan for the long term because short-term business needs force them into a more reactive mode, especially in the economically stressed UK market.

"If cooler heads prevail, then we stay the course. If not, then we vacillate from the strategy."
—*VP of sales and marketing at US automotive organization*

› **Chinese marketers focus on maximizing profitability to invest in long-term brand growth.** Chinese marketers are taking a longer view than their Western counterparts. In this rapidly growing economy, maximizing profitability is an important goal, but so is building their brand for the future. Chinese marketing leaders strive to strike a balance between short- and long-term approaches.

"The three priorities in my mind are ROI, brand, and the goals that focus on the long-term benefits, which our company thinks highly of. In short, it is to balance the long-term achievements and short-term profits."

—*Marketing director at Chinese high-tech firm*

"Brand is very important to us. We are always making efforts to create our own brand."

—*Marketing director at Chinese high-tech firm*

"We set an annual revenue target this year. If we achieve the target, we will invest 30% to 40% of the total revenue in one of several projects."

—*Marketing director at Chinese high-tech firm*

FIGURE 3

CMOs Focus On Proving Business Value

Marketing goals or objectives are most directly aligned to:

- Meet revenue targets — 54%
- Meet profit targets — 16%
- Increase shareholder value — 13%

Top three marketing objectives are to:

- Acquire new customers — 63%
- Increase brand awareness — 40%
- Launch new products/brands — 33%

Base: 212 global marketing leaders with 88 B2B CMOs and 83 B2C CMOs

Source: Q3 2013 Forrester/Heidrick & Struggles Evolved CMO Global Online Survey, Forrester Research, Inc.

AGENCIES REMAIN A CRITICAL PARTNER, BUT ACCOUNTABILITY REMAINS SUBJECTIVE

Marketers rely heavily on their agencies to help them navigate the rapidly evolving digital marketing space. But performance evaluation has not evolved. Most marketers evaluate their agencies by a more subjective assessment of doing a good job rather than on direct business outcomes. Our study shows that:

> **Most marketers still depend on agencies to guide digital choices.** For most marketers, agencies continue to be marketers' most-trusted partner. They are a source of best practices and help guide strategic decisions because they have a wider view of the market. Many marketers view their agencies as an extension of their own marketing team. Forrester reports that agencies can play a key role in helping marketers make sense of their data, because their own in-house skills are insufficient.[6]

"Agency is intertwined with everything we do."
—*VP of sales and marketing at US automotive organization*

"When it comes to making a better decision, they play a role."
—*eMarketing manager at Dutch healthcare organization*

> **Agency performance is evaluated based on project objectives.** Relationships, not business results, dictate marketing-agency partnerships' longevity in Europe and the US, but in China, agency relationships are more formally linked to business performance. In Western markets, accountability is more qualitative than quantitative, and few marketers tie remuneration to market performance. Agencies are expected to deliver on project objectives, and some marketers conduct annual

reviews. For some, renewing the relationship is its own measure of success. But China marketers institute more formal contracts that link their agencies' revenue to their own, with both upside and downside potential.

"There's no way to hold someone accountable in an environment that changes on a semiannual basis."
—*Marketing manager at US retailer*

"There are changes in payment plan year by year. . . . If the effect is better than expected, we will pay according to a certain percentage."
—*Marketing director at Chinese retailer*

Marketers Must Make Digital Actionable and Measurable to Prove It Works

To show how digital can help CMOs master today's marketing environment requires an investment that takes the organization to new levels of insight and success. The three components of that investment are:

> **A digitally savvy organization.** Digital marketing works when it is driven by marketers with not just digital skills, but a digital mindset.

> **An adaptive insight-driven digital process.** The fast-changing digital world requires a more flexible approach to marketing planning and execution that rewards rather than penalizes change.

> **People who can leverage tools and technology to measure what works.** Investing in customer insights and analytical tools is a baseline requirement. But these tools are nothing without the right teams to turn data insight into measurable actions.

CREATE A DIGITALLY SAVVY ENVIRONMENT

To create a leading digital brand requires a digitally savvy mindset. CMOs must surround themselves with internal and external digital resources. To do this, marketing leaders must:

> **Develop their marketing team's digital IQ.** Elevate the digital bench-strength of your teams in terms of skills, mindset, and aptitude. When hiring, look beyond the skills applicants have today and instead hire for a digital-first mindset and an adaptive insight. No new headcount budget? As natural turnover opens up new positions, hire people who are more digitally savvy, whatever the role—whether it's PR, product, or promotion—and raise the digital game of your existing team. One marketer ensures all new hires are digitally savvy and states preference for digital experience in all hiring ads. Another sets clear skills and aptitude expectations as part of each employee's development plan. Those who are unable to adapt get managed out. Several firms are focusing on upgrading skills of existing team members through both training and project assignments.

"It is important to invest in marketers' education, getting them to sign up for the latest courses and stay current. If you stop investing in your teams, there's always a chance that the team will not be the right team."
—*Senior marketing manager at global high-tech firm*

"It is important that it is part of individual objectives, otherwise it becomes part of a to-do list."
—*Senior manager of online marketing at global telecommunication firm*

"I'd like to put in more resources internally. Not necessarily into the digital marketing team but into other teams to think digital . . . [the] marketing organization has to have a fundamental understanding of digital."
—*Senior manager of online marketing at global telecommunication firm*

"We can teach the staff we hire techniques, but they must have the necessary mindset first."
—*Marketing director at Chinese retailer*

> **Hire for data enthusiasts and interpreters, not just data processors.** Digital marketing provides a wealth of data never before available. But data without insight will not move business forward. You need two types of data-savvy hires. First hire for people who can mine the data you have to turn it into valuable business-building insights. Then hire for data-friendly marketers who can take those insights and turn them into action.

"We need to understand data and its relationship to see the opportunities that data provides. . . . It's not just data mining, but data interpretation."
—*VP of digital marketing at US financial services organization*

> **Treat your agency as an extension of your team, and measure their performance the same way.** Agency partners complement your marketing team's depth of business knowledge with a breadth of insight into digital trends and best practices across multiple businesses. Marketers we spoke to get the most out of the relationship when they treat agencies as an integral strategic partner, not an execution arm at the end of the process, and hold them accountable for results. Take a cue from Chinese marketers who link their agencies' success directly to their own. Create aligned, measurable goals that sync your agencies' objectives to your team's objectives.

"Ultimately, it's not a one-off ad hoc relationship. They are more of a right hand. Treat them as . . . part of your team instead of us versus them."
—*eCommerce manager at US retailer*

"The payment is according to contracts that we sign in advance. If sales are better than the goal, we will pay more. If sales have not reached basic goal, we will pay less."
—*Marketing planning manager at Chinese insurance organization*

"I don't comment too much on media spend. . . . Rather I say we need to hit X in sales and I need to know if we are not hitting it. They don't like it, because before they weren't held accountable for anything."
—*Director of digital marketing at US automotive firm*

DEVELOP AN ADAPTIVE INSIGHT-DRIVEN DIGITAL PROCESS

Compel your team to operate with flexible, data-centric processes that can morph to changing needs. These processes must:

> **Set actionable, measurable objectives for each and every project.** Shift your organization from panicked reactions to adaptive strategies when the data points the way to new opportunities. Be clear at the onset of each project what you want to accomplish and how it will contribute to your top-line revenue goals. One firm we spoke to sets KPIs at the onset of each project—KPIs that align with the overall corporate vision. And ensure those KPIs ladder up to business results like lead generation or revenue growth.

> **Prepare to pivot with changing market and customer needs.** Old cumbersome processes no longer keep pace with consumer expectations and actions. A global brand building officer at a leading consumer product company believes that "constant change is the new reality."[7] Create a process and a mindset that allows for creating communications plans that are flexible enough to adapt to real-time market and consumer changes. Begin to shift the focus from rigid one-and-done annual plans to more adaptive planning that flexes to accommodate new opportunities as they arise. Start by allocating a portion of your budget for opportunistic events. One firm test pilots new technologies and channels to determine if they need to be there and what the benefit will be to the business, be that to gain a competitive advantage, maximize ROI, or support a strategic initiative.

INVEST IN PEOPLE WHO CAN LEVERAGE TOOLS AND TECHNOLOGY TO MEASURE WHAT WORKS

Digital is more complex than past marketing efforts. But investing in another analytical tool will only provide data, not a solution. CMOs must invest in hiring the right people who can use the tools, analyze data, and find the right insights to optimize marketing budgets. With these people in place, marketers must invest in tools and technology that:

> **Provide ongoing customer understanding.** Become obsessed by deeply understanding who your customer is. Stay connected to existing and prospective customers' changing media behaviors and needs. Seek tools that help you interpret mountains of data to bring customers to life. Forrester Research believes that firms must invest in real-time data sharing for actionable customer intelligence, such as integrating data sources, building predictive algorithms, and developing multidimensional views of the customer.[8] Forrester recommends a blend of customer analytics methods for a more complete customer understanding, noting that "no one method provides complete analysis of customer behavior. Applying multiple methods in concert can improve the accuracy of predictions."[9]

> **Measure performance to prioritize actions.** Invest in systems that help you analyze and optimize your marketing spend to ensure you are getting the best result from your digital choices. Ensure you have analytics tools in place to help you understand what is and is not performing. Try different things for different audiences to see what works.

"We know from analytics what drives revenue, and we do a good amount of testing to see what works and what doesn't work. . . . We are always testing."
—*Director of digital marketing at US automotive firm*

"We recently introduced a CRM package to track leads and calculate ROI. . . . We have detailed weekly report outs. . . . We drive calls to actions to specific microsites to analyze traffic."
—*Global marketing communications manager at large European CPG firm*

"To optimize, we will pilot run certain strategies in a particular region [and] track through the database to see if we are getting desired results. We also do message testing ahead of time."
—*Global innovation and strategic marketing manager at UK pharmaceutical organization*

FORRESTER®

Key Recommendations

Keep sight of your objective—to obsessively understand what your customers need and to then effectively deliver on that need to win their business. To make your digital marketing work toward this goal:

> **Build digitally savvy teams that thrive on change.** Digital skills are less important than a digital and adaptive mindset. Change doesn't come easy to teams built on functional skills. Reward rather than penalize a change of plans. One marketer commented that in her lean marketing team she needs "someone who can accept change and be flexible."

> **Align marketing performance with project KPIs that ladder up to overall business goals.** Don't treat digital as an experimental silo; ensure it is delivering your business results. Apply the discipline of annual business planning goals to every key project, with KPIs that ladder up to your overall business goals. Align marketing team goals to business goals at the beginning of a project, or tie them to a specific business cycle.

> **Hold all your agencies accountable for delivering results.** Apply the same measurement discipline to your agencies as you do to your business and your teams. So much of marketing is now measurable, there's no excuse for not connecting your critical marketing partners' work to results. Ensure agency remuneration is tied to market performance such as revenue growth or lead generation.

> **Set aside opportunity budgets to drive innovation.** Develop a budget that balances established strategic priorities and opportunistic possibilities. Balance time and dollars between building proven marketing programs, nurturing emerging methods that are starting to gain traction, and testing new opportunities. For example, shift 5% to 15% of your team's time and budget to improve projects or try new opportunities. A leading beverage organization adopts a strategy that assigns 70% of budgets to proven, established programs; 20% to nurture developing initiatives that show promise; and 10% to test new opportunities.

Addendum A: Methodology

In this study, Forrester conducted 25 interviews with marketing decision makers at organizations in China, EMEA (predominately the UK), and the US to evaluate how CMOs are quantifying the benefits of their digital marketing efforts and what resources, processes, and technologies they are using. Topics for the research included their strategies, successes, and obstacles for digital marketing initiatives. The study began in April 2014 and was completed in April 2014.

Addendum B: Demographics

FIGURE 4
Survey Respondents—Geography, Industry, Job Title

Geography	Industry	Job title
China	High tech	Marketing director
China	Retail	Marketing director
China	Insurance	Marketing planning manager
China	Retail	Marketing director
China	Hospitality	Marketing director
Netherlands	Healthcare	E-marketing manager
Switzerland	Telecoms	Senior manager, online marketing
UK	Hospitality and leisure	Marketing director
UK	CPG	Marketing manager
UK	High tech	Senior manager, marketing
UK	CPG	Global marketing communications manager
UK	Pharma	Senior director, global innovation and strategic marketing
UK	Insurance	Global marketing manager
UK	Hospitality	Marketing director
US	Telecoms	Director of channel marketing
US	High tech	Senior VP—Canada/LATAM
US	Automotive	VP—sales and marketing
US	Automotive	Director of digital marketing
US	Retail	Director—marketing
US	Financial services	VP, digital marketing
US	Retail	Marketing manager—digital and social media channels
US	Healthcare	Marketing director
US	Financial services	Advertising director
US	Financial services	Director—marketing
US	Telecoms	Director—product development

Base: 25 marketing decision makers

Source: A commissioned study conducted by Forrester Consulting on behalf of POSSIBLE, April 2014

Addendum C: Endnotes

[1] Source: "Understand The Digital Business Landscape," Forrester Research, Inc., April 16, 2014.

[2] Source: "The Digital Business Imperative," Forrester Research, Inc., March 26, 2014.

[3] Source: "Understand the Digital Business Landscape," Forrester Research, Inc., April 16, 2014.

[4] Source: "B2C Marketers Must Turn Fragmented Marketing Budgets Into Business Budgets," Forrester Research, Inc., December 12, 2013.

[5] Source: Garett Sloane, "This $35 Billion Company Will Spend 50% of Ad Dollars on Digital," *Adweek*, June 15, 2014 (http://www.adweek.com/news/technology/ 36-billion-company-will-spend-50-ad-dollars-video-158317).

[6] Source: "The Next Act For Agencies: The Post-Digital Agency Landscape," Forrester Research, Inc., December 6, 2013.

[7] Source: Eti Nachum, "Cannes Lions Festival Recap," Geektime, July 8, 2014 (http://www.geektime.com/discussion/cannes- lions-festival-recap/).

[8] Source: "Competitive Strategy in the Age of the Customer," Forrester Research, Inc., October 10, 2013.

[9] Source: "TechRadar™: Customer Analytics Methods, Q1 2014," Forrester Research, Inc., February 25, 2014.

DUMB WAYS TO DIE: DETAILED ANALYSIS OF CLAIMS

INTRODUCTION

In November 2012, McCann Australia and Metro Trains, an extensive and highly utilized suburban rail system in Melbourne (Australia), released a video and website campaign titled *Dumb Ways to Die*.

The video became an international sensation, with more than 100 million views and numerous parodies. By some, it has been called the most successful ad campaign in history. This Appendix examines the claims around the impact of the campaign—and its true impact and success. In the end, we conclude that for all its popularity, it is impossible to say with any certainty that the campaign was effective.

DATA SOURCES

Most of the data used comes from Transport Safety Victoria (TSV). Established in 2010, is "Victoria's integrated safety regulator for bus, maritime and rail transport." Its purview includes Metro Trains (http://www.transportsafety.vic.gov.au).

Additional historical data comes from the Australian Transport Safety Board, the organization responsible for safety reporting before the creation of TSV. (http://atsb.gov.au/media/4042317/rr2012010_final.pdf).

Note: The ad was released in November 2012. We have measured the effects using yearly published data. Our assumption is that if the campaign was effective, we would see a difference in incidents between the full year of 2012, before the ad was released, and the full year of 2013, after it was released. Statistics released by McCann Australia and Metro Trains do not reference published time frames. We also focused on "incidents" rather than just "deaths," as the number of deaths were small and had large fluctuations over the years. And even a change of a few in a year would throw the data off considerably (but would not be statistically significant). The campaign was targeted toward helping people make better decisions and be safer around the trains. There were also concerns (covered later in the analysis) around suicide deaths and trains that led us to look at the overall incident types to truly understand the impact of the campaign.

CLAIMS OF SUCCESS

Metro Trains and its agency made at least three different claims for success over the course of the campaign and its aftermath:

1. In February 2013, Metro Trains claimed that the number of near misses on Metro Trains had dropped 30% for November through January 2012–13, compared with the same period a year earlier.
2. They later said the campaign had "led to a 20% reduction in risky behavior."
3. The official case study by McCann claims "Metro Trains noticed a 32% reduction in accidents and deaths on its network."

EXPERT QUESTIONING

In spite of these claims for success, a number of observers quickly demurred.

1. In September 2013, Adam Carey and Craig Butt, writing in *The Age*, noted that something was amiss: "Transport Safety Victoria recorded 81 close calls between a train and a pedestrian between January and June this year, and 85 near misses with a vehicle—166 in total, almost one a day," they wrote. "That was a 14 per cent jump on the 143 documented near misses in the second half of 2012, and a 9 per cent increase on the first half of last year. The numbers were lower still in 2011." (http://www.theage.com.au/victoria/safety-message-may-be-falling-off-20130914-2trrr.html)
2. Communications specialist Karalee Evans weighed in on the 20% claim. Her opinion is significant because she had worked for Metro Trains in the field of safety messaging. She flatly declared the 20% was "social media bulls**t." She questioned whether the data had been correctly attributed to ensure that any changes were solely due to the ad. She called out a number of specific steps that safety experts usually take to isolate the

effectiveness of a public service campaign, none of which had been carried out. We'll quote her words in full:

> "Was the campaign (read: video) evaluated on a random sample of Christmas holidays commuters to ascertain prompted and unprompted message awareness at comparable stations benchmarked for incidence of risky behaviour over the same time period? Was the messaging measured against motivators and detractors of said behavioural change outcomes? Were environmental factors such as Christmas holidays, station and facility upgrades, weather et al. included?" (http://mumbrella .com.au/dumb-ways-to-die-and-social-media-bullshit -138887)

3. Communications specialist Marie Claire Ross pointed out a number of problems with the video. Among them:
   a. The video contains only 12 seconds of actual safety messaging.
   b. The website contained some safety messaging, but focused more on selling the video's song.
   c. Studies have repeatedly shown that entertainment does not produce behavioral change. (http://www.safetyrisk.net/5 -dumb-ways-communicate-train-safety/)
4. The TSV itself released information about an increase in level crossings incidents in April 2014. It stated:

> "Transport Safety Victoria (TSV) is reminding pedestrians to take greater care around railway level crossings as it reveals that 2013 saw more near miss incidents than in any of the previous four years.
>
> The latest incident statistics from the rail safety regulator show that there were 182 reported pedestrian near misses at level crossings last year, a figure which represents a 66 per cent increase on the previous 12 month period." (http://www .transportsafety.vic.gov.au/__data/assets/pdf_file/0005/1205 87/Safety-regulator-issues-warning-to-risky-rail-track -crossers.pdf)

CHERRY-PICKING

TSV segments data in many different ways. Each of the claims made about success is based on a different segment of that data.

We always have many options for measuring the impact of something, and very often you can find a way to measure something that works in your favor. In this case, TSV reports on nine different collision or accident types in the Heavy Rail category, which covers the Metro Trains. Those nine incidents types are:

1. Collision with Person
2. Collision with Road Vehicle
3. Level Crossing Collision with Road Vehicle
4. Level Crossing Collision with Person
5. Level Crossing Near Miss with Road Vehicle
6. Level Crossing Near Miss with Person
7. Slip, Trip or Fall on Train
8. Slip, Trip or Fall at Platform
9. Slip, Trip or Fall in Station

Below, you can find the full annual 2013 Annual Incident Statistics for Heavy Rail, as reported by TSV. It also compares the changes from 2009 to 2013 across all nine incident categories:

Collision with Person

YEAR	INCIDENTS	CHANGE
2009	29	—
2010	26	−10%
2011	18	−31%
2012	17	−6%
2013	15	−12%

Level Crossing Near Miss w/ Road Vehicle

YEAR	INCIDENTS	CHANGE
2009	174	—
2010	164	−6%
2011	146	−11%
2012	171	17%
2013	174	2%

Collision with Road Vehicle

YEAR	INCIDENTS	CHANGE
2009	4	—
2010	2	−50%
2011	6	200%
2012	5	−17%
2013	6	20%

Level Crossing Near Miss w/ Person

YEAR	INCIDENTS	CHANGE
2009	91	—
2010	105	15%
2011	123	17%
2012	121	−2%
2013	182	50%

Level Crossing Collision w/ Road Vehicle

YEAR	INCIDENTS	CHANGE
2009	13	—
2010	9	−31%
2011	17	89%
2012	17	0%
2013	13	−24%

Slip, Trip, or Fall on Train

YEAR	INCIDENTS	CHANGE
2009	72	—
2010	58	−19%
2011	73	26%
2012	59	−19%
2013	86	46%

Level Crossing Collision w/ Person

YEAR	INCIDENTS	CHANGE
2009	10	—
2010	5	−50%
2011	7	40%
2012	4	−43%
2013	5	25%

Slip, Trip, or Fall at Platform

YEAR	INCIDENTS	CHANGE
2009	303	—
2010	319	5%
2011	254	−20%
2012	246	−3%
2013	218	−11%

Slip, Trip, or Fall in Station

YEAR	INCIDENTS	CHANGE
2009	444	—
2010	548	23%
2011	672	23%
2012	894	33%
2013	834	−7%

In this case, there was a drop in some of those nine measurements year over year. But some also increased. When analyzing the nine categories comparing the incidents from 2012 to 2013, we can see that two recorded fewer incidents, three recorded more incidents, and four remained roughly the same (+/– 3 incidents). Added together, we see 1,534 incidents in 2012 and 1,533 in 2013.

When you take those nine categories, select the ones you want, and then compare carefully selected time periods, you should easily be able to find metrics that work in your favor. Looked at together, the picture is considerably less clear.

Note: During this time period, patronage—measured by boardings—increased by approximately 1% per year. In order to expose exactly where the data comes from, we have not adjusted the table above to normalize against that 1%. But you can see that 1% would not make a significant difference.

SMALL NUMBERS, BIG PERCENTAGES

Thirty-two percent sounds impressive, until you realize how few incidents occur on Metro Trains lines. In some of the categories there are just a handful of incidents a year. A change of just one or two greatly affects the percentage.

That also allows you to find persuasive numbers that don't actually indicate large changes in raw data. For example, when looking at the TSV data of Heavy Rail Collisions with Person, there were 26 incidents in 2010, 18 in 2011, 17 in 2012, and 15 in 2013. That shows a downward-leading trend into the campaign, but the numbers are very small. When comparing 2012 to 2013, a reduction from 17 to 15 shows a decrease of 12%. Depending on the words you choose, you could describe the changes as a "marked improvement" or a "slow trend." But it's only two collisions in total.

On the other hand, we could look at something like Heavy Rail Level Crossing Collisions with Person. That increased from four in 2012 to five in 2013, which could be called an increase of 25%, even though it's only one more incident.

STATISTICAL SIGNIFICANCE

Based on the great fluctuations in the data, we had our analysts assess their statistical significance. By looking at the changes in the data points over time, they were able to determine a typical or expected fluctuation in the metrics. This is done through calculating the standard deviation, which measures the variation from the average. In other words it allows you to understand if things are inside or outside an expected range.

We found that each of the nine incident measurements fluctuated a great deal year over year leading up to the launch of the campaign. Each time, the analysis concluded that—based on the public data from TSV—we were not seeing a statistically significant impact that supported a positive (or negative) narrative of the campaign in any of the nine categories or with all of them combined.

LONG-TERM IMPACT

The claims for *Dumb Ways to Die* often cited specific, short-term time periods. However, it makes sense to look at 2014 and beyond to understand the long-term impact. As of the completion of this book, the 2014 data is not available in its entirety publicly. When it is, we will continue the analysis and share that online to keep an eye on the long-term impact.

Anecdotally, however, the year is not off to a great start:

1. On June 14, 2014, a teenager died after breaking into a train's rear compartment and leaning out of the moving train in Melbourne's southeast (http://www.theage.com.au/victoria/teenager-dies-after-leaning-out-of-moving-train-in-melbournes-southeast-20140614-3a3pa.html#ixzz3IoRb5Qvq).
2. On June 27, 2014, a street artist was killed performing what many believe to be a stunt on top of a Melbourne train (http://www.theage.com.au/victoria/tributes-for-street-artist-electrocuted-while-train-surfing-20140628-zspnu.html).

3. On July 1, 2014, the *Daily Mail* published an article, "The Spiderman Gang: Terrifying Footage Emerges of Melbourne Daredevils Scaling Buildings and Train-Surfing" (see http://www.dailymail.co.uk/news/article-2676247/Footage-emerges-training-surfing-Spiderman-group.html#ixzz3IoOARzpS). It stated, "But what has alarmed Victoria Police the most are the group's train-surfing antics, where they are seen jumping off station platforms and latching themselves onto the outside of moving trains as well as breaking into the train driver's compartment." The video can currently be seen on YouTube (https://www.youtube.com/watch?v=Ofyzxf8HLa0) or by searching "Public Enemy Melbourne."

4. On July 15, 2014, the *Daily Mail* declared coupler riding, or riding on the unused coupler at the back of a train, "Australia's stupidest new craze" (http://www.dailymail.co.uk/news/article-2693799/Coupler-riding-Australias-stupidest-new-craze.html).

SUICIDE

A different perspective comes from social psychologist Dr. Rob Long, who pointed out that carelessness and recklessness are not leading causes of death and injury on the Australian railway system. In fact, 80% of all deaths are suicides (see: http://www.theage.com.au/victoria/suicide-main-cause-of-rail-deaths-20121101-28luk.html). He wrote that the campaign is "a classic example of a failure to think about the trajectory of a goal and trajectory of a discourse. The *Dumb Ways to Die* campaign and its self-assessed success (based on hits on the Internet) demonstrate just how superficial and short sighted the campaign is."

He decried the focus on fun and how it took away from a more serious discussion of the real problem. "The *Dumb Ways to Die* discourse is also about fun, entertainment, jingle and the myth of stupidity. Strangely enough the research indicates that the hidden discourse behind deaths on the rail network is mental health, depression,

isolation and loneliness." (For more information, see: http://www
.safetyrisk.net/dumb-ways-to-discourse-a-failed-approach-in-safety/.)

It's also worth pointing out that if you were suicidal, the video
suggests numerous ways to kill yourself and emphasizes the effectiveness of stepping in front of a train for that purpose.

DEATH BY OTHER MEANS

Whenever we create a campaign that produces fear about something,
we should also examine the alternative. A growing movement in
public transportation safety circles is urging transit systems to pivot
away from an emphasis on danger in safety messaging. The reason
is that public transportation is much safer than alternatives like cars
and bikes. By riding public transportation, people are less likely to
have an accident by other means. For example, a 2014 study by the
Victoria Transportation Policy Institute states:

> Despite its relative safety and security, many people consider
> public transit dangerous, and so are reluctant to use it or sup-
> port service expansions in their communities. Various factors
> contribute to this excessive fear, including the nature of public
> transit travel, heavy media coverage of transit-related crashes
> and crimes, and conventional traffic safety messages which
> emphasize danger rather than safety. (For more information,
> see: http://www.vtpi.org/safer.pdf.)

GOALS AND TARGET AUDIENCE

Most in the industry defined the campaign's success based on views,
pledges, app downloads, and song purchases from around the world.
And no one would deny that all of those were huge. The problem is
that the campaign seems to have been designed to be viral—not effective. Its goal was not to reach a Melbourne audience with a safety
message, but to get as wide an audience as possible. As a result, most

of the people the video reached were outside of the target. They have never been to nor will ever visit Melbourne. Even fewer of them will step foot on a train in Victoria.

One could claim the video made an impact on society overall by making everyone around the world safer and more aware around trains. There are two problems with that argument:

1. Metro Trains, which funded the campaign, spent money to improve safety around their trains in Melbourne. Their goals should have had nothing to do with global train safety.
2. If the campaign does not seem to have made a statistically significant impact in Melbourne, there is no reason to assume it would have an impact elsewhere.

ATTRIBUTION

In making its claims for success, other factors were ignored that may have contributed to improvement. Before the campaign Metro Trains was already working on improving safety in two major ways.

1. **TrackSAFE.** In early 2012 Victoria became a partner in a new national public awareness campaign, TrackSAFE, which aims to cut rail deaths, including suicides. (For more information on TrackSAFE, see: http://tracksafefoundation.com.au/.)
2. **Transport Safety Victoria.** This agency was established under the Transport Integration Act of 2010. Since its founding, it has helped drive many safety changes including upgrading technology, training for conductors, fencing to keep people out of certain areas, and improving crossings.

Both of these should have an ongoing positive impact on rail safety in Victoria, including Metro Trains.

A SAFE SYSTEM

The campaign was often claimed to be in response to an alarming increase in safety-related incidents. In fact, statistically, the Victoria system is on a par with Europe in the most significant and easily compared metric: deaths per million track miles. Thanks to the efforts of TSV, safety appears to have been improving for some time.

Fatalities per million train km travelled for Europe, USA and Victoria

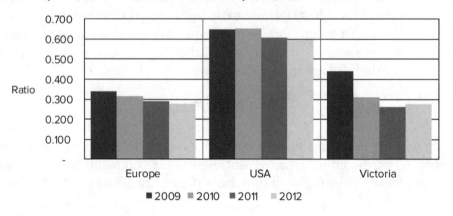

Sources: European Railway Agency and Federal Railroad Administration

CONCLUSION

Given all these factors, it is impossible to say that the *Dumb Ways to Die* campaign had a significant impact on train safety in Melbourne. While we cannot say with certainty that it had no effect, the creators did not take the necessary steps to prove that it was effective. The metrics they have used to support their claims are cherry-picked, not statistically significant, and lack proper attribution.

Overall, Metro Trains should be proud of its record and its serious efforts to improve passenger safety and reduce suicides on its lines. Passengers should have every confidence in using Metro Trains.

When writing this book, we decided to interview some of the most insightful people we knew in the digital space. We've included their ideas throughout the book, and in this sectio you can find out more about them.

McGregor Agan

Director of Marketing Corporate Affairs Group, Intel Corporation

In 20 years at Intel, McGregor has held numerous senior management roles and worked on everything from video conferencing and streaming media to environmental performance.

Andrey Anischenko

CEO, Grape Digital (a POSSIBLE agency)

Andrei helped grow Grape into Russia's top full-service, strategic digital agency. It serves a local client base while gaining the attention of the global digital scene.

Dean Aragon

VP CX Brand and CEO, Shell Brands International AG

Experienced in helping large global organizations grow their brands, Dean spent eight-plus years in senior leadership roles at Unilever and is now leading brand efforts at Shell.

Ali Behnam

Cofounder, Tealium Inc.

Ali cofounded Tealium in 2008 and has since led the design and launch of the company's enterprise tag management platform.

Emily Brooke

Founder & CEO, Blaze

Emily is a designer and entrepreneur who created an innovative laser bike light to improve rider safety and built an online business to support it.

Darin Brown

CEO EMEA, POSSIBLE

After a career that included executive positions at CP+B and Razorfish, Darin now drives POSSIBLE's business strategy and leads expansion efforts in Europe.

Yonca Brunini

VP, Marketing, Google EMEA

After stints at Unilever and Yahoo, Yonca now leads marketing efforts for Google across 30 countries, including some of the world's hottest locations (literally).

Jason Brush

Executive Creative Director, POSSIBLE

A Cannes Lions Gold winner, Jason Brush oversees both POSSIBLE's Los Angeles creative team and user experience design for the agency globally.

Dmitria Burby

Global Director, Performance Marketing COE, POSSIBLE

Dmitria leads the Performance Marketing Center of Excellence at POSSIBLE, helping clients to improve their business by integrating data-based insights into their decisions.

Ted Cannis

CEO, FordSollers, Ford Motor Co.

A longtime employee of Ford, Ted has held executive positions in general management and marketing in Argentina, the United States, Turkey, and, most recently, Russia.

Jason Carmel

Global SVP, Marketing Sciences, POSSIBLE

Over the last 14 years, Jason has worked with Fortune 500 clients to evolve digital experiences based on real-time feedback and behavioral data.

Doug Chavez

Global Head of Marketing Research & Content, Kenshoo

With 20 years' experience at the intersection of media and technology, Doug now leads Global Marketing Research and Content for Kenshoo, a leader in predictive marketing software.

Jim Chesnutt

UK, Managing Director, POSSIBLE

At POSSIBLE since 2007, Jim Chesnutt has overseen client engagements for global brands that include Shell, Coca-Cola, Sony, and Microsoft.

Dana Cogswell

Executive Director, Targeted Marketing & Customer Lifecycle Management, AT&T

With AT&T for 12 years, Dana leads the team responsible for targeted customer acquisition and customer lifecycle marketing. He has also worked for Merrill Lynch and iXL/Scient.

Andrew Connell

CMO, Western Europe, Devices Business, Huawei Technologies

With CMO-level digital roles at Nokia, American Express, and Huawei, Andrew specializes turnarounds, sales and marketing, and managing major transformations in a global context.

Marc Connor

Managing Director, Brand, Build-A-Bear

While new to Build-A-Bear, Marc has a long career on both the agency and the client side, specializing in innovation as well as the sales and marketing of consumer goods and services.

Justin Cooke

CEO, UK, POSSIBLE

Justin came to POSSIBLE through the acquisition of Fortune Cookie, the 200-person agency he founded. Today he focuses on harnessing digital's power to change the world in measurable ways.

Sam Decker
Chairman, Clearhead and Entrepreneur, Investor, and Board Member

As the founder of Mass Relevance and founding CMO of Bazaarevoice, today Sam is an angel investor, growth advisor, and Executive Chairman of Clearhead, a digital optimization firm.

Mike Dodd
Partner, Austin Ventures

At Austin Ventures, Mike focuses on investments in early and expansion-stage software and web-enabled business and consumer services. Prior to this, Mike was Omniture's SVP of Corporate Development.

Mike Fridgen
President & CEO, Decide.com (acquired by eBay)

An entrepreneur with more than 15 years' experience building consumer Internet companies and products, Mike is currently General Manager of Seller Insights at eBay.

Brad Gagne
Regional Director of Marketing Sciences, POSSIBLE

Brad leads a large digital-marketing analytics team that helps realize his ROI-driven approach to marketing for clients such as Microsoft, Intercontinental Hotel Group, and Ford.

Kieran Hannon
CMO, Belkin International

Kieran manages every facet of the Belkin's marketing organization globally including eCommerce and Customer Advocacy (Care). *Forbes* recently recognized him as "one of the most influential CMOS on Twitter."

Curt Hecht
Chief Global Revenue Officer, The Weather Company

Curt is responsible for the overall strategic definition and management of Weather's domestic and international business development, local platform development, and ad sales revenue.

Martha Hiefield

President Seattle, POSSIBLE

Martha's leadership in growing POSSIBLE's unique culture was recently rewarded with an *AdAge* Best Place to Work and 3 Cheers Award from the 3% Conference. Her life motto is "10% what happens, 90% how you handle it."

Brent Hieggelke

CMO, Urban Airship

Brent is the CMO of Urban Airship, which enables the world's top brands to earn and maintain a presence on their customers' mobile devices through mobile relationship-management solutions. Previously, he spent a decade in executive marketing posts at WebTrends, TouchClarity, and Omniture.

Grace Ho

Managing Director, Marketing, SAP Asia Pacific Japan

With 18 years' sales of sales and marketing experience in the technology industry and a strong perspective on Asia, Grace heads up SAP's marketing efforts for the region.

Diane Holland

Global Chief Financial Officer, POSSIBLE

Diane is responsible for POSSIBLE global financial and operational management, leading the agency's planning and growth, including mergers, acquisitions, and partnerships.

Phyllis Jackson

VP, North America, Consumer & Market Knowledge, P&G

Phyllis is an accomplished, visionary insights senior executive with over 30 years of fast-moving consumer products goods experience.

Josh James

Founder & CEO, Domo

Prior to working at Domo, Josh was CEO of Omniture, the web analytics powerhouse he cofounded in 1996, took public in 2006, and sold to Adobe in 2009 for $1.8B. From 2006 to 2009, Josh was the youngest CEO of a publicly traded company. He was recognized by *Fortune* as one of its 2009 "40 Under 40" top business executives. Josh was again recognized as one of *Fortune*'s "40 Under 40: Ones to Watch" in 2011. The World Economic Forum named him a Young Global Leader in 2012.

Steve Jarvis

VP, Strategy Global Tour & Transport, Expedia, Inc.

Steve serves as vice president of strategy for Expedia's Global Tour & Transport Group, handling the car, cruise, and insurance businesses for the world's largest online travel company.

Denise Karkos

CMO, TD Ameritrade

Denise is responsible for the overall management of TD Ameritrade's marketing, including segment strategy, brand and advertising, social media and content marketing, marketing analytics, and operations.

Avinash Kaushik

Marketing Evangelist, Google & Market Motive, and author of Web Analytics 2.0

Known for his blog, *Occam's Razor*, and his bestselling book, Avinash has become recognized as an authoritative voice on how executive teams can leverage digital platforms and data to out-innovate their competitors and achieve superior financial results.

Chris Kerns

Director of Analytics/Research, Spredfast, and author of Trendology

At Spredfast, Chris leads thought leadership and research around social data, exploring the value that can be found on Twitter, Facebook, Instagram, and other social networks.

Paul J. Kerr

CEO, Small Luxury Hotels of the World

As joint Managing Director for Hill Goodridge & Associates Ltd and CEO for Small Luxury Hotels of the World, Paul leads the growth of a brand that now has 520 hotels in more than 80 countries.

Nick Leggett

Associate Director of Marketing Sciences, POSSIBLE

With 15 years in the Internet and software industry, Nick manages user research at POSSIBLE, providing guidance for clients on all measurement disciplines, including analytics and optimization.

Brian Lesser

Global CEO, Xaxis

Brian is Global CEO of Xaxis, a digital media company that programmatically connects advertisers to audiences across all media channels. He was featured as one of *AdAge*'s "40 Under 40" in 2014.

Scott A. Lux

VP eCommerce & Multi Channel, Diesel

Having worked for both brands and agencies, Scott has deep experience in e-commerce, digital strategy, marketing, and analytics. He has led e-commerce and digital initiatives for Kiehls, AmEx, and Morgans Hotel Group.

Halina Lukoskie

Sr. Digital Analyst, POSSIBLE

Halina specializes in optimizing digital experiences and improving ROI through data-driven analysis for clients that include Adidas, TD Ameritrade, and Purina.

Lars Madsen

Business Strategy & Development Director, Canon Europe

An experienced international strategy and business development director in the EMEA region, Lars is responsible for identifying, scoping, and implementing new growth initiatives at Canon.

Jean-Philippe Maheu

Managing Director, Global Brand & Agency Strategy, Twitter

Since joining Twitter through the acquisition of Bluefin Labs, Jean-Philippe (JP) has led the company's global agency partnership and brand strategy teams.

Justin Marshall

Business Development Director, Americas, POSSIBLE

With a background in design and brand strategy, Justin is passionate about social innovation and has consulted for B2B and consumer clients, including Microsoft, Janus, Chase, and Sony.

Matt Mason

Chief Content Officer, BitTorrent, Inc.

Matt serves as CCO at BitTorrent, which provides innovative technologies to deliver large files over the Internet. He is also the bestselling author of *The Pirate's Dilemma: How Youth Culture Is Reinventing Capitalism.*

Alicia McVey

Cofounder & Chief Creative Officer, Swift (a POSSIBLE agency)

Alicia cofounded Swift in 2007 with a singular vision: to create the advertising model that authentically connects brands with people at the speed of life.

Jon McVey

Chief Creative Officer, POSSIBLE

Over the last 20 years, Jon has specialized in applying brand strategy across varying media, creating award-winning work for brands that include Apple, Converse, Tazo Tea, and National Geographic.

John Mellor

VP, Business Development & Strategy, Adobe

With over 25 years of experience in the technology industry, John now advances growth and market leadership strategies for Adobe's Digital Marketing business unit.

Eddy Moretti

Chief Creative Officer, VICE Media Worldwide

An accomplished screenwriter, producer, and director, Eddy is responsible for content across all VICE's media channels, including serving as producer with Shane Smith and Bill Maher on a new original series for HBO.

Kunal Muzumdar

Managing Director, POSSIBLE

A passionate storyteller and avid technology buff, Kunal has crafted strategies for some of the world's most iconic brands, including Ford, Levis, Disney, Audi, and Chanel.

Elaine Ng

Operations Director, Asia Pacific, POSSIBLE

Elaine leads a team that helps plan, manage, and execute digital marketing activities, including campaigns, websites, and e-commerce in the AIPAC region.

Deep Nishar

SVP, Products & User Experience, LinkedIn

With 20 years of experience managing large, global organizations that create insanely brilliant and simple products, Deep now leads overall product strategy and user experience for LinkedIn.

Richard Nunn

Brand & Web Director, Legal & General

In marketing since the days of mass direct mail, Richard remains passionate about growing brands around their core purpose through quality experiences and engagement. He's won a number of awards, the highlight being the Grand Prix at the DBA Design Effectiveness Awards in 2012.

Nick Nyhan

CEO, WPP Data Alliance and Chief Digital Officer, Kantar, a WPP Company

Since 2009, Nick has been the Chief Digital Officer for Kantar, and since 2011 has cochaired the WPP Data Alliance. A frequent speaker at industry events, he has also been quoted in major newspapers and other media outlets.

Tonya Peck

Chief Talent Officer, POSSIBLE

With a diverse background that spans plastics, people, and pixels, Tonya is responsible for attracting, retaining, and growing talent worldwide.

Lucas Peon

Executive Creative Director, POSSIBLE

Lucas is an Argentinian creative director who has lived in France, Chile, Brazil, Mexico, and the United States. Today, he is Executive Creative Director for POSSIBLE London, leading a creative team over key global accounts such as Shell, Peroni, Canon, Danone, Skype, and Coca-Cola.

Jonah Peretti

Founder and CEO, BuzzFeed

Jonah Peretti is founder and CEO of BuzzFeed, the social news and entertainment company that provides a pioneering mix of breaking news, entertainment, and shareable content.

Mark Read

CEO, WPP Digital

Mark Read is CEO of WPP Digital and Chairman of Wunderman. His primary focus is strengthening the Group's digital capabilities across all of WPP's operating companies, developing its technology capabilities, and building strong relationships with key partners in the digital technology industry. He has been a member of the board of WPP since 2006 and became Chairman of Wunderman in June 2014.

René Rechtman

President, Maker Studios

A former CEO of AOL's Be On division and SVP of AOL International, René has led Maker Studios' rapidly expanding international business.

Mike Reeder

SVP, Brand Strategy & Insights, POSSIBLE

The current leader of POSSIBLE's Creative Intelligence team, Mike has worked on everything from TV to print campaigns and has crafted digital media and creative strategies for leading global brands.

Ben Reubenstein

President, POSSIBLE Mobile

Ben leads a team of highly dedicated, mobile-centric professionals to create engaging consumer experiences. Previously, he was the CEO of Double Encore, which was acquired by WPP in 2014.

Guido Rosales

Europe Group Integrated Marketing Director, The Coca-Cola Company

Guido is responsible for the Coca-Cola Company's communication strategy across the European region, ensuring that integrated communication platforms are developed and executed across all consumer touchpoints.

Anders Rosenquist

PhD, Director of Emerging Media, Strategist, POSSIBLE

Anders focuses on developing multiscreen and multiplatform strategies for a range of clients, including Alaska Airlines, AT&T, Fortune, CNN Money, Norton, Hard Rock Hotel, and Pella.

Chris Scoggins

CEO, National Rail Enquiries

Chris has led National Rail Enquiries throughout its digital life, transforming the business from a pure contact center to 99% online with 17 million customers. NRE was recently rated the number one UK brand for its use of Twitter.

Joe Shepter

Freelance Marketing/Advertising Writer and Strategic Consultant

A journalist and award-winning copywriter, Joe also helps global executives refine and bring their ideas to a wide audience.

Andrew Solmssen

Managing Director, POSSIBLE

With 18 years of experience creating apps, products, and campaigns, Andrew is Managing Director for POSSIBLE, where he runs the agency's Los Angeles market.

Paul Soon

CEO Asia Pacific, POSSIBLE

Paul heads up the Asia Pacific region for POSSIBLE. As a digital veteran in the region he has worked with global and local brands in Singapore, Hong Kong, China, Indonesia, Malaysia, Thailand and Vietnam

Thomas Stelter

VP, Emerging Solutions, Americas, POSSIBLE

With over 20 years of digital strategy experience, Thomas now focuses on developing partnership and services on established and emerging platforms, such as Amazon and LinkedIn.

Krisztian Toth

CEO & Chief Creative Officer, Carnation Group (a POSSIBLE agency)

At Carnation Group, Krisztian has won numerous creative and professional awards and served as a regular member of international judging panels, including the 2014 Cannes Mobile Lions.

Danielle Trivisonno Hawley

CCO, Americas, POSSIBLE

Danielle has been integral in developing POSSIBLE's beyond-the-site initiatives, most notably leading award-winning work in the social space. Her work has been recognized by Cannes Lions, One Show, Communication Arts, and AdCritic.

Liz Valentine

Cofounder & CEO, Swift (a POSSIBLE agency)

Since 2005, Liz has led Swift, a digital advertising agency that serves global Fortune 500 clients, including Starbucks, Nestle, Teavana, HTC, Microsoft, and Disney, among others.

Michael Watts

Associate Director of Performance Marketing, POSSIBLE

With a decade of experience in big data and digital marketing, Michael leads some of POSSIBLE's larger client engagements and works across disciplines to come up with actionable recommendations.

Gus Weigel

Chief Financial Officer, Americas, POSSIBLE

With over 25 years of experience in finance and accounting, Gus led finance and operations during the sale of ZAAZ to WPP. Previous employers include General Motors, Dreyer's Ice Cream, and USWeb/CKS.

Adam Wolf

Chief Technology Officer, Americas, POSSIBLE

Since joining POSSIBLE in 2001, Adam has touched nearly every major project. In his current role, he supports software development processes regionally, connects them globally, and evangelizes the agency's technical offerings.

AUTHORS' NOTE:
CONTINUING THE CONVERSATION

We would like to continue our discussion of Does it Work? Over time, we will expand the conversation by sharing stories we find in the press, looking at award-winning projects that work, and examining topics readers bring to our attention.

To join in the discussion, see updates, and share your views, please visit:

www.DoesItWorkBook.com

or

www.POSSIBLE.com/DoesItWork

You can also join the conversation on Twitter, using the hashtag:

#DoesItWorkBook

ENDNOTES

INTRODUCTION

1. Quoted in Stephen Couchy, "No Dumb Luck: Metro Claims Safety Success," *The Age Melbourne*, February 14, 2013.
2. Adam Carey and Craig Butt, "Safety Message Seems to Be Falling Off," *The Courier*, September 15, 2003.
3. Deborah Gogh, "Suicide Main Cause of Rail Deaths," *The Age Victoria*, November 1, 2012.
4. Please see Appendix B for more information on train surfing.
5. Karalee Evans, "Dumb Ways to Die and Social Media Bulls∗∗t," mUmBRELLA. retrieved November 13, 2014, http://mumbrella.com.au/dumb-ways-to-die-and -social-media-bullshit-138887.
6. Dr. Rob Long, "Dumb Ways to Discourse, a Failed Approach in Safety," Safety.net. April 9, 2014, http://www.safetyrisk.net/dumb-ways-to-discourse-a-failed -approach-in-safety/.
7. Todd Littman, "Safer Than You Think! Revising the Transit Safety Narrative," Victoria Transport Safety Institute, May 22, 2014.
8. Policy Statement: Emergency Life Support, https://www.bhf.org.uk/~/media/files/ publications/policy-documents/els_policy_statement_june2012.pdf, British Heart Foundation, June 2012.
9. Ibid.
10. Buttrick Matt, "IPA Effectiveness Awards Submission," Grey London, 2014.

CHAPTER 1

1. Source: "The Million Dollar Homepage" Wikipedia, retrieved December 4, 2014, https://en.wikipedia.org/wiki/The_Million_Dollar_Homepage.
2. Sarah Jacobsson Purewal, "Groupon Nightmares (and How to Avoid Them)," *PC World*, May 20, 2014, http://www.pcworld.com/article/212328/how_to_avoid_ groupon_nightmares.html.
3. Source: Yelp. Data retrieved October 2013.
4. One Ford Mission, http://corporate.ford.com/innovation/innovation-detail/ one-ford, Ford, retrieved May 20, 2014.
5. Data retrieved October 12, 2013.

CHAPTER 2

1. "NOAA N-Prime Mishap Investigation Report," NASA, September 13, 2004.
2. Forrester Consulting, "What CMOs Need to Make Marketing Work," September 2014.
3. All of these can be found on multiple online forums dedicated to this topic. Among others, see Susan Gunelius, "5 Infamous Social Media PR Disasters and How to Avoid Them," Sprout Social, February 22, 2012, http://sproutsocial.com/insights/social-media-pr-disasters/.

CHAPTER 3

1. Doug Bowman, "Goodbye, Google," Stop Design (blog), March 20, 2009, http://stopdesign.com/archive/2009/03/20/goodbye-google.html.
2. Felix Richter, "15 Years of Google—How the Search Giant Dominates the Web," Statista, September 27, 2013, http://www.statista.com/chart/1502/15-years-of-google/.
3. Ibid.
4. Atchison and Burby, *Actionable Web Analytics* (Wiley: 2007), 21.
5. "Microsoft Confirms It Originated iPod Box Parody Video," iPod Observer, March 3, 2006, http://www.ipodobserver.com/ipo/article/Microsoft_Confirms_it_Originated_iPod_Box_Parody_Video/.
6. Source: IMDb, retrieved October 15, 2013.
7. Marshall Kirkpatrick, "Netflix's Big Data Plans to Take Over the World," Readwrite.com, July 26, 2011, http://readwrite.com/2011/07/26/netflixs_big_data_plans_to_take_over_the_world
8. Todd Spangler, "How Netflix Uses Privacy to Pick Its Programming," Variety.com, September 14, 2013, http://variety.com/2013/digital/news/how-netflix-uses-piracy-to-pick-its-programming-1200611539/.
9. David Carr, "Giving Viewers What They Want," *New York Times,* February 24, 2013, http://www.nytimes.com/2013/02/25/business/media/for-house-of-cards-using-big-data-to-guarantee-its-popularity.html?pagewanted=all&_r=0.
10. Andrew Leonard, "How Netflix Is Turning Viewers into Puppets," *Salon,* February 1, 2013, http://www.salon.com/2013/02/01/how_netflix_is_turning_viewers_into_puppets/.
11. Alistair Barr, "Amazon Kills 'Zombieland' TV project, Backs 'Alpha House,'" Reuters, May 17, 2013, http://www.reuters.com/article/2013/05/17/entertainment-us-amazon-tv-pilots-idUSBRE94G0YH20130517.

CHAPTER 4

1. The *Economist* Intelligence Unit, "Outside Looking In: The CMO Struggles to Get in Sync with the C-suite" (report), November 9, 2012, http://www.economistinsights.com/analysis/outside-looking.

CHAPTER 5

1. This section is repurposed from Shane Atchison, "Ten Signs a Company Has a Serious Culture Problem," Forbes.com, May 2014, http://www.forbes.com/sites/forbesleadershipforum/2014/05/19/10-signs-that-a-company-has-a-serious-culture-problem/.
2. For a summary of the research, see Sara Robinson, "Bring Back the 40 Hour Workweek," *Salon*, January 2012, http://www.salon.com/2012/03/14/bring_back_the_40_hour_work_week/.
3. Jessica Stillman, "Sheryl Sandberg Leaves Work at 5:30. Why Can't You?" *Inc.*, April 2012, http://www.inc.com/jessica-stillman/facebook-sheryl-sandberg-can-leave-early-why-arent-you.html.
4. Richard Lapchick, "White Men Continue to Dominate Advertising Agencies: A Study of the Super Bowl 2011 Ads," University of Florida School of Business, July 2011, http://www.tidesport.org/MadAve/MadisonAvenue2011_FINAL.pdf.
5. "See It Be It: New Women's Initiative at Cannes," Newscorp Australia, retrieved June 4, 2014, http://www.newscorpaustralia.com/see-it-be-it-new-womens-initiative-cannes.
6. "The Top 30 Stats You Need to Know When Marketing to Women," *The Next Web* blog, retrieved June 4, 2014, http://thenextweb.com/socialmedia/2012/01/24/the-top-30-stats-you-need-to-know-when-marketing-to-women/.
7. Ibid.
8. Research is ongoing in this field. Among others, see Scott E. Page, *The Difference: How the Power of Diversity Creates Better Groups, Firms, Schools, and Societies* (Princeton University Press: 2008).

CHAPTER 6

1. For a lengthy discussion of the evaluation process used by the foundation, please see http://www.gatesfoundation.org/How-We-Work/General-Information/Evaluation-Policy, retrieved May 16, 2014.
2. "How We Work," Bill & Melinda Gates Foundation, http://www.gatesfoundation.org/How-We-Work, retrieved May 16, 2014.
3. Melinda Gates, Facebook post, September 1, 2010, https://www.facebook.com/billmelindagatesfoundation/posts/150003875023953.

CHAPTER 7

1. Nicola Kemp, "Coke's Guido Rosales Talks Global Marketing, Brazil-Style," *Marketing Magazine*, June 2013, http://www.marketingmagazine.co.uk/ article/1183261/cokes-guido-rosales-talks-global-marketing-brazil-style.
2. Liat Kornowski, "Celebrity Sponsored Tweets: What the Stars Get Paid for Advertising in 140 Characters," *Huffington Post*, May 2013, http://www .huffingtonpost.com/2013/05/30/celebrity-sponsored-tweets_n_3360562.html.
3. Contact Babel, *The US Contact Center Decision-Maker's Guide 2013*, http:// www.contactbabel.com/pdfs/apr2013/US%20Contact%20Center%20Decision -Makers%20Guide%202013.pdf.

CHAPTER 8

1. Thomas Gilovich and Amos Tversky, "The Hot Hand in Basketball: On the Misperception of Random Sequences," *Cognitive Psychology* 3, no. 17 (1985): 295–314.

CHAPTER 10

1. Art de Vany, *Hollywood Economics: How Extreme Uncertainty Shapes the Film Industry* (Routledge: 2013).
2. Jon Steel, "Prove It," *The Wire*, October 2013.

CHAPTER 11

1. For a firsthand account, see Caroline Zielinski, "Father Pays Tribute to his 'Beautiful Boy,' Killed near Malvern Train Station," *The Age*, June 16, 2014, http://www.theage.com.au/victoria/father-pays-tribute-to-his-beautiful-boy-killed -near-malvern-train-station-20140616-zs8tq.html.
2. Lucy Thackray, "Is 'Coupler Riding' Australia's Stupidest New Craze?," Mail Online, July 14, 2014, http://www.dailymail.co.uk/news/article-2693799/Coupler -riding-Australias-stupidest-new-craze.html.

INDEX

Split testing, 211
Staffing, for innovation, 271–272
Starbucks, 167
Statistics:
   and customer service, 115–116
   respect for, 217–218
Steel, Jon, 278
Stelter, Thomas, 333
   on evolving digital landscape, 227
   on innovation, 282
Stories:
   product, 72–74
   in touchpoint mapping, 67
The Straits Times, 62
Strategic failure (in targeting), 241
Strategy:
   in consumer-action mapping, 71
   for innovation, 263
StubHub, 62
Subjective interference, 87–88, 210–211
Success:
   achievement as, 55, 121
   completion as, 55
   Culture Predicts Success and Failure
      (principle 5), 14, 289, 292 (*See
      also* Culture)
   defining, 262
   of digital marketing, demonstrating,
      300–301
   long-term, measuring, 169–171
   methodologies for evaluating, 294
   and opportunities for mistakes, 33
   of terrible culture, 136
   up-front definition of, 286
Sumerians, 87–88
Sustaining innovations, 266–269
Swift, 252
Swinmurn, Nick, 278
"Sword and shield" metaphor, 95

T

Target, 245
Targeting, 215, 228–253

   and behaviors, 235–236
   bland messaging, 232
   commonsense marketing, 231–232
   contributors' thoughts on, 249–254
   digital technology for, 235
   Google algorithms for, 83
   inadvertent, 232–235
   lazy, 243–245
   masking, 246
   One Size Fits No One (principle 9), 16,
      290, 294
   and personas, 238
   in physical world, 247
   principles of, 241–243
   privacy paradox, 245–246
   profiles, 236
   reasons for not, 240
   rewards of small changes, 239–240
   strategic failure in, 241
   technological failure in, 241
   types of customers, 237
Team goals, 28
Teams:
   building, 134–135
   and competition for digital employees,
      109–110
   differing goals of, 28
   digital IQ of, 305
   diversity of, 143–144
   goals of, 28
   investing in, 143
   managing culture of, 137
Technological failure (in targeting), 241
Technology innovation, 277–278
Tesco, 62
Testing, 206–227
   A/B/n, 211–212
   basics of program for, 217–218
   beyond creative changes, 214–215
   choosing areas for, 212–214
   contributors' thoughts on, 224–227
   and culture of optimization, 220–222
   at Google, 82, 83

ABOUT THE AUTHORS

POSSIBLE is a creative agency that cares about results. They back up every idea with real-world insights to create work that makes a difference—and makes a measurable impact. With more than 1,300 employees around the globe, POSSIBLE brings results-driven digital solutions to some of the world's most dynamic brands. These include Microsoft, Procter & Gamble, AT&T, Shell, and the Coca-Cola Company. POSSIBLE is part of WPP Digital.

@POSSIBLE
www.possible.com

SHANE ATCHISON serves as the Global CEO of POSSIBLE, where he leads the company's long-term strategic vision, helping businesses and nonprofit organizations realize the potential of digital technology. Shane has also written extensively on the industry in forums as diverse as Fortune.com, *Fast Company*, and *LinkedIn Today*.

@ShanePOSSIBLE

JASON BURBY serves as the President of the Americas for POSSIBLE. With 20-plus years of experience in digital strategy, he has become known as a passionate advocate for using data to inform digital strategies and inspire creative ideas that really work.

@JasonBurby